D1500335

For a Fundamental Social Ethic:
A Philosophy of Social Change

For a Fundamental Social Ethic:
A Philosophy of Social Change

by

OLIVA BLANCHETTE, S. J.
BOSTON COLLEGE

PHILOSOPHICAL LIBRARY

NEW YORK

Copyright, © 1973, by Philosophical Library, Inc.,

15 East 40th Street, New York, N. Y. 10016

Library of Congress Catalog Card Number: 73-77400

SBN 8022-2113-0

Manufactured in the United States of America

TO MY FATHER

who has lived up to his name, Delphis,
and whose reticent teaching has been more
eloquent to me than the words of many.

TABLE OF CONTENTS

ACKNOWLEDGEMENTS

This book has grown out of a double dialogue, one with authors, both classical and contemporary, and one with students, who have listened to me and challenged me to be relevant for our time. It makes little claim to originality, except perhaps as an attempt to develop a perspective as a whole for the articulation of moral judgments in actual history.

I acknowledge my debt to authors throughout the book and in the bibliography at the end. Here I would like to acknowledge my debt to my students, who have forced me to be more clear than I might have been otherwise, and to a friend and colleague with whom I first began some years ago to teach the course out of which this book has grown, Carroll Bourg, now doing sociology at Fiske University. Working with him in those early days of team-teaching not only helped to introduce me to what is best in the sociological tradition but also gave me a concrete sense of how the social scientists, for better and for worse, are really the ethicists of our day, though they often lack the philosophical perspective that would make them more truly and, if truth be said, more responsibly ethical in their outlook and in the influence they exert.

Also I owe a special word of acknowledgement and gratitude to Mary Raftery, whose typing and careful work did so much to make the manuscript for this book more than presentable.

May the book itself be not too unworthy of these and others who have contributed to it in many different ways.

INTRODUCTION

It should have been a somewhat embarrassing confession to make when some years ago, after a long and rather detailed discussion of developments in philosophical ethics in recent decades, a philosopher had to admit the analytical conception of philosophy had led philosophers away from practical social questions and we had to look more to religious ethicists for consideration of these.[1] But few among the professional philosophers seem to have been particularly bothered by this admission and the author himself had been satisfied to devote only a few pages, comparatively speaking, to this more concrete aspect of ethical reflection. Not long after, a book on *The Revolution in Ethical Theory* appeared,[2] but it hardly spoke of revolution in any real sense, certainly not with reference to any social context. It remained well within the abstract realm of linguistic analysis. It described only a palace revolution that stayed well within the realm of linguistic meta-ethics.

Since then, however, philosophy has taken some steps to break out of its narrow concern for only the abstraction of ethics. A cruel and mindless war and other matters of public policy have drawn its attention to a more historical task, as is evidenced by the appearance even of journals on philosophy and public affairs. But one could wonder whether philosophy, as it is still understood by many, is equal to the broader task of social criticism which it seems now more ready to take on, in keeping with a long tradition of philosophical ethics. One can well wonder if a broader, more concrete idea of meta-ethics than has been prevalent in linguistic analysis might not be necessary.

ix

Herbert Marcuse, himself long a social critic as a philosopher, has argued very persuasively against the so-called "logical positivism" in philosophy which, disclaiming any content of its own, has seen fit only to reflect the attitudes and values already established in language, whether ordinary or technical, and in society, and to work only at the clarification of the ideas contained therein. In this, according to Marcuse, it has failed to play the more positive, as well as critical, role it might be playing in the real, on-going revolution of history itself.[3]

The question is not whether philosophy should abandon its concern with meta-ethics, in favor of dealing more with concrete cases. That would only be passing from one form of abstractionism to another. The question is more one of how to do meta-ethics itself, so that it does not close itself off in an abstract discussion of ideas in morality, but rather opens the way to a more authentic and more complete exercise of moral judgment in history.

For this a purely analytical approach is not enough. It has to be complemented by a more dialectical method. This is not to say that a certain clarity about such basic notions as goodness, oughtness, obligation, and morality is not necessary. On the contrary, it is quite necessary: even a dialectical method presupposes and requires such clarity. But it goes beyond a merely analytical and conceptually fixed clarity. It seeks the further clarity which can come only in the interplay between ideas and reality, in the shock of ideas themselves that takes place in the relation between theory and practice, for it is only there that the ideas become historically clear, that is, really enlightening in the concrete.

The purpose of this book it to try to make this dialectical step toward the concrete in meta-ethics. It is not an attempt to work out a detailed social philosophy for out time, but rather to spell out an ethical perspective with which such a philosophy could be worked out. The focus of our attention, therefore, will be the concrete exercise of moral judgment in its dialectical structure: not just the elements of moral judgment taken in isolation nor anyone of its particular poles of concentration, but the living unity in which all these factors appear.

Perhaps the easiest way to make clear what is meant by this at this point is to look at two of the basic problems currently occupying some ethicists, if not most: that of situationism and that of the role of social science in moral judgment, and to see what kind of solutions they seem to call for.

In general the difference between an ethic of principle and a situation ethic seems to lie in the fact that the first speaks first of establishing principles and then of applying them to particular situations while the second simply refuses to approach any moral decision in such an abstract, aprioristic way, either because it fails to recognize any established principles at all or because it does not see any relevance of such principles to situations.

The case for situationism against principles could be made from a historical point of view. Principles could have seemed adequate and applicable in the past, when life and society were relatively simple. But the rise of science and technology, along with the new know-how as well as the new problems these have created for us, have made those old principles obsolete and have called into question the very possibility of formulating principles that would be valid for our new situation. Our knowledge in medicine, in psychology, or in demography, for example, has brought us to the need for decisions for which we have no known principles. We have reached limit situations, not just in the sense of the existentialists, who insist on the inescapable universality of suffering and death in this context, but also in the sense of a *world-wide* consciousness and a threat to our very existence. Such limit situations as the power of nuclear bombs and the possibilities of population explosion as well as genetic control loom very large in our moral consciousness and our "principles" seem rather paltry in the face of these new *world* problems and situations.

The debate has gone on over many particular issues, but it is not clear that it has advanced very far. Situationists tend to resort to a new style of casuistry, neo-casuistry,[4] but with little reflection on what precisely is meant by either principle or context. The old, abstract and aprioristic approach has hardly been trascended. Opposition to it has remained in the same genus, without effectively coming closer to the concrete in a significant way. In the words of Bonhoeffer, we have been left with "a casuistic system so unmanageable that it could satisfy the demands neither of general validity nor of concreteness."[5]

Actually, as was argued some time ago,[6] the debate has been misplaced. "Principle" and "context" seem hardly adequate to cover the differences that separate the participants in the debate. Depending on their own particular forms of emphasis with regard to the components of moral judgment, different authors draw up the sides in the debate differently.[7] But the fundamental question still centers in the meaning of "principle" and of "context" and, more importantly, in the relation between the two in the exercise of moral judgment. Can principle be understood apart from context? Can context be interpreted without principle?

Those who maintain the validity of absolute principles are perhaps exaggeratedly and too exclusively concerned with certainty and not enough with the true moral content of their principles. This appears against the background of an epistemology seeking a fixed objectivity in all things, a sort of "thing in itself" against which principles could be judged in their "absoluteness," without reference to the concrete.[8] Such reference comes only after the establishment of principles "in reason" or "in themselves," in a process of "applying" the principles, as if the principles could be understood adequately apart from their application. But this separation between principle and context, despite its seeming clarity, is fraught with confusion. It opens the way to all the ambiguity of casuistry, which never manages to put principle and context really together again

xii

and leaves us only with a "subjectively certain conscience" to fall back on in moral judgment. With this the ethic of principle turns out to be the most situationist of all, since, even when it is erroneous, the subjectively certain conscience is to be followed.[9]

It is back on this subjectively-certain-conscience that the situationist falls when he opposes the ethic of principle, a conscience that is no less abstract and a priori than the principle from which it has been set off, no less fixed and absolute. Situationists have shown little concern for forming and informing conscience. Almost any conscience has seemed the right norm, as long as it was "in touch" with its context. Little or nothing has been done to show how a *true* conscience is formed. Contextualism appears very dynamic exteriorly, but in essence it remains static with regard to conscience. It does not show how I come to a conscience that is dissatisfied with the possibility of error in the exercise of my judgment. I am persuaded that my conscience of today is more sensitive, more right, than, say, my conscience of ten years ago, even though I could not have had precisely this same consciousness and conscience ten years ago, for I am also persuaded that I have learned something *in conscience* over these ten years. With its insistence on context, situationism has said little of this *learning* in conscience so essential to the true exercise of moral judgment. It is in fact the ethic of principle that has tried most to deal with this problem of the possibly erroneous though subjectively certain conscience, with the theory of probabilism, for example, but it has done so only in a sort of extrinsic mechanical way, hardly in a way adequate to any form of real learning in conscience. Once again, "principle" and "context" find themselves in the same boat.

The dilemma as it has been posed is, of course, insoluble. One has to transcend the fixed opposition between the two poles. The experience of having learned something *in conscience* sets us on the way to overcoming this false dichotomy between principle and context. But learning is itself a complex and a social activity. One has to be willing to learn, not only from one's individual experience, but also from others, from teachers and from a whole tradition of learning, in short, from the community in which one finds oneself and to which one belongs. Judgment in the concrete as to what is right is part of a social activity.

This brings us to the second problem occupying ethicists mentioned above to exemplify the need for a basic reflection on the concrete exercise of moral judgment, that of the role of the social sciences. Here again we will find the same kind of abstract separation as we found between "principle" and "context," but the separation will take a different twist and lead us more deeply into the inadequacy of its abstractionism.

The first thing to note about the role of social science in the exercise of moral judgment is the reluctance with which social scientists are willing to serve as consultants. In all sorts of practical matters, including decisions on public policy, few are willing to admit they are exercising moral judgment in their expertise as such. Their discipline, they claim, is purely theoretical, that is, concerned only with what *is,* and not with what *ought* to be; or again it is purely "practical," that is, concerned with what is likely to come of some action, and not with the good or evil or the value of it. Such a *purely* "scientific" attitude is meant to leave room for the moralists, who presumably are something else than "scientific." But one could wonder whether social science can be so separated from real practice, the process of human decision and intentionality, as not to depend on it directly in the very subject of its investigation and not to affect the values implicit in any action it may recommend, so that human intentionality does in fact influence its conclusions while, in turn, its conclusions do influence the intentionality. *In the concrete,* theory and practice are inseparable and, to the extent that social science is concerned with the concrete, whether for purposes of investigation or of recommendation, it cannot escape from its responsibility for the real practice of society.

We could say that this is an essential part of its rational function. But why is social science so reluctant to accept this responsibility? Reinhard Bendix, a sociologist, has called attention to a strain of scepticism that runs deep throughout a large part of social research, especially where it is primarily statistical in its approach.[10] This strain can be traced back all the way to Francis Bacon and the preoccupation with "facts" as the sole means of overcoming bias. But it manifests an enduring naïveté with regard to what is meant by "fact," especially "statistical facts," and with regard to the methods of research for such facts. It is almost as if reason were not operative in these methods and in the conclusions arrived at through them. It is also almost as if reason, a creative form of reason, did not also have to be operative in practice and in policy making.

There are, of course, reasons for maintaining a certain separation between science and politics and these have been urged most cogently by one of the giants of social science, Max Weber. But Weber's point has been largely exaggerated or misinterpreted. There were very precise social conditions in the Germany of his day which led him to his position: given the kind of absolute authority which professors held over their students, they were not to use their chairs to do politics. Yet Weber himself saw a real connection between science and politics. He distinguished between an "ethic of responsibility" and an "ethic of absolute ends."[11] The latter he saw as too detached from real conditions of society and not concerned enough with learning what might be the consequences of this or that course of action. He preferred an "ethic of responsibility" precisely because he saw in it a greater concern for knowing human propensities before deciding on a course of action. This is why Weber refused to isolate politics from science, or science from politics, in his own appreciation of these two distinct yet historically inseparable "vocations."[12]

But perhaps the most profound reason for maintaining this false dichotomy between "science" and "moral judgment" goes back to a certain philosophical attitude with regard to morality in general. In this respect the social scientists may be only reflecting the formalism of moral philosophers themselves. The latter, as if in order to reserve an area proper only to themselves in the realm of human action, have tended to define morality as a reality other than that studied by social science as such. Thus in the face of "pure science" we are given to think of "pure morality." Each is either seen as more or less complete in itself or else the connection between the two is left totally obscure. This is why the social scientist seems justified to abstract from "morality," even though he is studying practice, while the moralist does his own thing by himself, apart from "science."

The origins of this formalism that afflicts social scientists as well as moralists in the Kantian idea of "pure practical reason" are clear enough, but it is interesting to see how it dogs any attempts to unify social science and moral philosophy in our day. To introduce a consideration of social science in moral judgment is somehow to move from "principle" in the direction of "context." Contextualism, however, is usually associated with the subjective pole of human action.[13] How can this be accorded with the claim that science is concerned above all with objectivity? Could we not say that, far from being an insistence on individual conscience, the appeal to social science entails a return to "principle," a concern for the laws that govern human situations rather than for the subject of moral judgment? Here we see how ambiguous the idea of "context" can be when it comes to moral reasoning. It seems to focus inside, on the subject of morality, and yet, if we accept the separation between social science and morality, it places us completely outside of that subject, in a law totally extrinsic to him.

This is where formalism leaves us on the side of social science. Let us see now where it leaves us on the side of morality. For this the situationist, Joseph Fletcher, can serve as a good example. In the "new morality" he proposes, love is the only absolute norm. Fletcher is opposed to legalism, but it is difficult to follow him because his idea of "law" is not clear. On the one hand he seems to reject the idea of law, without saying precisely what is meant by that, but on the other hand, in his opposition to antinomianism, he introduces ideas of "guidance," "demands," "web of life," and other such metaphorical expressions, all of which seem to be translations of what is meant by law.[14] Moreover, when he speaks of love as a norm, it is difficult to see how "norm" differs from "law," especially since Fletcher does not hesitate to speak of "love" as a "category."[15] Even if we admit that love can indeed be a norm, a principle, not a rule[16] — it still remains to be seen how this norm or principle operates in the concrete exercise of moral judgment. One is especially wary of any "absolute norm of love" when one remembers Weber's distinction between an "ethic of absolute ends," of which the "ethic of the Gospel or Christian love" is cited as an example, and the kinds of ruthless action that such absolute principles can open the way to when they remain abstract or isolated.

Fletcher does try to bring his norm of love down to the concrete when he connects it with justice. In fact, Fletcher refuses to distinguish between love and justice, as Reinhold Niebuhr does.[17] He sees the two as one and the same thing and, when he comes to the historical exigency for care, prudence and calculation in love, love disappears in a rather cold formalism with little of the sensibility one usually expects from love and which constitutes a very concrete norm of action for us. The abstraction of love ends up being a denial of something that seems quite essential to love. "Justice," Fletcher writes, "is Christian love using its head, calculating its duties, obligations, opportunities, resources. Justice is love coping with situations where distribution is called for. On this basis it becomes plain that as the love ethic searches seriously for a social policy it must form a coalition with ultilitarianism."[18] One could interpret this as an appeal to join morality with social science in policy making, but one could hardly be satisfied with such an extrinsic denomination as "coalition" for a unity that has to be much more dialectical. Nor does Fletcher speak of the social sciences precisely, but rather of utilitarianism, another form of abstract formalism when it comes to the social dimension of moral judgment.

All of this leaves us with the impression that, try as it may, abstract formalism is incapable of unifying the exercise of moral judgment in the concrete. On the side of social science, which is in many respects where our *real* practical and, therefore, moral judgments come from today, we are left with a realm of morality that remains outside of its competence. On the side of morality, we have a norm of evaluation that does not reach the real world without betraying itself. How, then, are we to understand the exercise of moral judgment if we are not going to remain hung up between the two horns of this dilemma? Analysis can only clarify our dilemma, not take us beyond it in the concrete.

An important step forward has been made by Gibson Winter in his *Elements for a Social Ethic* to take us beyond this impasse.[19] In this book Winter starts by working out a fundamental humanistic perspective with the help of George Herbert Mead on the one hand and Alfred Schütz on the other, a behaviorist with a penchant for philosophy and a phenomenologist with a special interest in the social sciences. From this perspective he examines various schools of sociology and their relation with one another as they focus on the phenomenon of man as a whole. He situates each school in an order ranging from behaviorism, through functionalism and voluntarism, to his own more intentional approach. In this way he presents a means of ordering all of them together in the exercise of judgment concerning social process and public policy. Winter does not succeed in pulling together all the loose ends, but he does propose an interesting model for relating various methods of social science in determining what is to be done in practice. A lot more needs to be done along the same line to bring in more of the social sciences.

But besides this step forward into the realm of the social sciences, there is a need also for stepping back from the immediacy of judgments to be made in practice to have a closer look at the dynamics of such judgment. This is what we propose to do in this book.

Hopefully, through a more historical and dialectical approach, we will be able to bring together in an organic unity what the various kinds of abstract formalism can only leave in a state of separation and, therefore, of confusion. For example, we will distinguish between justice and friendship, but at the same time we will insist on their dialectic unity in the exercise of moral judgment. We will speak of them as virtues, elements of our moral sensibility, but we will also see them in their dialectical unity with reason. All of these constituents of moral judgment in the concrete will be seen in their relationship to one another as well as in what is specific to each.

Our purpose will not be to establish principles as such, apart from the exercise of judgment, but rather to examine how principles actualy operate in our real judgments and how they are assumed in our free activity. Situationism as such is not enough to account for all that goes into human action. In any human situation, any context, there is only one reality, one order, which, in its very transcendence of context as merely given, embraces and immerses itself in its particular orders, so that any moral judgment on our part is totally transcendent and totally immanent at the same time, totally absolute and totally relative. Contextualism, like its opposite, the ethic of "absolute principle," is still too absolute in its abstraction and purity. It cannot escape its involvement with principle in the concrete.

But what precisely is this principle? This is something we will have to attend to very carefully when we come to speak of the good of history, for the good which is the principle is very difficult to conceive positively as well as concretely. This too we will have to approach dialectically. Here, however, it is enough to indicate why the ethic we propose will have to be a *fundamental social ethic*. We spoke of a need to form and to inform conscience and how this has to take place through reflection on experience, that of others as well as our own. This is to say that individualism of any sort, whether existential or utilitarian, will not do. The principles that are operative in any concrete exercise of moral judgment are the principles of a whole, the social whole of which any person is a part. Whether that whole be the City, as Aristotle thought of it, or the State, as Hegel thought of it, or a global Society, as some think of it today, those principles can be summarized only under the idea of the Common Good.

What we will argue here, therefore, is that any ethic in the concrete has to be social, not just adventitiously, as in most forms of utilitarianism and Kantian formalism, but fundamentally and from the very beginning. Indeed, we would even object to the idea implicit in the title of one of Reinhold Niebuhr's books, *Moral Man and Immoral Society,* inasmuch as it tends to oppose individual and society and to suggest that an individual can be free and moral independently of his society. Granted that there is a special weight attending society as a whole and granted that not everyone in a society is equally "moral" or "immoral," still it is clear that ethics is always a matter of the whole from the start and this "whole" is always something more than any individual taken in isolation. One's coming to ethics is always a function of one's community. An ethic is a place where man takes his stand humanly, that is, with understanding, freedom and responsibility, and such a place cannot be found except in a community of persons.

The ethic we would propose, then, is something akin to that of an Aristotle or of a Hegel, but without the specification of either "city" or "state" which each would add respectively. We wish to take man in the universal sweep of his history. Aristotle thought of man only in terms of the *polis.* Hegel thought the

State was the ultimate political term of history. For him love was too immediately bound with nature: it pertained only to the family, not to the political realm. Beyond the State or any particular people there was a World Spirit, but that Spirit called for no further political organization beyond the State. War remained an inevitable and necessary dimension of international relations. Though we share much of Hegel's view of ethics, we share neither of these restrictions concerning the extension of love or the proper expression of the World Spirit. It is perhaps these restrictions that have tended to harden Hegelian philosophy into a kind of totalitarian system, when it was intended to be essentially liberating. In any case, by arguing for a certain universality of friendship along with justice, as we shall do, and by looking for a universal form of politics beyond that of the nation-state, we shall be trying to go beyond the Hegelian idea of ethics into something more authentically universal as well as personal. This will appear both in the dialectic of the common good and in the dialectic of justice and friendship.

To do this we shall follow the movement of moral judgment itself as it grapples with the world in an effort to humanize it. It is a basic supposition of the book that the fundamental notions of ethics cannot be understood properly in isolation, apart from their dialectical interplay with one another in the concrete exercise of judgment. In this our effort is akin to that of Marxism, especially in its attempt to "realize" Hegelian philosophy in history as a whole. But we will distinguish ourselves from Marxism by showing how the end, which is the good of communion, not "communism", has to influence the choice and the quality of means in the present, something Marxism tends to neglect in its *Realpolitik*.

This is where we find ourselves at variance with Marcuse also, though we agree wholeheartedly with his effort to broaden the scope of philosophy to include a properly historical task. There is lacking in him, as in Marxism in general, a well articulated view of the good of history. To be sure, in his critique of established society and in his discussion of alienation, there is implicit an idea of that good. But that idea is hardly, if ever, expressed positively. It appears only as a power of negative thinking.[20] Worse still, that idea, however positive it may be in itself, does not seem to play any positive role in the concrete exercise of moral judgment for Marcuse. This judgment, negative as it is, derives its content solely from the system to which it is opposed. Thus, it seems almost inevitably to fall into the same shortcomings of that system with its violence and injustice. It is hoped that with a more positive idea of the common good playing a more positive role in the concrete exercise of judgment we will be better able to avoid these pitfalls.

The plan is, therefore, to get to the fundamental dimensions of moral judgment. We will begin by a reflection on responsibility as the actual form of our moral consciousness in our new awareness of social order. From there we will move on to discuss the fundamental principle of moral judgment in the concrete, the good of history or the common good. In close connection with this will come the dialectic of justice and friendship which will appear as an internal means of concrete specification for the common good in the here and now. Along with this will also appear the realm of authority and law as that of external means to be used in all responsibility for the common good, but means which can be radically corrupted in totalitarianism or radically transformed in revolution. The argument of the book will center on the common good, justice and friendship, authority and law, as principles of judgment or as a dialectic of principles, but it will begin and end in a more contextual framework of responsibility and revolution.

Of itself a fundamental social ethic cannot fill out the idea of the common good. This is something that can be done only historically, not just philosophically. But a fundamental social ethic can work at keeping the idea as open as possible to every dimension of history. If we can succeed in doing this to any degree, in a truly historical way, our effort will not have been in vain.

For a Fundamental Social Ethic:
A Philosophy of Social Change

CHAPTER I

RESPONSIBILITY AND
THE SOCIAL ORDER

Fundamental ethics as we understand it here is not concerned with principles as such, whether primary or secondary. We do not question that there are in fact principles operative in human action, nor that some of them can be proper norms for evaluating right and wrong, good and evil. But it is not our task to examine what these might be in truth nor what they mean in themselves. Rather we are concerned with how principles are known and how they are used in the concrete.

Our consideration will not have to do immediately with the here and now. Hence in a sense it will be general, but not in the sense that we will have to do with general principles which will later on have to be applied to particulars. I do not find the consideration of moral principles in the abstract particularly helpful in moral discourse, at least not taken in themselves nor as a starting point in moral reflection. The Cartesian clarity usually associated with such consideration more often than not hides a radical ambiguity that becomes quite evident as soon as the question of application arises. We have only to think of the volumes upon volumes of casuistry to realize how difficult it is to "apply" principles, no matter how supposedly clear and distinct they are in themselves. Indeed, can we know the meaning of moral principles apart from their application? Is it not in the "application" that we discover their real meaning? There is something misleading about supposing that we can start with moral principles in the abstract and then proceed to the concrete, as if the concrete were not the primary focus

1

from the start — a procedure that denies the hermeneutical circularity at the foundation and the heart of all moral judgment.

In what sense, then, can we speak of a concrete fundamental ethic not dealing immediately with the here and now? We can do so only if we understand that we are trying to thematize the fundamental outlook present in our moral reasoning and striving, an outlook found only in the concrete but which we will try to bring to expression as much as possible, recognizing that the expression, abstract as it will be inevitably, has to be essentially open to the concrete and absorbed with it. Here most philosophers would insist that this kind of ethic is not normative, and I would agree, but not completely. Our aim is not to discuss rules for action or for evaluating action. But there remains another aspect of the picture which we should honestly recognize. What we will say will imply certain norms on how to go about making moral judgments and in this sense our fundamental ethics will be normative, not directly but indirectly with regard to moral action as a whole, and even directly with regard to the exercise of moral judgment and moral reasoning as an essential part of this action.

The only place for an ethic such as this to begin, therefore, is the actual exercise of conscience, our historical consciousness. We do not appeal to some kind of privileged position for ourselves in doing this. What we appeal to is something to be found in some way or other in anybody that has given serious thought to the meaning of his own action and of human action in general. By insisting on historical consciousness we may be underlining something that seems characteristic only of our contemporary conscience, but this characteristic has never been totally absent from reflection on action in the concrete and such reflection is surely not the prerogative of contemporary man. There have been many views of history, some explicit and some only implicit, some full-blown theories and others mainly underlying frameworks, but history has always been at the heart of human existence, the existential which specifies man's essential being better than anything else. Man is rational animal, symbolic animal, productive animal, but above all this and including it all, he is the historical animal. His being is essentially historical and history can be defined only in terms of his being and his action. In our historical consciousness, therefore, we stand in the place where life begins for us, where it is ever beginning, in the actual exercise of understanding and freedom.

To describe what this conscience actually is, therefore, is to explicate *how* man goes about being what he has to be, doing what he has to do in the world. It is to unfold the fact whence all moral reflection has to begin. This is what we propose to do in this chapter.

To do so we shall speak mainly in terms of responsibility and the social order because these have come to have a special significance in our own historical consciousness. They are intimately bound with one another and they have come to the fore together in function of a new awareness of our world that has been developing especially since the early part of the nineteenth century. Responsibility implies some reference to the social order and the social order becomes a matter of conscience primarily in terms of responsibility. After reflecting on the nature of moral judgment, therefore, or more precisely on the relation between theoretical and practical judgment, which is where our historical consciousness can be most properly situated, we shall discuss the meaning and the structure of responsibility and its ramifications in the social order. We shall then examine how the social order itself affects responsibility and how it enters necessarily into any moral reflection that is not stunted by infantilism or individualism.

I — *Historical Consciousness*

The subject of ethics, as of any moral reflection, is human

3

action. This means something more and something less than what is frequently understood by "ethics." It means more because it includes everything that has to do with human action, the "practical" and the "political" as well as the "moral." We do not start off, whether generally or here in particular, by opposing the moral to the practical or the political. Inasmuch as all three have to do with action, we identify them. It is only as a result of a secondary reflection, and a rather formalistic one at that, that moralists begin to separate the moral from the practical. The practical is then restricted in meaning to a limited and abstract perspective that is not coextensive to the moral, though it might come under it, if one does not push the formalism too far. The outlook of Aristotle in this regard, which we will make our own, was quite different from this: he viewed the political and the practical as the more universal category and the ethical or the moral as contained in the political, as only a propaedeutic for the political, which is really the realm of human action in its fullest sense. For Aristotle, however, who did not have to think too much of what was beyond the walls of the Greek city-state, or at most beyond Greece itself, when he thought of politics, this subordination of ethics to politics was perhaps relatively easy. The growing complexification of our political life, which now embraces states that far surpass any Greek city, or Greece itself, in size and in cultural diversity, has made it difficult to keep this ancient view of politics. We have been somewhat overwhelmed by the bigness of modern politics, economics and management and we have settled for a "purer" view of morality, but one which is really less genuinely moral to the extent that it is impractical, while at the same time we have given an equally narrow meaning to the "practical" and the "political." When we speak of action as the subject of ethics, therefore, we mean to restore the *primordial* unity of the moral, the practical and the political.

It should be clear, however, that in doing this we mean something "less" than what is ordinarily understood by ethics.

4

"Ethical" usually refers to the ideal, over and above the real. It may or may not include the real, but in any case it is understood to refer to something more, the aim of human life, the end to be achieved. We are not concerned with defining the content of this ideal here. We recognize that human action is in view of an end, that it has an aim beyond the present and the merely given, that its present perfection is ever in view of a further perfection, a first perfection in view of a second perfection, a first act in view of a second act, but here we stop at this recognition and seek to draw out its implications without trying to determine what precisely the end or the final perfection will be, or even what it ought to be.

But if we do not insist on a fully developed teleology for human action at this point, neither do we expect a complete archaeology of the human subject. The roots of my action are sunk deep in the gloomy recesses of my psyche and even in the physiology and the chemistry of my being. They go back also down the ages of my ancestry as well as the determinisms of my cultural and economic antecedents. I could never retrieve all these ontogenetic and phylogenetic influences and bring them to the clear forum of conscience. Nor do I need to do so.

What does it matter what these dark recesses have been? The fact is that I have come to consciousness and that is what is important for me here and now. I am well aware that my origins and my past might contain the key to a significant part of my behavior. It would be good for me to undergo psychoanalysis, no doubt, and also to understand all the subtle ways in which economics determines me even in my very consciousness. Freud and Marx surely would have a great deal to tell me about myself. But this is still not the essential thing about me as a subject, as a human agent. It has to do only with the conditions of my being such an agent as I am, but not with being an agent as such. Indeed, my recognition that there are certain conditions to my being a true agent in the cosmos, that there are certain determinisms at play in my very action, presupposes not only the idea of liberty, as Kant surely would have allowed, but even the experience of liberty. The claim that everything is determined in human action can only be made if one supposes liberty in act.[1]

Of course, this does not mean, that human liberty, my liberty, for example, simply soars above all determinism or outside influence, whether present or past. Human liberty is rooted in determinism and necessarily emerges from such determinism. This is what it means for me to *come* to consciousness. We do not affirm liberty as a formal and somehow disembodied act any more than we allow for an ethic divorced from the practical and the political. What we wish is simply to work and to reflect within the light of consciousness that is given to us here and now and to push the shadows that press in upon us back as much as possible so that we may act as freely and as creatively as possible.

Hence we do not say that all investigation into the origins of the subject is futile. We say simply that such investigation, as necessary as it may be in certain instances of illness, for example, is not the primary thing, and that it always remains subservient to the actual light of consciousness, whatever it may be here and now. Only in the case of mental illness, or fixation, or obsession, does analysis of the psyche seem required as a first step, in order always to release the light of consciousness. But then one could ask: who is not sick?

We cannot go into this somewhat technical question here. But it does point up precisely what kind of ethic we must think of, if we consider human action in the concrete as its proper subject. Once we abandon the ideal of liberty as simply given here and now, but see it more as something to be realized through actual liberty, we cannot any longer fall back on some sort of categorical imperative of pure reason, nor even on some sort of natural law that is discoverable by a simple analysis of human nature in the abstract. We can only fall back on what is usually ignored or relegated to some secondary realm

6

by such an aprioristic outlook, that is, on prudence, the ability to plan and to provide in the concrete for what I want to become or what I want the world to become. Prudence is not oblivious of imperatives, obligation, law, and so on, but it sees these within the broader framework of human action as a whole, as means more than as ends.

Prudence looks more to the future, before looking to the past, because human action is above all a project. It is prospective before being reflective, and it is reflective only the better to assess the real possibilities open to me in the concrete. If Kant thought less of prudence than we do here, it is because he thought primarily of small-minded calculation, an excess of "prudence" which is not genuine prudence at all.

We find in prudence, that fundamental human virtue of which no man is ever willing to admit he is totally deprived, the true locus of our historical consciousness. It is not split between future and past, as if the two were to be viewed in the same way and in competition with one another. It looks to the past by reason and in function of its openness to the future. It does not separate theoretical reason from practical reason. It is theoretical for practical reasons and it finds theoretical enrichment in practice itself. It lives and grows by the mutual complementarity of theory and practice. It is the reason of *praxis*. It has to do not just with the ways and means of human life, as Aristotle was wont to suggest, but with the whole quality of life, the end to be realized through the means as well as the means. Whatever else may be said about historical consciousness, if it is not this, it is nothing.

Our knowledge of history has grown immensely in the past century or so. We have stretched the limits of the past almost to infinity, both in distance and in depth. And our historical consciousness has grown apace. But the heart of historical consciousness, no matter how far it extends in time and space, is always in the human present, the *now* that is open to the future above all and foremost, the *now* that is a project seeking realiza-

7

tion in fear and trembling but with every means at its disposal. This is prudence and it is not to be spurned as something merely calculative and self-seeking, for the final evaluation all depends on how we actually calculate and what we really seek.

At this point in our reflection at least, we are in no position to say what this entails, for we are only trying to say what is the case with human consciousness and conscience, which has been aptly defined by Pieper as "the living unity of *synderesis* (the presence in the mind of "universal principles") and prudence."[2] The dimensions and the quality of our conscience may have changed in recent times, but it continues to turn on the hinge where theory and practice meet so that it always requires a better knowledge of reality and further realization of the good. Moral judgment always entails a critical reflection on the order, or lack thereof, given in oneself and in the world, followed by a certain deliberation in view of an end to be achieved by one's action. This is why prudence, the virtue that rectifies reason in practice, remains crucial even for the most sophisticated historical consciousness.

II — *Responsibility*

But perhaps prudence is not the best term to use today to convey the positive and essentially forward-looking aspect of genuine moral judgment. For us prudence has come to connote a certain do-nothing attitude rather than an attitude of enterprise. We think more in terms of commitment and better still, because it keeps the rational aspect of commitment more clearly in the forefront, of responsibility. This is not something apart from prudence properly understood, but it does force us to bring into view the broader, more universal dimensions of our world which a more limited understanding of "prudence" might leave out. "Responsibility is a total response of the whole man to the whole of reality."[3] It mediates between conscience and social order.

The idea of responsibility, familiar as it may seem to us today, gained prominence in moral reflection and discourse rather late in Western thought. If one looks for an equivalent to our term responsibility in antiquity or even in the middle ages, one will find nothing corresponding exactly to what we mean by it. One will find elements of the idea, such as imputability, or accountability, or voluntariety, but nothing of the positive social dimension we associate with the idea. To be sure, responsibility is not a totally new idea. It is made up of elements that have long been in our moral tradition. It has developed from the Greek ideal of the "reflected life," the only one humanly worth living, and from Aristotle's analysis of the internal structure of human action, but only under the pressure of a new concern for the practical and the political. It has brought old elements together in a new constellation more suited to our modern world. Whereas earlier moral focus had been on self-fulfillment, or on duties and rights, now it is in the idea of answerability. The old elements have not necessarily been dropped from sight. They have been regrouped around a new symbol having to do with the interaction of men with the world and among themselves rather than just with men taken by themselves.

It will be instructive to review briefly how this new idea of responsibility came to be as we understand it today.[4] While some forms of the adjective, "responsible," can be found in one language or another going all the way back to the thirteenth century, the noun, "responsibility," seems to have been forged for the first time in both English and French around the year 1787. Alexander Hamilton was the first to use it in the Federalist Papers. The German equivalent, *Verantwortlichkeit,* seems to date only from the nineteenth century with the poet Heinrich Heine. What is significant about this origin is that, from the beginning, responsibility was a matter of government, of political answerability *for* a task defined in advance and *to* the people for whom the task was performed. The term was born at the time of the American and the French revolutions and it grew from there, stamped by the events that made the new idea a necessity.

In the nineteenth century the term came to be used widely and its meaning spread to embrace not only the formally defined political order, but also any socio-cultural system and even the moral order as a whole. As the term became more universally applied, it also became more interiorized. At first it had pertained only to the external order, but now it is understood to be applicable in the moral order on the level of conscience as such. We are responsible for our deeds not only before the law, nor only before public opinion, but also before ourselves, before our conscience, and, for some at least, before God.

The easiest meaning of responsibility to grasp, and therefore the first one to come up for reflection, is the juridical meaning. This is how it was in the practical order at the time when constitutions and laws were being established and this is how it was also when John Stuart Mill first introduced the term as a substitute for punishability. From this point of view we can easily see where the roots of the idea can be found in the Western tradition.

But an important transformation should be noted. For ancient Greek philosophy in general and for Aristotle in particular, "justice" had been the link between ethics and politics. Justice originally implied a certain order either discerned by wisdom or established by convention and it was in function of this order that one judged imputability and accountability. With the rise of Stoic philosophy, and with Zeno in particular, a subtle change took place. "Duty" came to take the place of "justice" as the link and the norm for distinctions and oppositions. This entailed a rather significant reversal in the mode of analysis that had obtained previously. What is discerned first in Stoic philosophy is not order but a drive found in human action and in nature as a whole. There is an order to be recognized, but it is an order of drives, and the question is to establish the right order of these. Ethics thus became a matter of "natural law" and "duties," and not of "justice," though one could read back into the ancient texts the new perspective, inasmuch as one did find there such ideas as "moral necessity," "natural inclination," "principles" and even some notion of things that were "due."

Significantly enough, it was this kind of Stoic ethics which dominated the scene among philosophers at the time when the idea of responsibility began to crystallize near the end of the eighteenth century. It was the framework for empiricists like Hobbes, Locke and Hume and for rationalists like Puffendorf, Wolff and Kant, though they adopted different views with regard to the relation between freedom and necessity in human action and the capacity of man to be truly a cause of something in the cosmos. Hegel and Marx tried to rethink the relation between freedom and necessity, but they did not succeed in completely superseding the Stoic "natural law" framework. In the meantime, however, the idea of responsibility was taking its own course in the practical and the political sphere. Hegel and Marx did succeed in reactivating the long-lost political idea of ethics, without, however, doing enough to restore the idea of personal initiative and creativity in human reason itself here and now, something that is essential to real responsibility.

But if the philosophers were slow to discern the importance of the new development in the moral consciousness, the social thinkers of the time were perhaps better attuned to it. Many of them, like Marx, though often in opposition to him, were deeply concerned about the breakdown of the old order and the seeming chaos as well as the inhumanity of the forces emerging after the industrial and the French revolutions.

It is from a social scientist, Max Weber, that we have one of the best approaches to an ethic of responsibility in an essay quite fittingly entitled "Politics as a Vocation." After reviewing the rise of the modern day politician and what characterizes him either as a charismatic leader or just as a party technician and bureaucrat, Weber presents "passion, responsibility and proportion" as the three most important qualities of the good politician and then goes on to discuss the *ethos* of politics as a cause. He is quite rightly not interested in laboring on the question of responsibility with regard to the past; he is concerned more with responsibility towards the *future*. Though there is some value in trying to clarify whatever guilt there may be for the past, in establishing responsibility for a war or for war crimes, for example, this can become a sterile exercise and it could well keep the politician or the responsible citizen from looking to the future where action is to be taken.

But how are we to go about thinking for the future? There are those who think primarily in terms of principles, absolute ends to be achieved at all costs. These tend to ignore that "politics operates with very special means, namely, power backed by violence."[5] Politicians, on the other hand, operate in terms of these means and are more concerned with getting real results, with the precise effects their action is likely to have. If they are not men of principle in any way, they will be prepared for any kind of compromise. Even if they are men of principle, they will be inclined, not to sacrifice principle, but perhaps to interpret it in a different way than the absolutist might.

Rightly understood responsibility thus focuses neither just on the end to be achieved nor just on the means available for action, but on both at the same time and on the relation between the two. The absolutist can be irresponsible either by totally absenting himself from the political scene or by refusing to take into account the ambiguity and the danger inherent in any intervention in the interplay of power backed by violence. No purity of intention can ever totally exonerate the blunders perpetrated against people for the sake of some abstract ideal. On the other hand, however, the politician, whose concern is first of all the manipulation of power, can also be irresponsible by failing to reflect upon the quality of life that he is likely to bring about by his action and whether such a life might not be in direct contradiction to any ideal of the good life he might have. The truly responsible man is neither just an "absolutist" nor just a "politician" but both at the same time, and something more. "What is decisive is the trained relentlessness in viewing the realities of life, and the ability to face such realities and to measure up to them inwardly."[6]

Weber's own preference is not for an ethic of absolute ends nor an ethic of responsibility independently of one another. He is for both in different ways and at different times, as is clear from a passage well worth quoting at some length here:

"One cannot prescribe to anyone whether he should follow an ethic of absolute ends or an ethic of responsibility, or when the one and when the other. . . I am under the impression that in nine out of ten cases (of people who invoke principle and refuse responsibility for the consequences presumably due only to the stupidity or the immorality of others) I deal with windbags who do not fully realize what they take upon themselves but who intoxicate themselves with romantic sensations. From a human point of view this is not very interesting to me, nor does it move me profoundly. However, it is immensely moving when a *mature* man — no matter whether old or young in years — is aware of a responsibility for the consequences of his conduct and really feels such responsibility with heart and soul. He then acts by following an ethic of responsibility and somewhere he reaches the point where he says: 'Here I stand; I can do no other.' That is something genuinely human and moving."[7] The passage is worth pondering over, for it seems to characterize not just the man whose vocation is "politics," but any responsible man living in a democratic society.

It is not by mere accident that the idea of responsibility has emerged at the same time as modern democracy. The sense of responsibility is intimately linked with the experience of personal participation in government and the movements that shape society. It is a strange paradox that the possibility of this experience as we know it today has been due in no small part to the individualism of the seventeenth and eighteenth centuries. In earlier times there had been a strong sense of belonging to a society or a community, of being involved in one way or another, but the feeling was never very widespread that one had to participate actively in the shaping of this society. This seemed to belong only to a privileged few. Whatever one did, one understood it to be a part of the social order as a whole, and that's all there was to it. Even if one was not a fatalist, one did not think much on one's responsibility to change the order of things. Before this could become a matter of clear conscience, the individual somehow had to be emancipated. He somehow had to assert himself as free from the social conditions of his existence and then recognize his responsibility with regard to these conditions and the other individuals in society with him. The emergence of a general sense of responsibility was intimately connected with a revolutionary spirit that began to pervade society as a whole.

Understood properly, however, the sense of responsibility goes far beyond individualism. It is not just a return to the ancient sense of community and belonging, of the political as the locus for the ethical. The Age of Reason and Individualism has brought about a transformation of that ancient sense into something much more active for all concerned, not just those who are at the top of the hierarchy or the few who qualify as free men in the city while the masses remain more or less slaves.

What then is the essential meaning of responsibility? From the foregoing review of its emergence as an important category in moral reflection and behavior, it is clear that it is associated with the rise of the democratic spirit, but at the same time it is opposed to the individualism that has accompanied and continues to accompany this spirit in so-called bourgeois society. Responsibility is the moral category corresponding to the new kind of social awareness that has been developing since

14

the beginning of the nineteenth century. In his book on *Elements for a Social Ethic* Gibson Winter spontaneously brings responsibility into the center of his ethical style, which he calls "historical contextualism." "There are other understandings of responsibility within other ethical styles," but his own is the one that "fits historical contextualism."[8] The reference to "contextualism" may not be entirely felicitous by reason of the ambiguity that surrounds the term nowadays. But the meaning of Winter is clear: "Responsibility was, in this sense, the ethical corollary of man as a maker of history; placed in a world where he had to fashion his future, man identified himself as the one who was answerable for that future. The term was likewise the corollary of a democratic tradition in which men took responsibility for the decisions which affected their interests by participating in the making of those decisions."[9]

If we ask how it is that responsibility is the "ethical corollary of man as a maker of history," the moral category corresponding to our new social awareness, we shall have to return to what we have taken to be the essential characteristic of man's being, his historical consciousness. This consciousness has two sides: it is at once a consciousness that one is made by history and that one is a maker of history. The now, the moment of freedom which is hedged in by past and future, is the moment of responsibility which has to assume the past and proceed to the future. One does not choose to become responsible. One simply comes to an awareness, where one inevitably adopts an attitude, which no less inevitably has practical consequences. To refuse one's responsibility is to act irresponsibly and to be liable, responsible, for this act. Responsibility is at the pivot which unites future and past in a present of conscience because it is at the pivot between theoretical and practical reason. It is conscience itself taken in the concrete as a whole.

Understood in this way, responsibility is further open not only to many situations in one and the same historical context, but to any number of socio-cultural contexts. This does

15

not mean that one can belong to many contexts at the same time, at least not if we take "context" in the full sense of the term. It means that, from within one's own context, one can be in a position to assimilate and integrate what comes to one's awareness from another context. In other words, one can enter into dialogue with others, no matter how strange they may seem at first, and learn to form and enrich one's life better through this interchange. For, as McKeon writes, the enlarged concept of responsibility "provides, so far as theory is concerned, a way to discuss moral problems of individual action, political problems of common actions, and cultural problems of mutual understanding, without commitment to a single philosophy or to the expression of values traditional in a single culture, and thereby to diversify and deepen the values of men by exploring possible common bases and interrelation of philosophical assumptions and cultural traditions. It provides, so far as practice is concerned, a way to appreciate the history of the development and the present circumstances of responsibility as it emerges from application to material needs and individual interests to applications which advance the common good and build an understanding."[10]

Thus, no less personal than conscience itself, responsibility draws us out from our individuality into the broader understanding of others as well as ourselves and in this way opens us better to the universal and more radical principles of human action. This is why, when we speak of moral reasoning and the "norm of morality," we shall have to make ample room for dialogue, not just interdisciplinary but also intercultural.

In his book on *The Responsible Self* H. Richard Niebuhr has tried to set off his ethic of responsibility against two other ethical styles, the teleological and the deontological. The teleological starts off with man as a maker, *homo faber,* and is concerned with the *good* to be achieved. Its symbolism is that of technology. The deontological starts from man as a citizen, *homo politicus,* and is concerned with the *right* to be maintained. Its symbolism is that of politics. Each of these outlooks has its own peculiar difficulties: with regard to the first, we do not control the material of our decisions nor the future, and with regard to the second, we may be dealing only with a particular cultural symbol. An ethic of responsibility could cope with these difficulties with more success perhaps. Such an ethic starts from man as an answerer, *homo dialogicus,* and is concerned with what is *fitting* in human action. It works under the symbolism of interaction.

While this is an interesting presentation of the ethic of responsibility, the opposition with the other two styles of ethic may not be as pronounced as Niebuhr makes it out to be. Have we not seen that insistence on responsibility has emerged in conjunction with a new and more generalized awareness of man as politician? And is there not a way of insisting on rights and duties that is quite divorced from politics? Does not the connection between rights and citizenship exist more on an extrinsic and juridical level than on a genuinely internal and moral level? Furthermore, is not responsibility first defined in terms of the future and is not teleology precisely a category of the future?

There are many ways of slicing the pie of moral discourse and these questions bring out the complexity of any way we choose. One thing they do point up, it would seem, is that responsibility should not be conceived as being in opposition to the other styles, but rather as transcending them and reorganizing them in a new perspective. Responsibility is not indifferent to rights and duties, but it approaches these from the viewpoint of the whole of man in the whole of the world. Responsibility looks to the good, but not just to the good given in the present. It looks to the good of the future, to the future as the place for the good to be realized, for it recognizes a lot of imperfection and evil to be overcome in the present.

But most important of all, responsibiliy recognizes all this as a matter of interaction and in this Niebuhr saw quite exactly

17

what is of the essence. "The idea or pattern of responsibility, then, may summarily and abstractly be defined as the idea of an agent's action as response to an action upon him in accordance with his interpretation of the latter action and with his expectation of response to his response; and all of this is in a continuing community of agents."[11] This view of the moral life, as Niebuhr adds later on, "holds in the center of attention the fundamentally social character of selfhood."[12] It is not enough to speak of answerability *for* the future. We must also speak of answerability *to*. . . To what? To whom? If we follow Niebuhr, we will have to say, to the other selves who constitute a community with me.

We shall have to ask eventually who these other selves are in the concrete and this question could lead us down many different ways. Strictly speaking "answering" presupposes a call of some kind or other. One could think of this call only as something vague given in the world, but this would be to water down the idea of responsibility into something like the Stoic idea of duty, a response to the "call" of nature or of some world-spirit. Properly speaking one responds to the call of another, another self, another person with whom one has ties, even if it be only the tie of a common humanity that brings us together in history.

Ultimately the question of whom we are responsible to could lead to the question of God, not as the metaphysical law-giver but rather as the one who calls, the one who summons me from the future. But fundamental ethics is not the place to go into this theological question. We mention it here only as an open question, recognizing that a theologian like Bonhoeffer can well think of responsibility as the point of insertion for the call of God.[13] For us here it can also be the call of other men coming to meet us in our situation and summoning us to our historical task. There is, of course, no opposition between the call of God and the authentic call of other men. In fact, for a Christian the two become one and the same call in Christ. The question is always to discern what is the true call as well as just who is calling. This, however, cannot be done without a more precise understanding of the social order,[14] the objective correlative of responsibility.

III — *Social Order*

There are many ways of considering the social order. One is to reflect upon the nature of man to bring out his essential intersubjectivity. Another is to argue to the necessity of this order *a priori,* starting from the needs of man, his inclinations and his potentialities. Still another is to look for the principles of this order in its origins and its development. Here, however, it is not our purpose to do precisely any of these things. It is rather to reflect upon society as we experience it and perceive it historically. Our first concern in a fundamental ethic is with the fact, and in reflecting upon this fact we must follow the lead of the social sciences, whose first concern is to understand the various relationships, the different patterns of interaction between people.

What we have seen of responsibility, its emergence as a dominant moral category in conjunction with a heightened social awareness, its symbolism of interaction among selves in a community, already makes this clear. But if we go one step further, back to the very subject of our consideration, human action, we shall see it even more clearly. For society, as given in its actuality, is constituted in the concrete by praxis, by human action.[15] Human action is indeed the bond of society. It comes as man's second perfection, but this perfection does not come to be fully without reaching out to embrace somehow the whole of historical reality, the reality that sustains it as it presses down upon it, the reality that is to be lifted up and transformed by it. Human action is a function of the whole.[16] Historical consciousness is thus social consciousness by the mere fact of its being human, and this is the fact from which we start.

How, then, is this fact to be understood? To begin with, we

19

should distinguish two dimensions in the fact, two aspects, one external and the other internal. The first corresponds more or less to the realm of the social sciences, while the second has more to do with the realm of consciousness as such and the reponsibility proportionate to it, that is, the realm of ethics.

To be sure, the two cannot be properly conceived apart from one another. Human action is at once internal and external. Nor can one be seen as social while the other is considered merely as individual. This is a mistake we often make in the face of external social pressures, when we take refuge in our private consciences, not realizing that the internal dimension of human consciousness is no less social than the external. This is already clear from what we have seen of responsibility as a fundamental moral category. But it can also be seen from the new communitarian sense that is developing in the face of the powerful and often overwhelming structures of our technological society.

This new sense is not always clearly seen as communitarian. It is often expressed in terms of "respect for the individual," almost as if he were to be taken in isolation, set off against the mass of society. But the concern is not really with individuals as such. Rather it is with persons and with personal relationships. More and more, technological society seems to be crowding in on these relationships and the cry is for more room, *Lebensraum,* to live these personal relationships. More than rugged individualism, this new sense of community is looking for new ways, more personal ways, of being with others, reaching out to others, beyond the merely functional way of getting things done, whether this be in communes, hippie or otherwise, sensitivity grouping, or just plain mutual acceptance of one another in our daily living.

It is not for us to analyze the varying modalities of this phenomenon. It is enough for us to recognize its essential characteristic as both internal and social at the same time. This communitarian sense, of course, has its external dimension precisely in the different modalities it takes, the structures it assumes in opposition to the established and oppressive structures. But as an internal reality it transcends these structures, to which it is opposed or in which it expresses itself; it is free, at least relatively, not to separate itself from all structure, but to shape as well as be shaped by structures, in communion with others. True, genuine, personal communion, mediated by external structures, is the act most proper to this internal social realm. Whatever external or structural modalities it takes can only be means, more or less good, more or less effective, for this essential act.

We will have more to say of this act of communion when we speak of the common good. Here, however, let us attend more to the distinction between the internal and the external aspect of social reality. If it is understood that the two are essentially social and inseparable from one another, it should also be understood that they are irreducible to one another. They are found always in relative tension with one another, a dialectical tension which we shall call the *historical tension* of man's social being.

Perhaps the simplest way to bring out this tension will be to start from the social sciences, from what is accessible to them and from what is not. Undoubtedly, it is the whole of society that is the object of these sciences. There are not two social orders, one hidden away in some internal order and one manifest in external structures. There is only one which, internal as it may be, exists only in its external manifestation. Nevertheless, that internal aspect of society is not directly accessible to analysis by science or manipulation by management. The internal dimension of the social order is one of freedom and transcendence, which begins in recognition and personal respect and ends in love. No one will claim that such an internal reality, as internal, can be properly the subject of social anlysis. Those who make exhaustive claims for scientific analysis as such usually end up denying the reality of freedom and transcendence or separating anything like recognition, respect and love from the social order they intend to study. Such gratuitous claims, however, and the dualism consequent upon them, need not detain us here. In a sense it is futile to argue against such claims because the argument depends upon an experience, the experience precisely of freedom and transcendence in mutual acceptance and love. It is not that those who make such claims have no such experience; it is just that they refuse or fail to recognize in it anything relevant to their scientific activity. They are right, in the sense that science can deal directly only with the external aspect of the social order, where it becomes increasingly proficient and penetrating; but they are also wrong-headed in thinking that this external aspect exhausts the reality of the social order or in thinking that the internal aspect has nothing to do with the reality they are studying.

What the social sciences deal with, therefore, is only one aspect of social reality, an aspect that is in tension with another, a more internal and personal aspect. There is perhaps no greater manifestation of this tension than the malaise we feel in the presence of any mass society. But the tension, the distintion and unity, can be seen also by reflecting upon two different meanings of the term "community" and the connection between them.

In social science "community" (*Gemeinschaft*) is used to designate a special type of society, something more familiar and intimate, more spontaneous and natural, in opposition to "association" or "society" (*Gesellschaft*), which is often more complex and remote, more rational and calculated.[17] "Community" thus represents one extreme in a typological analysis, an ideal type opposed to another ideal type on the same analytical continuum. For the sociologist a "community" may seem less structured than an "association," less artificial and externally articulated, but it is still conceived only in terms of structure, in opposition to other structures. For example, in a "community" there is always a pecking order and an authority structure, though these are established and perdure in quite different ways than in "associations."

22

This use of the term "community" by the sociologist tends toward the more spontaneous use of the term based on a more immediate experience, the experience of community, whether primitive or more sophisticated. Yet, though it tends that way, it can never adequately cover the experience because, on the one hand it remains affected always by the abstraction of the scientific method, and on the other, the experience itself is always both more immediate and more transcendent than any analysis can be. Thus the experience of community says more than can be grasped by analysis, though this experience can be elucidated and even heightened by analysis, and the idea of community necessarily transcends the sociological category that goes by the same name.

Evidence for this can be found not just in the sort of spontaneous reaction often found in any society against mere analysis and manipulation, but also in the procedures of social science itself. First of all, while Tönnies, who first made extensive use of the *Gemeinschaft-Gesellschaft* typology, tended to think of the first, the more primitive one, as more human, another sociologist, Durkheim, who made a similar distinction, thought of the first as more mechanical, less free and hence less human, and of the second as more organic and hence more human.[18] Both, of course, can be perfectly correct, from different points of view. But the difference points up a certain distinction, a certain transcendence, of the order of human values with regard to social structures. These values can take shape in "communities" or in "associations," in either extreme, or better still in composition with different combinations of each extreme. It is really for the community, in the fundamental sense of the term, to find its own proper expression in appropriate social structures, whether communitarian or associational.

This brings us to a second consideration to bring out the transcendence of the idea of community with regard to the sociological category. From the viewpoint of mere typological analysis it is quite unthinkable that "community" should become "association" or that one should be valued more than the other. These are simply categories of structure, opposed but neutral in themselves, each with its own properties and functions, advantages and disadvantages. This is not to say that in the concrete a particular society cannot pass from one type to the other, or that one type might not be better suited to a people than another. But it is precisely here that the transcendence of lived community appears most clearly, inasmuch as it cannot be reduced to either one form or the other even while existing in either the one or the other.

It is entirely possible that one type of social structure may be more suited to one living community than another or that a community may pass from one type to another, from "community" to "association" or from "association" to "community," to elicit only extreme examples that would be difficult to find in their typological purity. But this very possibility depends upon the living reality of community that transcends any given structure, even the structure that has been given by the community itself. In other words, living community is not restricted to any type of structure. Tönnies characterized the ideal type, "community," in terms of nature and instinct as opposed to reason and calculation. But reason itself, as we shall see, is no less constitutive of community than nature and instinct, and genuine community can find its expression in an associational type of structure no less than in "community." This is why Durkheim could take a stand diametrically opposed to that of Tönnies in his evaluation of the different types. The apperance of reason does not mark the end of community. Indeed, through recognition, respect and eventually love, it raises it to a higher level, which may continue to express itself in the more natural kind of social structure, "community," or may find it necessary to devise new social structures for its purposes, "associations" rather than "communities."

We can speak here of progress in the development of social structures from *Gemeinschaft* to *Gesellschaft,* but we can also

24

see that such so-called progress, which would proceed in defiance of nature as expressed in "community" and in the absence of any real mutual acceptance of persons, any genuine, living community, could also become the worst of aberrations. This is precisely where the notion of historical tension comes in. The passage from one social structure to another can be viewed along a horizontal continuum, which may or may not entail real human progress. This cannot be judged on the basis of the horizontal dimension alone. There is need also of an internal dimension of community which appears as a sort of vertical dimension in the evolutionary continuum of structures, ever present in all of them, relativising them always in the here and now, and always transcending them, opening the way to revolution in social structures. Historical tension is this crossing of the two dimensions in the here and now of society.[19]

Given social structures are always a relic of the past, but at the same time they are an expression of a community on the way to being formed while being already formed in part. As such these structures have a certain dynamism within them, coming from the internal reality of community, urging any given society to transcend itself and possibly even to replace the old structures with totally new ones. Yet, on the other hand, no matter how transcending and revolutionary the spirit of community may be, it will always need to find expression in social structures, for it has no reality apart from *its* expression. History, the movement of man's social being, thus moves by the dialectical tension between these two dimensions, a tension that should not be reduced to mere opposition, as we shall see in speaking of the common good, but a tension that is creative only if it is seen as transcendence and not sheer destruction.

With this tension clearly in mind, then, how can we define society? Clearly, the first thing to be said is that it will have to be something personal. This has long been clear in the classical tradition of social philosophy, but it has been somewhat obscured by the rise of the new social sciences which, by

25

their methods as well as their results, have brought out the natural or the animal side of man, his subjection to a vast array of determinisms. The validity of these results is surely not to be denied, but they should not blind us to the fact that man remains more than a brute animal, that his historical existence transcends mere nature. Even Marx, who surely cannot be accused of unduly separating man from nature or minimizing the determinisms that constrain him, recognized this when he distinguished human labor, for him the primordial fact of history as such, from the activity of other animals such as ants and bees, who act in groups but not out of imagined or projected ideas.[20] Mere animals act out of mere continuity with their antecedents in nature. Man has the power of denying these antecedents and imagining new possibilities; he can create something new, which nature alone could not produce, that is, he can make history, and it is only at this level that society as such appears. Society is constituted by man's historical action.

In this social and historical order, however, nature is not abandoned or left behind. It is transformed and remains an existential of man's social being. Nature becomes qualitatively different — still subject to scientific analysis, but at the same time assumed into a higher, social order as it becomes properly historicized. This will become evident if we reflect upon the passage from the merely animal to the properly human, the passage from nature to history, which did not take place just once upon a time in a process of evolution but which takes place constantly in human existence.

This passage can best be seen in terms of the master/slave relationship. Aristotle, like most of his contemporaries, thought that some men were by nature free while others were by nature slaves; some had the function of reason in society while others had more the function of brute animals, beasts of burden, though slaves were more than mere animals because they were already capable of language, the first sign of human sociality. They were somehow intermediary between brute animality and reason. But this relationship was seen by Aristotle as more or less permanent, a function of nature itself.[21]

Hegel, however, came to conceive the relationship in a more dialectical and historical fashion, as a sort of beginning both of thought and of all social relations.[22] Man becomes man when, over and above all biological functioning, he begins to seek recognition, when he begins to value something more than life and is prepared to risk his life for that basic human dignity, recognition. He thus enters into a life and death struggle, the outcome of which can be death for himself or for his adversary or for both. In that case, nothing is accomplished, for there remains no one to be recognized or no one to recognize. Man has not yet apppeared historically.

But if in the struggle for recognition one of the opponents decides that it is better to live without recognition than to die for it, then the struggle gives way to a master/slave relationship. One of the protagonists begs for mercy and accepts enslavement as ransom for his life. The other, who was willing to risk his life to the end, accepts and so is constituted master by this act of recognition from the slave. Thus a first social bond is constituted along with a first sign of self-consciousness.

Little by little this relationship develops, for it is historical and dialectical, as the slave struggles with nature at the service of his master. In this struggle the master learns nothing — he only enjoys the fruits of the slave's labor; but because the master takes away from him the fruit of his labor, the slave begins to grow in reason by this forced detachment from the immediacy of nature and, as he begins to recognize the form he gives to nature as his own, he develops a new mastery over nature. This new mastery will in time be turned against the master himself, as the slave begins to demand recognition himself. But through this mediation of labor, beyond any mere struggle unto death, we see the emergence of reason and the fullness of recognition in the mutual recognition of human persons. Such recognition is not just given, like a thing of nature; it is worked out in a struggle between man and man and between man and nature.

This master/slave relationship does not give us the last word of social reality. There is also another dialectic at play in the constitution of a human community — a man/woman dialectic which is more closely related to language itself than to labor.[23] But the master/slave dialectic shows how man is both implicated with nature and transcends it in his social relations. The slave is the eventual bearer of reason because he has to struggle with nature; but he is the bearer of reason only because he is the one to overcome nature, while the master remains a child of nature.

This brings us to a second essential aspect of society. Besides being personal, or more exactly, because of this personal character, society also has to be conscious and deliberate. Here again there is not a sudden leap from nature to history, much less a leap out of nature. There is a passage from the one to the other. There are needs, forces of nature, that draw men together. But these alone, even if they are economic, are not enough to constitute society in the fullness of its historical reality. This requires man's own conscious and deliberate assumption of these needs in his project as maker of history. Out of his needs, and in tension with them, man imagines new possibilities for himself in his relationship with others and with nature. At first this may be just the originating act of the slave recognizing his master, but it also runs the gamut of creation all the way to the most sophisticated act of mutual recognition in a contract among equals. Here we find the historical tension we spoke of above taking the shape of a tension between the natural and the artificial, the spontaneous and the calculated, the necessary and the voluntary. But the tension is not just a stand-off between opposing polarities. It is a dialectical relationship opening the way to new social relations, both conscious and deliberate. Man enters into society as he begins to form his own projects in consort with others or, put another way, society in the concrete is constituted by a community of projects.[24]

The third essential aspect of society is closely connected with this idea of project. It is purposefulness. The child has to learn that he cannot always have immediate satisfaction for his desires. The slave is forced to renounce the enjoyment of the fruits of his labors. By this forced renunciation, however, both child and slave eventually learn to put off into the future some of their pleasures and ends and to work in the meantime in view of these ends. They develop a sense of purpose. This sense goes beyond mere recognition, the originating act of thought and society, but it is no less a part of social reality. Men may come together by chance or nature, but they do not stay together historically just by chance or nature. Social bonds are *created* with a purpose, in view of some idea or ideal which men formulate together, in view of a good they want to achieve together. Indeed, one wonders whether a man could ever form a project in his own mind apart from society, apart from others to draw him out of the immediacy of his nature and his pleasures. Human purposefulness seems to be essentially social and social being seems to be an essential part of man's purpose.

All of these three aspects of society, however, its personal aspect, its conscious and deliberate aspect and its purposeful aspect, have to do primarily with the internal dimension of social reality. We have tried to keep the relation to the external dimension of society clear as we reflected on them, but no definition of society would be complete without explicit reference to the external dimension, to the *structure* that lends a certain stability to the social order. Social purpose or purposeful sociality can be realized only in time. Man must be able to rely upon himself and upon others if he is going to realize any of his projects. This supposes a certain interior fidelity to the projects, but it also supposes certain ways of acting and doing things that come to be accepted and expected, certain external relationships that come to be established, informally at first but in time also formally, structures that need not and should not become static but that can serve as means for achieving projects and realizing community. These accepted ways, these expectations, are based on past experience, even if that be the outcome of a struggle, and though it may be felt that new social structures are called for at different times, it is always realized that something in the nature of structures will be required for the future. Only the anarchist, not the true revolutionary, would deny this. But the anarchist may simply be oblivious of man's social nature, let alone his social history.

There is, inherent in social structures, a tendency to become static, overly established, to solidify in their own right, so to to speak, independently of and even against their essential purpose. They become things in themselves, ends in themselves. But this is not in keeping with their true nature as an expression of community. It is like taking social structures outside of the historical tension in which alone they exist, something that may seem to succeed at times, but only for a time, since history eventually has its revenge. Social structures, by reason of their relation to the internal reality of community, have to be dynamic and ever expressive of the new community that is in the making through them. They are the essential *means* of history for bringing about man's fulfillment. They cannot take the place of the fidelity and personal reliability which are at their source and give them their true meaning, but neither can this fidelity and reliability exist historically, and hence in reality, without them. Without a spirit structures can only be alienating, but without structures a spirit can be little more than velleity.

Thus we see in what way the social order is the objective correlative of responsibility. It is not objective in an impersonal, inhuman way, though it can be viewed that way, abstractly, and it can become that in fact. It is objective in the sense that it draws the individual subject out beyond the privacy of his own self into the more universal realm of community and society. Responsibility appears in the historical tension between communion and social structure. It flows out of a sense of belonging with others, the communitarian sense, and is aimed at the social structures which serve as expression and means for community. To act responsibly is indeed to personally assume one's own role in the historical drama of the social order.

IV — *Levels of Mediation in Society*

In conclusion of this discussion of our starting point for a fundamental social ethic in responsibility and the social order it would be good to reflect briefly on the content of what is meant by the social order. So far our reflection has remained somewhat formal. What do we have in mind when we speak of the social order? Do we mean just one all-embracing system of relations or do we mean a multiplicity of more restricted systems? Are there many social orders or is there just one, with a diversity of subordinate systems? If there is diversity in the social order, what is the nature of this diversity?

There are many ways of studying social reality — economic, political, ethnological, cultural, sociological, ecological, etc. These can give rise to different ways of dividing the social order. But one division seems to deserve attention more than all others, the threefold division between the familial, the national and the international. This division appears in all other divisions as the most fundamental. Each of these particular orders seems to constitute an irreducible whole with its own specific dynamism, structures, relationships and exigencies that cannot be met except on their own level. They are sort of "natures" in the social order or, more exactly, they represent specific levels in the historical tension between the internal and the external levels which have to be recognized each in their own right and have

31

to be respected in any adequately conceived historical action. Each has its internal spirit and its diverse structures.

Not everyone will immediately agree that these are three essential levels of the social order. Some will argue that there were times when only one of them could be found, like the family in primitive times, or that there could be times in the future when only one or two of the others could be found, like the nation or the international society. It could be, therefore, according to this line of argument, that our threefold division is appropriate only for our present historical juncture and that it might not hold for other times.

This kind of argument, however, seems to say too much and too little at the same time. On the one hand, it seems to suppose there can be one and only one external form for the different levels of society we distinguish, the one we can observe in our present historical situation or have observed in the past, in other words, the one that is given or has been given. On the other hand, it fails to take into account the movement of history as a whole, the convergence of all the various forms of society at every level into these three essential levels. What we are suggesting is not that we have reached a definitive form of society on any level. On the contrary, we clearly have a long way to go on the internal level, while both the familial and the national levels remain open to significant variations in the future, especially as we approach a better international society. Rather what we would argue for is that a valid historical development of society cannot be adequately conceived without taking into account each of these three levels of society, not in separation from one another but still each with its specific exigencies. In other words, international society cannot be properly conceived without the mediation of the nation in some form or other — even if we change the vocabulary and speak of a universal society instead of an international society; nor can national society be properly conceived without the mediation of the family. Each of the three levels represents a permanent element of society, a sort of end in the social order, or more exactly a constitutive part of the end, each essentially open to and mediated by the other levels but irreducible to any of the others.

Earlier we spoke of the social order in general, almost univocal, terms. Here we see that social reality is indeed analogous. Just as it does not exist apart from the individual persons that constitute it by their interaction, so also it does not exist apart from particular orders. Taken in its genuine, historical sense, the social order is not a leveller of distinctions; it grows by mediation and integrates a rich diversity of structures as well as experiences. The social order is not something abstract: it does not leap to the absolutely universal from the isolated individual without intermediaries. It is neither more or less than an order of families and nations as well as of individual persons.

In its particular form this order is fairly well delineated, but in each of these it is open to the more universal forms, the forms of history as a whole. Between the different levels there runs an analogy of forms, so that in certain respects one can serve as a model for the other. Thus we speak of the "family of man" or "international authority." This helps to conceive what an international society might be. But the analogy should not obscure the differences. A family of nations is not a family in the ordinary sense of the term, nor can the authority for such a family be merely parental authority, or even political authority as we understand it at the level of nations. International society, with authority, will have to be something quite *sui generis*. But the interdependence of the three levels and the dialectical relationship between them enables us to go from one to the other and to enrich the one with the other while maintaining each in its specificity or particularity.

The idea that we might one day learn to do without familial or national structures seems simply utopic. History cannot be without mediation, without what has been called subsidiarity, to justify, not just the family and the nation, but also many other sorts of particular associations formed to meet particular needs at particular times. Human reason cannot grasp the universal and the particular, the whole and the part, in the concrete at one and the same time without the dialectical interplay of different realms of society. The specificity of each level calls for specific judgments and specific prognostication. The future is indeterminate. It is to be determined by man. This he can do only gradually and by careful consideration on all levels of human action and interaction. Such is the demand of prudence and responsibility.

CHAPTER II

THE GOOD OF HISTORY

If a concrete fundamental social ethic starts from the fact of our historical consciousness, it cannot be satisfied with mere recognition of the fact as given. Recognition of incompletion in the fact itself is part of the historical fact as such. Prudence, the concrete unity of theory and practice, is openness to the future. Responsibility, beyond mere imputability or accountability for the past, is first and foremost a surge to overcome the past in a future that will be man's making. Even the recognition that grounds social being at the same time as it brings man to self consciousness is not just a retrieval of the past or of nature: it is a radically new venture, an entrance into history charged with purposefulness. The social order is a striving for the good from the beginning.

Thus even from a scientific and analytical viewpoint, to consider historical consciousness only as a fact would be quite inadequate. It would be to stop short of something that is given in fact, though it transcends mere fact. But from an ethical and more synthetic viewpoint it would be doubly inadequate, for the mode of moral judgment must follow the mode of human action, which is to be purposive, and it must encompass experience as a whole. Hence, having begun to unpack the fact of human action, we must now turn to what constitutes it as human, to the question of justification in moral judgment.

This question is often represented in terms of a dichotomy between fact and value. But this may not be exactly the best way of raising the question. If a distinction is to be made between fact and value, it must not be made as if one could separate the one from the other. In historical reality everything is always

35

both fact and value at the same time. Separation of the two implies a certain formalism in moral judgment and no really fundamental social ethic can settle for such formalism. We must therefore reach back to the point where fact and value coalesce as one and the same reality.

This is not easy to do. It supposes a complete reversal of the natural attitude, which claims to deal only with facts. Instead of starting from the merely given, from nature and from the past, it means that we start from intentionality and from the future as well. We must learn to speak of facts in terms of value, and of values in terms of fact, without confusing the two and without reducing the difference which they imply. Knowledge of facts alone does not constitute a moral outlook, but no moral outlook can long withstand the rigors of history without a solid hold on the facts of life, of nature, and of whatever else comes into play in human action.

Hence it is that we turn to the common good — an old idea, but one which remains crucial in any evaluation of historical reality — to elucidate the ultimate ground of moral judgment as such and to mediate the turn, the reversal in perspective, which such judgment implies. The common good will serve as the pivot for this essential turn in any ethic. The ground of moral judgment is not exactly the same as the ground for a factual or a scientific judgment, though it includes such grounds; it is more an intentional ground. But inasmuch as moral judgment is truly an exercise of reason, it has to be grounded. What we hope to show is how precisely the common good is that ground. This essential reference to the common good is what takes moral judgment beyond passing circumstances and makes it something transcendent with regard to any particular historical situation.

This does not mean that the good we shall speak of here somehow hovers above history. On the contrary, what we wish is to reflect on the common good precisely as the proper good of history. It does mean, however, that with the idea of the common good we are drawn not only beyond the merely given as such but also beyond the particularity of that given, toward a universal that is concrete — not the concrete universal of an absolute spirit, but the concrete universal of genuine communion between men, the spirit (which is not a thing!) that draws men together in social reality.[1] When we speak of the *common* good, we mean precisely this universality of the good in which men find communion.

We shall proceed in four stages. First we shall try to enter into the idea of the common good as the first principle of justification in moral judgment. This supposes a proper understanding of that good, something which is by no means easy to find. Secondly we shall consider the dialectical nature of this good: how it comes into play as the ultimate horizon of meaning in human action and in the excercise of moral judgment. Thirdly we shall examine the kind of reasoning which this good calls for in the determination of its concrete historical exigencies. Finally we shall try to see what can be said about the meaning and the end of history starting from our actual understanding of the common good.

I — *The Idea of the Common Good*

Resistance to the idea of the common good as the ultimate norm for moral judgment can often be very strong. Apart from the intrinsic difficulty of the idea itself and the self-transcendence it implies, much of this resistance can come from a misconception of the common good. To open the way to a better understanding of the idea, therefore, let us begin by looking at the misconception.

This misconception consists primarily in setting up an opposition between common and personal good. It can stem from the rugged individualism that has characterized modern man. It can come also from a sense of frustration in the face of sheer bigness and complexity in modern society, which seems so unwieldy and indifferent to persons and their good. But ultimately it seems to depend on a totalitarian view of the common good, wherein the relation between part and whole is conceived in purely mechanical or natural fashion. The totalitarian view is prepared to sacrifice any good, any individual or any part of society, for the "good of the whole," but the good it speaks of is not truly the common good. It is only a partial good, a good opposed to that of other parts, not the really common good at all. It may be the good of a particular tyrant, the good of a segment of society, or even the good of society as a whole at a particular time in history, but it is not the good of history as a whole, a good that remains always open to higher and better forms, ready to integrate, rather than destroy, all personal goods.

Totalitarianism is based upon a false identification of the common good with no more than a particular good. It is precisely this false identification which leads to the opposition between the common good and the good of persons. In a dictatorship this is fairly easy to see, especially if the dictatorship is maintained for the individual aggrandizement of the dictator himself. The common good has been reduced to *his* good and the good of others cannot but come into opposition with such a good. But even when higher principles are invoked, whether cynically or sincerely, the totalitarian view always reduces the good of the whole to a particular conception, even in a so-called democratic society controlled by the few at the head of a party or by a massive public opinion. It is always only a particular, often static, view of the common good that is considered final and absolute. If other views cannot be reduced to that particular one, they cannot be brought into composition: they have to be eliminated purely and simply. There is no room for a higher view that would integrate really opposing views into a real common good.

It is unfortunate that much of the resistance to totalitarianism has failed to criticize this view as such. While insisting on personal values against the oppression of totalitarianism, it has accepted the view of the common good on which totalitarianism is based, that is, that of a radical opposition between common and personal good.[2] Thus, in rejecting totalitarianism, it has been led to reject the priority of the common good in the moral order, or at least to neglect and minimize it. Totalitarianism tries to implement an abstract idea of the common good without the concrete mediation of the persons who constitute society. But in the face of this, absolute personalism tends to erect another absolute, that of individuals as such, which is no less partial and abtract, because it fails to take into the account the relations that bind persons together in their very personality. Thus, the opposition between common and personal good is allowed to persist and the best antidote to totalitarianism, a proper understanding of the common good, is lost. It is this opposition which must be overcome by the development of a better and more positive view of the common good.

To be sure, there is opposition in society, a real opposition between real goods — yours and mine, for example — or between different parts of society. But this is an opposition between particular goods, not between particular goods and the common good as such. This opposition affects the common good, but this good will consist precisely in a composition between the particular goods caught in a certain competition between one another. We shall try to see later on how this takes place concretely in a dialectic of reason and of sensibility which is at the same time a dialogue between persons. For the moment, however, let us try to see how the undeniable opposition between particular goods can enter into composition as the common good.

How is this relation to be characterized? Opposition gives rise to tension and struggle between different values, the struggle of history. It is often difficult to say which of the goods in competition should prevail, but hopefully the struggle should not be unto death or the elimination of any real good that comes into question, at least not on the personal level. Instead, opposition should give way to a certain composition. This does not mean an end to all tension. In fact, it would seem that tension itself will be part of the common good. Rather it means a *participation* of all the particular goods in what is to be the common good.

The common good is not something pre-established, apart from this participation. It comes into being only through it. It will be most fully what it should be only to the extent that each part will have realized its own good through active participation in the good of all. The idea of part here is, of course, nothing merely mechanical or functional. It is more akin to the idea of taking part in political or common action, something quite personal that supposes liberty and creativity. But in connection with the idea of the common good as such, the idea of part and participation seems to go even further than just taking part in an action. It implies a certain identity between the good of the part and the good of the whole. The part finds its good only in common with others. This gives a certain universality to each of the parts, a certain finality for any personal good, but this universality and this finality are not something to be reckoned apart from that of others.

Instead of opposition, therefore, we shall speak of participation, in an effort to forestall any false absolutization of particular goods, against the common good, or conversely, of the common good against the good of persons. What we wish to speak of is the good of each and the good of all at one and the same time. This is what is properly called the common good, a good that is at once personal and communal, a good that is only in the process of being realized and cannot be reduced to any particular conception of it we may have now. This good may entail a certain transformation of particular goods, what could be called a "sacrifice" for the common good, on the condition that this sacrifice be properly understood and not just imposed extrinsically in the name of some abstraction, but it surely will not mean the elimination of the real good essential to persons. It will always be the most crucial problem to decide what this sacrifice will be in the concrete, what is to be sacrificed, and how, as well as by whom. But clearly such a sacrifice can never be the simple reduction of a real good. It will have to be a passage into a higher good, an assumption of the particular good into the common good, a beginning of real participation in the real good of all.

There is yet another way of speaking of the common good which can lead to misapprehension about the common good. This good is often defined in terms of law and authority. While this can have a certain justification, inasmuch as law and authority have a special function in providing for the common good, it can also lead to an undue restriction of the good in question. Without reducing this tendency to totalitarianism as such, as some might wish to do in modern society, we must still recognize that it does represent the common good only in terms of established society. From there it is only one step to totalitarianism; and it is often difficult to see how an exclusive preoccupation with "law and order" differs in practice from totalitarianism. There is, however, an important difference, in theory if not in practice. Law and authority can serve the common good. Totalitarianism cannot.

But the difficulty with defining the common good in terms of law and authority remains. It is, of course, easier to define the common good, which we have not fully experienced, in terms of an order we have already experienced. It may even be justified at a later point in the development of a social ethic, once the relation between law and the common good has been clarified. But this could not be justified at this point. Fundamentally, it is not law and authority that justify the common good. Quite the contrary, it is the common good that justifies law and authority, or even their opposite, revolution, when they prove deficient. Here we have to elaborate a notion of the common good independently of any established order, because all justification in the social order derives from the common good itself.

This is the way we have to proceed, if we are going to be completely logical in our reflection. But to do so is also to free the idea of the common good from any undue restriction coming from established society. Better still, it is to provide a better means to escape from these limitations as well as from all absolutism of a "law and order" mentality. Law and authority are in fact totally relative to the common good. The reason for their existence, as we shall see, lies in that they are means, necessary means perhaps, but still only means, to the common good. Thus, a properly conceived common good cannot be enslaved to any particular idea of "law and order." It transcends any such idea and should open the way to a new and better understanding of law and order as serving the community of men.

But even if these misapprehensions about the common good were overcome, it could still be thought that there is no need to bother with the idea. This, however, would constitute another misapprehension, which also has to be overcome. The common good is not just another idea which might help in the elaboration of an ethic, a ground among others for exercising moral judgment in history; it is an idea we cannot do without. It is a necessary idea for the liberation of man. To illustrate this necessity, let us reflect on the Marcusean critique of contemporary one-dimensional society.[3] This critique is opposed to reductionist thought; it is for a form of negative thinking, a capacity for dissent, that will allow us to break out of the limitations into which one-dimensional thought has trapped us. It calls for a transcendence of the social structures in which we find ourselves, in view of a better society. But it has no positive doctrine of the common good, and in the absence of such a doctrine it fails at the most crucial point of its criticism.

Thus, for example, Marcuse takes so-called positive thinking to task for settling into the accepted patterns of thought in ordinary language or in the given social systems, for analysing and clarifying these at great length, but for caring little about any radical criticism of the accepted system. The a priori of such thinking is found in a principle of verifiability concerned with nothing beyond the *fait accompli.* In place of this, Marcuse wants

42

to introduce a broader a priori that will take in the originality of history as such. "The range of verifiability in this sense grows in the course of history. Thus, the speculations about the Good Life, the Good Society, Permanent Peace obtain an increasingly realistic content." But the conclusion to which Marcuse comes appears disappointingly empty: "on technical grounds, the metaphysical tends to become physical."[4] We are left with a more historical form of reductionism, but nonetheless a reductionism. Technology does in fact transform history, the result of human initiative. But to say this tells us very little about how we are to deal with it in view of man's own good. Marcuse is reluctant to go further than his negative stance with regard to established, one-dimensional society, even while insisting on a need for historical transcendence, because he is afraid of verging into anything like an unhistorical metaphysics. But this fear stands in the way of his developing a real anthropology that might be more successful in escaping the trap of reductionism. This is why he leaves us with a very ambiguous stance in the face of the very thing which is the source of our problems as well as our power, technology. Our concern with the common good here is an attempt to deal with this ambiguity in a positive way. Without flowing over into any sort of theology or so-called unhistorical transcendence, we would like to develop the sort of anthropology that is necessary for realizing a genuine historical transcendence.

To focus our attention, let us say immediately what will be our essential proposition. The common good is to be viewed as the ultimate good sought in all human action, to the extent that every other good in the moral order can only be a participation in that good. This is to say that the entire social order which has come into question for us here falls under this good and is to be judged in terms of it. It is also to say that any human action, any moral judgment, that does not somehow reach the common good cannot be thought of as fully moral and that any action that excludes this good is essentially immoral.

This can only be a formal statement at this point. It needs to be given a content in the concrete. Our task is to see how we go about giving this content in the exercise of moral judgment, more immediately, with regard to the common good as such, and subsequently, with regard to the dialectics that derive from that good and lead back to it, so to speak.[5] To think of the common good is to think in anticipation of what, according to the expression of Marcuse, "grows only in the course of history."

How does such thinking of the good emerge in human life? It appears as a concern for the Good Life, whatever that may be, and it implies some form of transcendence, even if it be only an unwillingness to let the good already achieved be dissolved. I may not want much more than what I have right now, but I certainly do not want to let it go at that, because I run the risk of losing everything. Moral judgment, like human action, is a function of the whole given in experience. Life is seen not just in the here and now, not just under this or that aspect, but as a whole stretching into the future, unto death, the end that totalizes life.

In all that I do as a man I ask myself what sort of being I want to be in the end. I think of what I am to decide as a particular way of becoming what I want to be. When we speak of transcendence in connection with the moral order it is to this wholeness of life that we refer primarily, not some detached realm of formal Reason. It is transcendence with regard to particular acts that constitute a man's life in the flow of his existence. But this transcendence is also an integration of particular acts into a totality, a man's life. It is also transcendence with regard to particular orders that we abstract from life as a whole, such as the physical order, or the psychological order, or the sociological order, or even the moral order taken apart from the other orders, but which eventually have to be seen as part of one and the same whole with the moral order, an order of life and action which is the realm for the concrete exercise of moral judgment as such.

Here we see the importance of thinking in terms of participation rather than opposition. The transcendence implied in moral judgment cannot be properly understood apart from participation, for the moral order is not something apart from the particular orders that constitute experience as a whole. It is real only in that experience where man is decisive and creative. In his decision he assumes the various aspects of life into a totality that would not be without him. Transcendence refers to this act of totalization.

But the participation in question goes far beyond the life of just an individual. We see this, as a matter of fact, in the way each individual is influenced by others even in formulating his idea of the Good Life as well as in working out the details of that life. But more than that we have to see it also as a matter of principle, as a matter of fundamental conception of the good. The Good Life is not something to be thought of primarily in terms of individuals. Most fundamentally, it has to be thought of as the common life of all.

Individualism and utilitarianism here constitute the greatest obstacle to a proper conception of the common good. It is not that they have no thought for the social dimension of the good; it is just that this thought arrives too late and with too little. Utilitarianism, with its basic individualistic presupposition, starts with the idea of self-interest. At first such an interest may be naïvely selfish and fail even in its selfish interests. Little by little, as it faces up to the presence of others in the world, this self-interest becomes enlightened. This enlightened self-interest entails a certain "healthy" respect for others and their good, but that respect never goes as far as genuine *recognition* or acceptance of that good as part of its own good. The good of others always appears as something adventitious to its own good, something to be taken into account, but never part of the primordial interest.

In the utilitarian perspective, the social order thus appears always as something merely extrinsic to the real interests of man. Each man seeks his own good and, somehow or other, whether it be by some "invisible hand" or some pre-established "harmony of interests," both of which have long since stopped being credible as really operative in history,[6] still somehow or other all are supposed to find their good in the end. There is no thought of working out that common good from the beginning. Utilitarianism does try to take this social dimension of the good into consideration with its principle of "the greatest happiness for the greatest number," but it continues to think of individuals only in isolation and it gets lost in its calculations, largely quantitative, as to what constitutes the greatest happiness. Is it a large amount in a few individuals or is it a small amount in many?

What is at issue here is a complete reversal of this perspective, a recognition that such questions are not only futile but also based on a false supposition. The good is what is to be done — *bonum est faciendum*. This is the first principle of all moral reasoning. The good in question, however, is not the good of any individual in isolation, but the good of all, the good of men in community. Ignoring this, because of its individualist supposition, utilitarianism brings us to a dead end. No contrivance of "invisible hands" can extricate us from the impasse. In a sense there is no argument against individualism, apart from its own inadequacy even from a utilitarian viewpoint, for in the end it does fail to provide a norm for practical judgment. The only way to get beyond the difficulties it has raised is to recognize that we have to start on a completely different ground. It is as if dissatisfaction with utilitarianism as it has been understood, its own inability to bridge the gap between the good of each and the good of all, were a sign that what is first is not that utilitarianism as such has to be rejected, for the common good requires that we be eminently practical, but rather that we must find a higher form of utilitarianism. Individualism takes the partial good as a criterion and a measure for the whole. It attempts to escape its narrow individualistic outlook by adding up partial goods. But it fails to recuperate the wholeness of life which it left out of its consideration from the outset. Our task is to recuperate this wholeness which is more than just a sum and to restore it in its primordial unity. It is to recognize this wholeness as already realized in the world of our experience and as the starting point for moral reasoning. What is first is the whole. Analysis and utilitarian calculation appear only in a second order of consideration. To reverse this order is to take from moral reasoning its first and ultimate ground in the concrete.

We are not, of course, claiming that the first and only idea of the good will always be that of the common good. In fact, it is quite clear that the child's first idea of the good is quite self-centered. The child is the individualist par excellence and his self-interest can reach very high levels of enlightenment, especially when childhood is prolonged into advanced ages. The child, however, is called to be a man, not to remain a child. When this takes place, a new idea of the good begins to take shape for him. He finds that his action is not just his own, but that it is a communication with others. In spite of his self-centered interest, he finds that he is already communicating with others and that the good is really something bigger than just himself alone. This is what we call coming to the age of reason, coming to maturity, or more exactly coming to the age of responsibility. At first we think that the only thing which lies between us and our fulfillment is our own action. Eventually we discover the action of others, and others themselves, as they come into our purview, and only then do we learn that the fundamental good, that is, the good we were seeking from the start, is the good of communion.

What we are claiming, therefore, is that once this new vision of the good is reached in coming of age, the old vision simply has to be reversed. Though the latter may have been first in time, it ceases to be first in outlook once the properly moral sphere has been reached. One might say that individualism has to give way to communism, but the latter term might open the way to much misunderstanding as well as undue fears. Communism as a movement, international and otherwise, has been far from doing justice to the idea of the common good. With all its announced good intentions it has only managed to reduce it to a very restricted, not to say purely totalitarian, view of human liberation. It is better to avoid locking ourselves into any form of *ism* and try to keep the idea of the common good as open as possible. To give some concrete shape, however, let us say that the common good is that good which a man discovers in communion with others, whether that be in his family, in his neighborhood, in a gang, in a people, or whatever. These, of course, are not exclusive of one another in the common good. In fact, the more normal thing is to discover the different levels of the common good in a living symbiosis of different communities. The thing to note is that no particular community can embody the fullness of the common good by itself, even though any number of such communities can open the way to such a good, as long as they do not become closed in upon themselves. In doing so a particular community ends up closing the individual in upon himself, or upon itself, after having opened the way for him to a broader perspective. The second form of "self-interest" can be much worse than the first, because it benefits from reason and the combination of strength which have intervened between the first and the second.

Finally, in this first approximation to the common good, let us make a distinction between common good and common needs. One of the restrictions which the communist movement has imposed on the idea of the common good has been precisely to reduce it to a matter of needs and labor to satisfy these needs. This follows from Marx's conception of history as constituted only by human labor and production.[8] Such a conception collapses the ancient distinction between *praxis* and *poiesis*,[9] between human action and production, into one and the same thing and loses sight of the qualitative aspect of human life which transcends the mere satisfaction of needs. There are many ways of satisfying needs, but not all of them are considered fully human. Man is not satisfied just to eat, for example; there are amenities to be observed which are no less, if not more, important to him. Leisure, the basis of culture, as Josef Pieper argues,[10] is no less constitutive of history than labor. It cannot be just the good of a privileged few, but has to become the good of all, both as a means as well as an end. There is a certain need for leisure in historical existence, but leisure itself takes us beyond the realm of needs and represents a certain form of transcendence in the common good, the possibility of a person to be himself, not just a cog or a function in a social system. Unless this possibility is preserved and maintained, not individually but communally, any appeal to the common good will stunt man in the process of his liberation and thereby betray the common good itself. Even the good of communion can be perverted without this transcendent sense of leisure. Attempts to communicate become sticky and oppressive as manipulation and a subtle form of "communal" functionalism take over, allegedly to overcome the resistance of individuals, when it may well be that the supposed resistance is really a desire for leisure, not just to be left alone, but to enter into real communion with others.

With this transcendent sense of leisure we are brought to the broadest dimensions of the common good. When we speak of this universal good in terms of common needs to be satisfied, it is still possible to give the idea some immediate representation, complicated as that may be. But when we add to this, not a dimension, but a qualitative sense which cuts through every aspect of needs and their satisfaction and reaches to the internal aspect of persons in community as well as the external aspect of social structure, then no immediate representation is possible. How could we adequately imagine the quality of a life where the good of all would be assured? It is impossible to conceive such a Good Life apart from the historical tension which exists between the two aspects, internal and external, of social reality. This is why we must turn to the dialectical nature of the common good and the way in which it presents itself historically.

II — *Dialectic of the Common Good*

It is difficult for us to see the common good as identically our own personal good. For a Greek citizen of classical times, at least according to Hegel,[11] it was easier to do so. But even then the good in question was the good only of a particular city, like Athens or Sparta, or of a particular culture, like Greece, not the good of the world as a whole, which would have included what were then called the barbarians — outsiders to the Greek world. One could see his own good in the good of a well ordered city. One could even risk his very life in war for such a good.[12] But one had to leave the good of large segments of humanity, even the largest segments, out of consideration. For us such exclusion, for practical as well as for ideological reasons, has become unacceptable. Hence the problem of the common good has become quite different and vastly more complicated. The society to which we belong is now a global society. War itself, as a form of relation between nations and as a way of consolidating a national spirit, has come into question along with the economic and cultural relations that bind nations together. How can we identify our own good with a good of such universal dimensions? And how can we do this not just in the abstract, but in the concrete?

If we admit the primacy of the common good and if we recognize its universal dimension, we are faced with a serious dilemma. In the exercise of moral judgment the question is always to decide a concrete course of action here and now. The universal good, however, appears so remote and hence so abstract that it is of little or no use in determining what is to be done here and now. We cannot give it an immediate concrete form nor can we derive from it any concrete determinations for action in the present. Yet, if it is to have any effect in human action, as it must, it will have to come down to particulars. How can we bring it to this without abandoning its universality?

The dilemma is of the very essence of the common good. We cannot leave this good in its purely abstract form, but neither should we think of it as simply a state of affairs to be reached once and for all at some point in the future. Historical tension is part and parcel of the good. We must not, therefore, think of the common good as something static, even though it is the end of history. If we think of it as having exigencies in the present, we must think of it also as open to the future. As a historical reality it has to be dialectical. The question then is: how do we go about dealing with it as such?

Here Aristotle, always a close observer of how we go about forming judgments in the practical as well as in the speculative order, can be of help to us. In the *Nicomachean Ethics,* his propaedeutic to the real science of ethics, which is the *Politics,* he asks how we come to know the good in the exercise of moral judgment. At first, he says, we see it in rough outline and then, in time, we work out the details; for, as he adds, time seems to be a good discoverer and a good co-worker.[13] There is at the core of human action an idea of the good. This idea takes many and diverse shapes at different times. It is frequently reduced to one form or another, such as pleasure or riches or honor, but with experience and a critical interpretation of that experience we learn to distinguish between the idea in its most fundamental sense and its different forms. It becomes clear that the ultimate ideal, the good that inspired our action from the beginning, cannot be reduced to any of the particular shapes we experience. Each of our experiences has given us knowledge of some good, but the good itself which appears in a diversity of forms is understood as embracing and going beyond each and every one of them.

We have, therefore, a certain knowledge of the good from the beginning of our exercise of judgment. Otherwise, how could we ever come to recognize anything in experience as authentically good? How could we ever come to distinguish between true goods and false goods? But this is only an exercised knowledge, so to speak, not a formulated knowledge. It is only a first knowledge which is far from complete. It may give rise to heated discussions about the good as such, as it often does among young people, but if it lacks real experience it does not lead to fruit-ful discussion. This is why Aristotle was reluctant to discuss ethics with young people: it wasn't just that passion often stands in the way of rational discourse for them; it was also because an important dimension of the good was lacking in their understanding.[14] Our first knowledge of the good is quite universal, but it is also quite formal, still too detached from life. As such it remains confused. In spite of its seeming clarity, formal reason alone cannot take us out of this confusion. Only historical reason can, that is, reason with experience. Without experience our understanding of the good can only hover above reality, never penetrate it, and hence stops far short of a true understanding of real good. Hence, though we find a knowledge of the good in our first exercise of moral judgment, we need experience before we can more adequately discuss and reflect upon the true content of that knowledge. In short, we still have everything to learn about the good.

The good, therefore, is both known and unknown as it appears to us in history. To overcome this strange paradox of knowing and unknowing, a natural law ethic falls back on what is referred to as the metaphysical and ontological nature of man, the analysis of which is said to determine a set of specific ends to be achieved by man.[15] In other words, the "natural order" is seen as determining the "natural ends" of man. But one could wonder whether this is not too quickly said and done, and whether it goes far enough. Even if we add to the merely philosophical analysis of human nature a knowledge of man as given in the social sciences, is this enough to determine what is to be done in the concrete?

The good is what is to be done — *bonum est faciendum.* This will be realized only by human initiative. Though this initiative depends on the natural order as well as the social order, as these are given in the present, it also goes beyond them in the future. It is constitutive of a specifically historical order. The question is: how is the good of the historical order to be determined? There is no question of doubting the existence of a natural law or the validity of a certain knowledge of that law, though many who propose a natural law ethic today tend to exaggerate the import of that law or the extent of its knowledge. There are surely necessary conditions to be observed in seeking the good of history, conditions of nature, which can be known and should be studied in all the human sciences as well as in philosophical ethics. But these conditions, and the knowledge of them, as perfect as it might be, are not enough to specify the exigencies of the good in the concrete. To say this is not to repudiate all natural law ethic or to attach no importance to such an ethic. It is surely a part of moral judgment to take such an ethic, as far as it goes, into account. But this must be done by assuming it into a dialectical and hence more historical form of moral judgment.

Natural law ethics often presents itself as a continuation of Aristotelian ethics and as a means of overcoming mere historicism in moral reflection. One can wonder whether it is not more an offspring of Stoic ethics and whether it does not break down at the very crucial point of historicity. With all its presentation and articulation of principles based on nature, it leaves off precisely at the point where the good is still to be determined. It says nothing historically. It tries to make up for this lacuna in the practical order by developing a casuistry on the side, but this casuistry never quite manages to bridge the gap between itself and the principles of natural law. As concrete as it might seem in its discussion of cases, it remains abstract, because it fails to get down to the concrete here and now, which is always much more than just a case. Surely the good at this fine point of historical actuality is not to be left as something arbitrary, without reason. Yet a natural law ethic is incapable of assuring this passage to the concrete in accordance with reason. It has too short a view of reason. Thus it leaves us always with the final essential element unexamined, unreasoned. It cannot reach the concrete of real moral judgment.

How does this question appear in the light of historical actuality? If nature alone does not completely determine man's end, if the realization of this end truly depends on man's own initiative and creativity, how can it be known in advance so that it may serve as a light for moral judgment in the present? We cannot do as if we were already at the end, as if we knew it adequately. This is the pretension which gives rise to every form of totalitarianism. Even if our intentions were perfectly clear in our minds, always a highly questionable matter in human affairs, we would still have to think of the distance which separates us from the end, and how the ways between now and the end can vary infinitely. Who can presume to know in the present all the possible ways he might go in the future? Who would be willing to foreclose on his originality or that of others in this way? Indeed who can presume to anticipate the originality of others in their response to his own initiative? Who is to say that we have nothing to learn in the future from our common experience? Yet the common good is to result from this historical initiative of men. How can it serve as an ideal in the present?

Thus, if we cannot, as it were, take our stand at the end of history in weighing what is to be done, how are we to proceed? Are we left only with a natural law ethic to fall back on? Are we to abandon simply all ideas of starting from the good, the end, in moral reasoning, as many have done in modern times, arguing only from nature and eventually, as nature seemed to dissolve in their hands, giving in to scepticism and relativism? Or are we not rather to recognize that, while the good is not something arbitrary, it is still neither realized as such in the present nor set down in any determinate way? It is something to be realized by man and it will have to be imagined creatively. This is no resigned abandonment of reason in the determination of what is to be done. It is an insistence upon the true and highest function of reason, which is not so much to set down negative conditions for attaining the good, but rather to create the positive content of that good as well as the means to it. In this Promethean task reason must remain modest, but it must not fail to see the full extent of its responsibility. Even with the best of intentions man will never be able to fully anticipate what the good will consist in in the concrete. He will always have to learn. But he will not be able to learn except through his own undertaking, as a result of his own initiatives. This is especially evident in the realms of economic and technological development. But practice will come as a revelation only if man remains truly open to learning in every sense of the word, qualitatively as well as quantitatively, ready to overcome the simplistic inclination of wanting everything to be settled once and for all and having every possible contingency figured out before hand. Man must be prepared to hand himself over, as it were, to experince, even to others in this experience, in order more completely to discover what is his own good.

In terms of moral reasoning, what this means is that man still starts from a consideration or a vision of the end in determining what is to be done, but at the same time he recognizes that his understanding of the end is always inadequate, never determinate enough to allow a simple, formal deduction. Further determination has to be sought in experience by a return to the present and even a reflection on the past. This is where a consideration of natural law and of other facts and laws known in the social sciences comes in — not as a first principle, but as a complement to man's primordial intentionality toward the end. Thus, though it is not first, the natural order retains an irreducible role to play in moral reasoning: it comes as a means for filling out some of the picture of what man only dimly sees of this end, a means of working out real possibilities for the future. The same would have to be said of the results of the social sciences, which give us a more complete and sophisticated knowledge of human nature in its social reality and afford a better means of prediction for the future, without however giving us the last word at any time, since man always remains free and creative with respect even to his own creations.

Yet even in this return to the present there is something which escapes both natural law and social science. As we saw earlier in discussing the internal aspect of the social order,[16] there is something that remains inaccessible to this sort of reflective analysis. There is the good of communion, a good already realized which at the same time is also constitutive of the final good as such, whose reality is unto the end. This is, so to speak, a presence of the end as such, though that end is still to be actualized fully. Thus, knowledge of the good is not just an intention, a project for the future, known only in outline, typically or figuratively. It is something already experienced in community, the beginning and the condition of our coming to maturity and to freedom here and now. It is just such an experience of the final good that enables us to transcend our historical situation, adopt a critical stance toward it, and seek to go beyond it, not arbitrarily or blindly, but with a real knowledge of the higher good to be sought.

With this intimate knowledge based on community, we have come to the dialectical core of the common good. The presence of the end in the present is not just the presence of a given as such. The end as such is not given — it is intended. Yet it is *really* present and its effect can be felt: it is what makes us dissatisfied with the merely given or the merely present. The good is something that *is* and that still has to be at the same time. It is only in function of a vision of the good that we can truly discern the evil of our time. It is only with the same vision that we can come to a genuine remedy for these evils. It is the good that gives rise to the historical tension of society we spoke of earlier more than anything else.

An old adage spoke of this tension, but it has not always been understood dialectically. *Quod prius est in intentione posterius est in executione.* Understood in a purely linear fashion, this could mean simply that what is first in intention comes last in execution; and it could be turned around, as is often done in Aristotelian philosophy, so that it also means, what appears last in the order of execution was first in the order of intention. But there is also an historical reading of the adage which is not linear. Intention and execution cannot be simply stretched out

56

on a continuum of duration. They are intimately bound together in the *now* of liberty. They are in a dialectical polarity which makes them flow into one another without confusion but with a priority of each that is irreducible in their very unity and distinction. Real intentions are discovered only in the execution of them. Execution thus transforms the order of intention. But on the other hand we cannot judge what we have done except in the terms of our intentions. Intentions shed light on the order of execution. Existentially speaking, intentions come first even in an order of execution. This is why we still have to discover what they really mean in practice itself. Our intentions are subject to the historical limitations in which they are formulated. This is why our actions always take us beyond where we intended to go, for better and for worse. But human existence is not just brute facticity. If we learn from experience, if the order of execution really brings something new to our knowledge of the good, it is because intentionality actively penetrates it from the beginning to the end. It is because our intentions are irreducible to what we have done that we adopt a critical stance with regard to it. Somehow or other our intentions always remain ahead of our execution. Beyond a linear interpretation, the adage thus expresses a certain dialectical circularity between intention and execution, where we find now one, now the other in advance of the other, as we draw closer to the final good. The common good would be the perfect coincidence between execution and intention, a realization of the highest intention which would totally adequate that intention. This, however, remains an ideal difficult for us even to conceive, let alone execute.

Nevertheless, with this dialectical aspect of the good, we are in a position to deal with our original dilemma concerning what precisely is the common good and how it affects the concrete determination of what is to be done here and now. The common good does not appear immediately in its universal form. It appears only in the dialectical interplay between intention and execution. Concretely it appears through the mediation of more immediate communities where our intentions

57

and our actions are mixed and bound up with those of others.[17] These communities have their own good which, in comparison to the universal good are particular, but which are genuine forms of the common good with regard to the individual. Long before man comes to think explicitly of the universal common good, he has experienced different forms of the good in common with others, first in more restricted circles like the family or the tribe, but also in ever broadening circles like the city or the state.

We could think not only of our childhood but also of the whole of past history as having constituted this sort of mediation, much as Hegel did. He thought of the French Revolution as the moment when man finally broke out into the universal dimension of liberty and the good in the Declaration of the Rights of Man.[18] But we would have to remember that this past experience is not something to be left behind. The experience of communion in the family or the tribe, for example, on which we relied so much to articulate a positive notion of the common good in its internal aspect, must continue to enlighten our thinking on the common good, even though it will have to be transformed. So too will our experience of the nation which drew us beyond the narrow pale of family or tribe.

Nineteenth century liberalism failed to recognize this need for mediation, a failure that has led to grave consequences. On the one hand it affirmed the "rights of man" in order to protect the individual against the incursion of the community or the state. But on the other hand it affirmed these rights on the basis of an abstract understanding of man. Over against the good of any particular society it proclaimed the good of individuals on the ground of universal and inalienable rights, duties and obligations. Thus it was appealing to the *community of the good,* above and beyond the *good of any particular community,* to justify the rights of every man. But the tension between good of community and the community of the good went unnoticed for the most part until it erupted into an opposition of ideologies in the twentieth century, that between Nazism and and Communism.[19]

Nazism opted for one pole, the good of community as found in the state and the "master race." Communism opted for the opposite pole, the community of the good to be realized in society as a whole. The aberration on both sides came from the exclusive attempt of each to foster one pole at the expense of the other. Nazism recognized only the particular good of a state and was prepared to sacrifice every other good and right to that good. Communism sought the higher good of universal society, but did so without giving due consideration to the mediating goods of particular societies as well as of individuals. In either case the dialectical relation between the good of community and the community of the good was ignored.

The reason for an oversight of such grave consequences goes back to liberalism itself and its failure to develop the higher viewpoint necessary to keep these two dimensions of the good in proper relation. Beyond the good of community and the community of the good as expressed in the Declaration of the Rights of Man there is the *good of communion* which permeates every level of the good, both personal and communal, individual as well as societal, and maintains the various dimensions of the good in dialectical tension. There was an intimation of that good in the idea of fraternity found in the motto of the French Revolution, but the idea, especially in its universal aspect, got lost in the laissez-faire attitude of liberal society. Fraternity remained an abstraction as far as most men were concerned, as did also liberty and equality; it did not become a vital part of the good to be sought in common by all. Had it become such, the opposition between the different goods of the individual, of the nation and of universal society might not have seemed so irreducible.

Marx tried to break out of the liberal perspective, but he remained a child of liberalism in too many ways. While criticizing the partiality of bourgeois society in view of driving toward a

59

genuinely universal good for mankind, he did not sufficiently attend to the need for a new vision of the common good. Granted the extreme difficulty of working out such a vision for historical consciousness, still, if we are going to transcend the actual limitations of any social system, something more than vague and ultimately abstract references to what true "communism" should be is necessary.[20] Marx got lost in his opposition to nineteenth century bourgeois society and, though he had much to say about overcoming the limitations of that society, he failed to articulate the dimension of the good implied in his idea of communism. For him, as for others, the idea of universal brotherhood remained too vague to become operative in any concrete exercise of moral judgment. The Good Life was put off to some indeterminate time in the future, while he concentrated on the contradictions and the alienation of the present society, to exacerbate them, in view of a universal revolution that was no less abstract and remote from real people in their historical situation.

How, then, is this higher good of universal communion to be understood, not just theoretically but also practically? By itself it seems both inconceivable and unattainable. We have seen how the idea emerges from experience in the ever broadening circles of the family, the city, the nation, until it reaches the universal dimensions of man. But it is not just an idea that emerges; it is also a real experience that becomes the ground for a further step at every instant. It is this experience that Marx failed to take into account in his critique of bourgeois society — the experience of communion that begins in the act of recognition and acceptance.

Our first experience of communion is very restricted; it is limited to a few individuals. But it is an experience that seeks to transcend its limitations. True communion is something that goes out to any person, to all persons as we encounter them. As I come to recognize others in ever broadening circles, I am thus drawn into new relationships. This expansion of the experience, however, does not take place in a straight line unmarked by the social circles in which I find myself. It takes place dialectically as I discover the good of particular communities in tension with the community of the good and as I discover this universal good in its tension with the particular goods of persons and particular associations.

All of this is based and finds its spring in the good of communion experienced in this tension. From that experience of a good that is actual, a presence of the end here and now, there arises the awareness of limitations in our present relationships and the capacity to criticize them fruitfully. From that experience also comes the discovery of new and real possibilities for the future, the ability to be truly radical, and not just destructive, in overcoming the obstacles to the universal brotherhood of man.

What in effect we have to do with here is a level of dialectic which can no longer be represented by the master/slave relationship as seen by Hegel and Marx. Taken by itself this dialectic leaves us only with the "liberal" ideology and a basic shortcoming concerning the common good, or else it opens the way to those two bastard sons of liberalism, Nazism and Communism. The master/slave dialectic, which starts in a life-and-death struggle, must be complemented by a higher form of dialectic, a man/woman dialectic, which entails recognition at a new and deeper level than in the master/slave relationship and opens the way to a deeper acceptance, a loving acceptance of others. It goes further than the life-and-death struggle and touches man even more intimately than the risk involved in that struggle; it involves the risk of accepting the good as the good of others as well as my own, of recognizing the good as communion among many.[21]

This dialectic does not replace the master/slave, which remains an essential aspect of historical existence and gives rise to relations of subordination in social structures. Rather it gives rise to other relations no less necessary in the constitution of society, relations of communication. Without the latter, the former would be intolerable in the long run. Thus the two dialectics complement one another in the relations between man and man and between man and nature, for the man/woman dialectic is rooted no less in man's unity with nature than the master /slave dialectic. In fact, it expresses this unity more perfectly, for the difference of the sexes is both natural and human at the same time. As Marx himself wrote, "in this *natural* species-relationship man's relation to nature is directly his relation to man, and his relation to man is directly his relation to nature, to his natural function."[22] But Marx failed to draw the consequences of this insight for his view of history. He continued to conceive history only in terms of a struggle unto death, whereas this loving struggle, if it is not once again reduced to a master/slave relationship, brings into play at the most fundamental level of human relationships, a desire of communion which is at work already in every act of recognition. Thus it introduces into historical existence a sense of the good which transcends and assumes all other goods, the good of communion. The dialectic of social existence is, thus, not just a confrontation, but a dialogue, an effort at communication, that is already an anticipation of the end inasmuch as it supposes, as well as advances, mutual acceptance in mutual recognition.

III — *Dialectic of Ends and Means*

With this idea of the common good we are led to a new and a more complete view of the prudence and responsibility we saw earlier, a view that is at once more positive and more dialectical, for if the good is what is to be done, and if what is to be done is for the communion of all men, then prudence will consist primarily in providing, as the term prudence itself suggests, for such a good, and responsibility will find in each situation a call to provide what one can.

We made no attempt earlier to explore the teleology of historical man or to specify the ideal toward which he is striving.[23] We were concerned more with the fact of historical consciousness and how prudence, responsibility and the social order arise as part of that fact.[24] Now, however, with the idea of the common good as the radical principle of moral judgment we see

62

quite definitely how the fact is informed by a teleology — not a linear teleology proper only to natural processes, but rather a historical teleology to be worked out through man's free initiative in his struggle with himself as well as with nature.

Such a teleology can only be termed dialectical. It gives rise to a dialectical use of reason in the exercise of moral judgment. The rational element of responsibility, as we saw,[25] has to do with the relationship between means and ends and their mutual implication in what we do. This implication cannot be static, nor merely formal. It has to be dynamic and living, with its axis in the good of history.

Here a twofold pitfall has to be guarded against, that of formalism and that of pragmatism. The Kantian idea of morality, in separating pure reason from prudence, has led us to think of the ethical as essentially outside the phenomenal order, uninvolved and unhistorical. Few people can be satisfied with this sort of dualism today, but it is not clear whether we have escaped from it sufficiently. The ideal of existentialism, or personalism, for example, often seems evasive, even angelic at times, when it comes to coping with the real complexities of our technological life. It only tries to escape from the burden of that life. On the other hand, pragmatism, whether American or Marxist, seems to be no less formalistic in its idea of morality. It is prepared to forego the language of ethics and it is satisfied to adopt purely and simply, the language of "science" and its determinisms, as if that could afford an adequate expression of human life as such. Opposed as they might seem, these two ideologies share very much in the same kind of capitulation of the moral before the pragmatic, or in the same kind of separation between the two.

Our point, however, is not to defend the moral against the pragmatic, if this means trying to restore a formalistic idea of morality. We have already insisted on the transcendent aspect of the moral order and we have tried to show how this is to be understood as part of historical reality itself.[26] Our point is rather to restore the dialectical unity between the immanent and the transcendent, between fact and value, which have been separated by both formalism and pragmatism.

Formalism fails to take historical man seriously, especially in his relation to nature, positing as it does a kind of special "nature" for man based on pure reason and abstract liberty. But man does not find his moral outlook ready-made; it is never given immediately. He has to grow into it both personally and communally. He has to develop it himself.

Pragmatism, on the other hand, tends to remain shortsighted and partial by restricting itself to one or the other abstract discipline or to a whole set of them. The ethical character of life, which consists in a sense of wholeness, has to be part of any human project, but the pragmatist frequently ignores this quality in making his plans for the future. His planning is based on an analysis of what the past has given, as if the wholeness were already established and not something to be created by man. Real creativity in social science and social planning is contingent on an authentic moral sense of life. This was the case with great social scientists like Marx or even Weber, and it can be seen at work in the development of all new theories that are socially productive. Great innovators in social science have always been moralists of a high order, though they have not always acknowledged this explicitly because of a false and formalistic idea of morality. Technocrats as such can furnish only part of any project for human *praxis* — the plan. The rest, the most important part, the quality of life implied in the plan, whether it be humanizing or brutalizing, sensitive or ruthless, comes from the man as such. Hopefully, history will be a composition of the two aspects of man, quantitative and qualitative, and not a separation.

There are both formal and pragmatic elements in every moral judgment. Ethical reflection is necessary to criticize the data and projections of science. Any model for human action entails value implications; these cannot go unexamined. The adequacy of a model must be measured, not just in terms of specific problems to be solved in our everyday world, but also in terms of our lived experience of the world as a whole. At the same time, however, science cannot ignore ethics or prescind from it; it must be critical of ethics, as Weber himself was, for example, to mention only one who was most anxious to keep science on an "objective" plane. Science must be willing to criticize ethics in terms of the regularities it has discovered in human *praxis*, the "laws" of human action, for this is the only way to focus on real possibilities for the future and avoid certain disaster from a too naïve conception of ideals. Both the ethical and the scientific thus intersect in the actual exercise of moral judgment, for better and for worse. In this historical now where we find ourselves, we assume a certain critical stance with regard to ourselves and our world as we look to the future in prospection of what we are to be.[27]

How, then, does dialectical reason come to the fore in this intersection of ethical and scientific thinking? It appears first as negativity, a "power of negative thinking," as Marcuse calls it.[28] Recognizing the inadequacies of the given order, it seeks to break out of these limitations. It refuses to accept the established order as the end, but sees it only as a means. It has to struggle against that order because establishment always resists the relativization that reason wants to cast upon it.

But reason is not merely negative thinking. If it were, it would derive its meaning and its content only from the establishment and, ultimately, it would be reducible to the very order it repudiates. The content of negation as such is derived from its object. Repudiation is not for its own sake, but for a greater good. Reason contains a positive orientation toward the good; and through this orientation, which is already, though only, a beginning of vision, it becomes anticipation based upon, and in dialectical interplay with, an actual experience of the good that is in the making, and hence already made in part, a good that must be fostered by overcoming present obstacles to its fulfillment. The good of the present is thus seen both as a presence of, and as a means to, the End, as a point of arrival and as a point of departure for the greater Good.

Dialectical reason also appears as calculation, a weighing of the good that is expected to come from a course of action against probabilities and consequences. But care must be taken about the kind of calculation that is called for. It is not enough to assert a principle of love on the one hand, as some theologians do, and a need for utilitarian calculation on the other,[29] without at the same time showing how the two are one in the actual exercise of moral judgment, without showing how the love has to inform the calculation and how the calculation has to specify the love quite concretely. Much less is it enough to calculate merely in quantitative terms; the good cannot be measured in such terms, though it is not independent of such measurement. The quality of the means we choose will affect the end we seek more than anything that can be numbered or amassed quantitatively, for the common good is not to be a reduction to the lowest common denominator. Reason's role is to highten the quality of life for all, not to lower it. The utilitarians who would object to this would still be measuring well-being too much in quantitative terms, whereas the good of communion is literally immeasurable and transcends all quantitative calculation.

Moral calculation thus entails an element of value judgment, since there are more than material forces that come into play. The anticipating vision of the good here and now makes the end really present, though not given, and that presence transforms the judgment we make on what is to be done, from the interior. The good is not something we can put off to some future date while we calculate the means for realizing its conditions here and now; it is something we begin to do right now in the very act of calculating what is to be done. This is why the quality of the means we choose is not less, but more important than the quantity.

Let us see, with the help of four basic propositions on the relation between means and ends in historical reality, how this works out in the concrete.

First, the end has priority in any exercise of moral judgment.

It is the end that defines any order of movement. It is the end that totalizes human action, makes a whole of it, a life, either by prospection or by reflection, depending on whether one is looking forward or backward. All subordinate orders of life are themselves defined by subordinate ends.

The end, therefore, is chosen first, but not absolutely, because it is not known determinately enough, especially when the ultimate good is at issue. Thus, though formally speaking the end is the absolute reference point in the exercise of judgment, its content is not known absolutely; and, since the content does affect the form, the decision on the end cannot be taken absolutely by historical reason.[30] There is a certain irreducibility of the present for us, even in the thought of the end, and hence an irreducibility of the means to be found.

Secondly, the means as such are totally relative to the end. They have a reality of their own, a nature and an activity proper to themselves, even a finality of their own, with a certain autonomy. Hence they cannot be absolutely relativized. They have exigencies which must be recognized. Yet as means they are strictly relative to the end and derive their meaning, their value, from that end. Their reality is assumed into the order defined by the end through a participation that allows for and even requires whatever autonomy is proper to them in their own order of reality. The order of the end grounds the very existence of the means as such in its ulterior reality.

Thirdly, it is from this grounding in the end that a sense of obligation and justification arises in historical consciousness. Obligation is not just a push from conscience, a categorical imperative. In the concrete, and with reference to what is to be done, it is a necessity that arises from reasoning as well — *ex suppositione finis,* from a sense of the end to be realized. Particular choices are made and are justified only in view of an end. There may be some who seem unconcerned with the justification of their action, but anyone who gives it thought will see that the question arises only because it takes an end to justify a means. Even when we say that an action has its own justification, this remains true because, formally at least, we are thinking of the action as an end in itself no less than as a means. To think of moral justification in any sense one has to distinguish between means and end, and the reason why most men are concerned with justifying their action is that they do make the distinction *in actu exercito,* if *not in actu signato,* between the end, the good which they seek, and the means they choose in view of that end. Choice is primarily concerned with means to an end.

If it is understood properly, this third proposition raises serious difficulties with regard to the idea of *intrinsically* good or evil acts. The idea of intrinsic good or evil is well grounded, if we admit the reality of means with their own nature and their own exigencies; and there seems to be no good reason for denying this, unless we are going to be total skeptics with regard to all human science. But all this is true only in the abstract. In the concrete we have to do with the whole, which is defined by the end. The good or evil, then, of any particular action cannot be determined apart from the end, no matter what it may be "in itself." Indeed, no human action can be "in itself." It is always a function of the whole. It can be judged only in function of the whole. This, of course, does not come as a brand new revelation, but it does suggest that the question of intrinsically good or evil acts might be a false starting point for the moral consideration of any act. Such a question should come in only in the second moment of reflection when we are concerned with the real possibilities in the present in view of our end, for that is where the intrinsic exigencies of the means comes into play and that is where their validity as good or as evil has to be judged. In short, the end can *never* be a *secondary* consideration in deciding whether an act is right or wrong in the concrete; the end has to come first and every other consideration, necessary and indispensable as it may be, has to be done with reference to the end. The error connected with the idea of intrinsically good or evil acts consists in wanting to reverse this order of moral judgment. It stems from a confusion between the abstract and the concrete in the exercise of that judgment.

Our insistence on the priority of the end, however, should not lead us into the error of what Weber called the ethic of absolute ends.[31] It is knowledge of the end, the good we seek, that enables us to judge, as far as we can, whether a particular act is good or evil. But our knowledge of the end is never so perfect that it allows us to judge without a good look at consequences, as these can be imagined from past experience and nature itself. Consequences do not take precedence over the end, but they do give us a better understanding of means and real possibilities toward the end and, in this way, open up for us a better insight into the end itself.

This brings us to the fourth and last of our basic propositions on the end/means relationship in historical reality: *there has to be a dialectical reciprocity of means and ends in the concrete exercise of moral judgment.* In other words, every human good within history is in a sense an end and at the same time a means for the Good Life. As an end it is final in its reality and cannot be rightly sacrificed to anything else. As a means, however, it is not final, but rather open to a greater good which calls for sacrifice, not of the good, but of the limitations and the partiality we cling to in the good.

Thus, as Kant saw rightly, I am an end unto myself and you are an end unto yourself. And yet, in my historical actuality, as Kant failed to see sufficiently, I am also a means for what I am to be and even for what you are to be; and in your historical actuality you are also a means for what you are to be and even for what I am to be. I cannot simply use you as a thing, nor can you use me as a thing. But we both have to use the present, our mutual presence to one another, as a way into the future, into liberation and the free development of all men. For historical reason, means and ends are not mutually self-enclosed realities opposed to one another; in their irreducible distinction and their irreversible relationship, they

69

interpenetrate in a sort of cycloidal movement where now one, now the other, seems to take precedence in a growing unification of the two.[32]

To put all of this in the terms of our main concern here, we could say that the common good is made up of the end of human life, the order defined by that end, and all the things that constitute that order, the means along with the ends. That is why the means as well as the end can be spoken of as *really* good.

To distinguish between ends and means, we could say that everything which pertains properly to the personal good of men belongs to the common good as *end*. This includes such things as human dignity, personal integrity, fulfillment, and last but not least, communion. The aim of history is the achievement of these ends for all. It should be noted, however, that some of the ends are already attained in part, at least for some. Hence the end is already realized as something not to be overlooked or sacrificed to any abstract plan for the future. But the end can only be partially realized in the now of liberty and hence becomes an opening, a springboard, a means toward greater liberation for more people through the sacrifice of its partiality — a real sacrifice, because our good is *really only* partial and as such must be given up if we are to enter into greater freedom and greater fulfillment.

At the same time, however, we must add immediately that anything which is necessary for or conducive to the greater personal good of all also belongs to the common good as *means*. This will include such things as the necessities of life and health, education, economic well-being, and real political power. The *necessity* of these things, based on the very nature of social reality, is the ground of their very goodness, which in history is never merely arbitrary. Hence the historical tension we find between liberty and necessity — liberty is never merely given; it is always something still to be achieved through the mediation of social reality. History does not stop: man has to choose; he has to use what is given or be used as a given, or rather he

70

has to accept both as a way toward fulfillment. The end is present in his historical actuality in the good he finds among persons, but the dignity, the integrity, the fulfillment, the communion he experiences is not final. Between the present good and its final realization the whole cosmos must be brought in as a means toward that end, disorder must be overcome and partiality must give way to communication from one end to the other.

IV — *The Meaning of History*

This by no means gives us a complete idea of the common good as the good of history, but it is not the task of our fundamental ethic at this point to elaborate in greater detail on it. Further on, other elements of it will be brought in, in conjunction with justice and friendship, yet in the last analysis it is for history itself, and the concrete exercise of moral judgment, to fill out the picture as well as it can at the various points along the way.

As a conclusion to this reflection on the common good, however, let us see what light it can shed on the meaning of history — a meaning that can be found only in terms of the end. To do this we do not need a completed view of the end, something that is radically impossible from within history; the form and the structure of the common good, along with what content we have been able to suggest up to this point, will be enough for what has to remain a very modest prospection.

We do not have to presuppose that there will in fact be an end of history; we can leave this an open question, though that will have some bearing on our understanding of the meaning of history. We speak of the end only in terms of the good to be realized in history, the *bonum faciendum*. Though there is a certain momentum in history, by reason of human forces as well as natural forces, this good will not come about automatically; it will be realized positively and creatively only by the initiative of men acting according to reason, that is, in view of an end, looking to the future primarily, and not just to the present or the past.

But there are two basic ways of viewing the end of history, one cyclical and the other linear, each with its own implications regarding the meaning of history.

The cyclical view is perhaps the most ancient but has many proponents even in modern times, not the least of whom were Nietsche and Whitehead, though with important differences. This view precludes an end of history in any strict sense. It may admit a diversity of epochs but never a point of absolute beginning or end. There are no last things, and hence no eschatology. In such a view the common good has to be radically relative. This is why modern readers are always surprised to find Aristotle so much of a relativist in his ethical views, for though he viewed the common good as the primary good he could never see an end to it. Hence, for him, it could never represent anything more than the best possible arrangement for a time of eternally interacting elements, something that could and did fluctuate with time. Any hierarchy of values one had in this view was locked into the cycle and, though one had to take the times into account in estimating the real possibilities in the present, one had no ultimate point of reference in the exercise of judgment.

The linear view has gained more general acceptance only in the past one hundred years or so because of the general idea of evolution that has come to prevail. The view is not tied to the idea of evolution, since the evolution we know can still be seen as characterizing only our particular epoch and not the coming and going of epochs as such. But more often than not evolutionism has led many to think of history along the lines of a model like that of a natural process leading to a determinate end. This has given rise to a new form of humanism, eschatological humanism. The switch from the circle to the line comes with the conception of an end that will consist of really last things. This in itself would not be so significant, if it were not for another switch that also takes place in the very exercise of moral judgment. For, unlike the cyclical view, this view tends to absolutize its judgments. If there is a determinate end in view, as it supposes, then there can be only one way of getting there efficiently. The problem is to find that way and then to follow it ruthlessly. Paradoxically enough, while supposing a determinate end, this view often fails to reason from the end; it reasons only from the efficiency of means, as we see in the many forms of social Darwinism, leaving the end to take care of itself, so to speak, by the interplay of forces. We are thus left with nothing more than a survival for the fittest, if not some form of historical entropy, rather than a concern for the quality of life and the much more positive good of communion.

Marxism does not stop at this plane positivist view, but it remains basically linear in its outlook, even with its dialectical view of history and its insistence on human initiative as constitutive of history. It situates the end beyond history, not unlike theologians do, or at least beyond what it terms, rather self-defeatingly, pre-history. Having done this, it then proceeds to deal with pre-history as leading inexorably to a determinate point, the end of pre-history or the beginning of history or, to speak more logically, the end of history as we know it. But this transcendence beyond actual history is seen only on a horizontal plane (— more of the same, only different —), not on a vertical plane, so that the end is still not seen as affecting or qualifying the judgment to be made in the present. We are left to judge only on the basis of forces given in the present, as in Darwinism, economic forces, no doubt, but forces that are conceived on the model of natural processes. With all its insistence on history as a distinct category from nature, Marxism still falls far short of a genuine ideal of dialectical reason.[33] Engels was among the first to make this evident when he undertook his *Dialectic of Nature* in which, influenced by Darwinism, he brought the Marxist idea of dialectic back to a linear process and found himself once again faced with the question of the eternal return, a circular view of history.

This paradox of Engels' own evolution is a sign that the two basic ways of viewing the end of history, the cyclical and the linear, cannot be separated in historical consciousness. But they should not be confused as they were in Engels. Without going more deeply into the vertical dimension of historical transcendence, which would take us into theology and beyond the fundamental ethic we are concerned with here,[34] we have to affirm the actuality of history here and now, and not just at some point in the future, an actuality that will change and be transformed by human initiative but nevertheless remains the beginning of history for us, an end that is only a beginning. The now of the future will not be the same, but it will be historical and it can be envisioned only from the present now. To say anything else would be to have recourse only to some abstract and univocal concept of history that has little or nothing to do with our actual history, the only one that is real, and our real historical consciousness.

History, therefore, should not be conceived as either cyclical or linear, but as both at the same time. This follows from what we said about the presence of the end in the now of historical actuality. The good is real now and only that good-real-now can bring us to any good in the future. History, as we have already suggested, follows a sort of cycloidal movement alternating between future and present, between the end and the means. It is not tied to any line inexorably, but it ascends in a sort of spiral which, ideally, will come to include one day all men in a good of well-being and communion.

Just what that "one day" will be, or even whether it will or can be a day in history at all, we cannot say at this point of our reflection. We can only say that, properly understood, the common good is the ground for developing a meaning of history, not the last word of history, but a word sufficient to orient ourselves here and now intelligently and critically in world-history, as we decide what is to be done. The common good can be such a word by reason of its very radical openness to the future and the positive orientation it entails for human action.[35]

CHAPTER 3

JUSTICE AND FRIENDSHIP

The common good, however, cannot be taken in just as a word of reason, dialectical as that word may be. We are repeatedly brought up against the difficulty of picturing that good in such a way that it will yield some specification for us here and now on what is to be done. We have tried to show how the difficulty can be dealt with in two ways: first, by a return to the present and a reflection on experience to uncover what real possibilities are open to us, and secondly, by a recognition of the end as already somehow present in our actual experience. But this is not enough to answer our difficulty. It is only the beginning of an answer.

We shall have to take a longer look at each of these two ways. The first will be explored, at least in some of its aspects, when we come to discuss authority, law and revolution, for the proper understanding of these depends very much on how we read our present and how we derive possibilities for the future from past experiences. But before we come to this, we must reflect more carefully on the actual presence of the end in our historical now, for only this actual presence itself can shed the proper light on the more external elements of the good life that come into play in the dialectic of authority, law and revolution.

Is it possible to arrive at a more precise determination of this actual presence of the end in the historical now? What would be the mode of this presence? This is where the notion or, more precisely, the exercise of virtue may come into play. Virtue, we are told, is its own reward. If it is so, it is because it is itself the end. Though it may not be as simple as all that, it may be that we do have in the idea of virtue an opening to what we are looking for at this point in our fundamental social ethic.

How can this be so? Let us not suppose that virtue is indeed its own reward, at least not in the present; it always remains too fragile in historical actuality. But let us see how its actuality in the present can help in determining the exigencies of the common good here and now.

Thus far we have considered the common good only from the vantage point of reason. This has led to one way of specifying the content of the common good — through a dialectic of means and ends. But this way remains somewhat formal, not to say abstract, by itself. Human action is not just an affair of reason and calculation, even taken in the best and most ample sense of that term. It springs as well from personal dispositions which, along with reason, are no less real "reasons" for action. A man cannot always explain or give a reason why he has come to think a course of action is good; he senses it in his being and this sensibility is what he goes on in deciding what is for the good. Virtue is precisely this sort of disposition actually found in a man's sensibility and it plays an essential role in historical consciousness in coming to know the good. Whether it is its own reward or not, it is a necessary means for the proper exercise of moral judgment.

Virtue is a sense of the good and it is something actual in the present. It is a sense of value here and now needed to complement reason. Without this living sense, reason remains detached, not just cold, but incapable by itself of finding the proper concrete specification of the good. In a way, therefore, virtue has to take precedence over reason; a man has to be sensitized to the good before he can judge properly, though his sensibility cannot become or remain genuinely oriented toward the good apart from reason and the fullness of its intentionality. This is why prudence, which informs reason, is itself a virtue, the proper disposition of reason toward the good,[1] and why also philosophy has the role Marcuse has assigned to it in its historical com-

76

mitment, to raise the chance of alternatives to the established order:[2] without a reason properly disposed to the common good, the sensibility, experience itself, would remain locked in its present restrictions or become too constrained in the future. Yet virtue, this sense of the good, is actual and irreducible and it is needed to arrive at a proper discernment of the exigencies here and now of the common good.

But there are virtues and virtues. It is not the task of fundamental social ethics to go into all of them, important as they may be for arriving at a good balance of dispositions in judging what is for the good.[3] Here we shall deal with only two of them, both of which are general and of special relevance for a social ethic — justice and friendship.

Justice and friendship have to do *directly* with the common good, each in its own way. As general virtues, like prudence, they inform every particular good act in its relationship to the common good. Particular virtues, like courage and liberality, also have to do with particular acts. But to serve the good as completely as they should they must be subsumed under or, better still, assumed by general virtue in view of the common good. Thus all particular virtues as well as particular acts must come under the general virtues of prudence, justice and friendship in order to be fully conducive to the good; without ceasing to be particular in any way, they must also transcend their own particularity and attain the universality of the good.[4]

We have already seen how prudence, which inheres in reason as such, plays this role with regard to the end and the choice of means to that end. Now we must turn to the other two, which inhere more in the will, the rational appetite,[5] though they cannot be separated from prudence any more than prudence can be separated from them. Each of the two, as we have just noted, has its proper relation to the common good, justice having to do more with social structure and friendship with communion, but there is between them a dialectical relationship; each has its own actuality and each is related to the other in its very relationship to the good of history. Thus, just as there is a dialectic of reason in judging what is for the good, so also there is a dialectic of the sensibility rooted in the tension between these two basic virtues of justice and friendship. Indeed, as we shall see, there is a dialectical tension within each of these virtues themselves, between an inevitable particularity and a necessary universality.

We will therefore consider each of these two virtues successively, beginning with justice, then friendship, and after we have seen each separately we shall reflect on the relationship between them.

I — Justice

Justice has to do with external actions and things.[6] As a virtue it is a disposition in men leading them to seek a right and proper arrangement of the world we live in. It has an economic aspect, inasmuch as that world is natural, and a political aspect, inasmuch as it is human. But it transcends each of these particular aspects and assumes them into the higher order of the common good. It gives history a positive orientation toward that good. Though it entails an internal disposition in men, its concern is with externals, the realm of means, institutions, social structures and relations. But inasmuch as the ideal in this realm is still to be realized, justice here and now is also concerned with the end; for communion itself always requires an expression in social structure and the proper structure cannot be realized apart from justice, a sense of right order in things to open the way for real communication and friendship.

Justice cannot be understood apart from social structures, apart from an objective order which is somehow real independently of man's internal disposition. Thus, if a man fulfills the requirements of an objective order, if he gives back what is not his, he is considered to have done the just thing, even though he may have no intention of being just in the case. He may not be doing all that justice demands, but he is satisfying justice in a minimal sense, even without intending it.

This is why the ancients set justice apart from all the other moral virtues. The measure for rightness in other virtues, like courage or liberality, ultimately lies in the subject, in the actual dispositions of each man in a historical situation. The courageous man, for example, will have to judge what might be too much for him as much as what would be too little according to the degree of his real dispositions here and now and the possibilities which they entail. Otherwise he might turn out to be a fool as well as a coward, and not courageous at all. But not so with justice: there the measure is in things, not in an individual's dispositions, in an order that is somehow prior to those dispositions, though that order is by no means restricted to the established order. Justice could very well call for an overthrow of the established order, but it would do so in the name of a higher order, still somehow independent of anybody's particular dispositions. Only the tyrant acts differently, but he can never be said to be acting truly in the name of justice.

This peculiarity of justice helps us to see how justice, along with prudence, has to enter into composition with all the other moral virtues. In exercising judgment, what we seek is a happy medium[7] between two extremes. Liberality, for example, lies somewhere between greed and waste. But this mean cannot be found concretely without a proper estimation of the objective order of things in the historical situation. This is where justice comes into play, along with prudence, because it has to do with the mean as specified by things, over and above subjective dispositions. Justice, therefore, is itself a subjective-objective structure drawing man out of the privacy of his subjectivity toward his historical confrontation with his fellowman. It does not allow him to settle for just what happens to be his present, subjective disposition; it summons him toward a coincidence between the subjective good and the objective good, from a merely subjective liberty toward an objective liberty, a real liberty in the common good.

The reason why this is so is that the proper subject of justice is not any one of the particular passions of man, but the will itself, the rational appetite as such. Passions, by reason of their sensibility, are always drawn toward particular things. It takes a universal faculty to be concerned with an order of relations between things — an appetite that can transcend or free itself from any particular thing and see it in its context with other things. The will is such an appetite precisely because it is the rational appetite; it can enjoy the universality of reason, on the condition that it free itself, not from the passions, for the human will is not real apart from them, but from the particularity of the passions. Justice, therefore, which as a disposition in man has to be proportionate to his real liberty, is a rule for prudence, just as it supposes prudence itself to arrive at the proper mean in things.

One final aspect of this peculiarity of justice as a moral virtue is closely related to the historical tension of consciousness. Other virtues presuppose the internal disposition and go out to action from there. An act is not courageous of itself; it presupposes a real quality of spirit in a man. The same external act that would be termed courageous for one man could be termed presumptuous or cowardly for another. The difference comes from a prior disposition of the subject. With justice, however, it seems to be the other way around. A man can be just without the prior disposition to be so. More than for any other virtue, the external execution of justice seems to engender the internal disposition. It is as if man could not really become just without first entering into the objective realm of justice where things take precedence over attitudes. To talk of justice as long as universal justice is not established in reality often sounds more like a perversion of justice. But to think of justice as an order to be realized, whether we like it or not, is the only way of entering into the proper disposition in this regard. This is why the exigencies of history appear so much as exigencies of justice.

Seeing this peculiarity of justice as a virtue, then, how is it to be defined? The classical adage, *suum cuique,* seems to hit the matter off succinctly, but it leaves too much unsaid and it

80

is open to any number of particular biases. It needs more precise interpretation.

The fundamental idea of justice has to do with equality, a certain proportion between things and persons, an order of relations. This in turn supposes altereity, other persons besides myself — *aequalitas alteri*. Justice is always *ad alterum*. Though one is an object of justice, one is never just to oneself in the strict sense of the term, except inasmuch as one considers oneself as other than oneself in action.

In a sense, then, if we accept the Greek idea of *politics*, which is an order that supposes equality as well as altereity — real liberty — we shall have to say that justice is most properly a political virtue.[8] It can be found in other orders, such as the family or the clan, but not in the full sense of the term. Children not only lack equality with their elders; they are also not completely other than they, at least not as long as they have not reached maturity, which is liberty and equality with them. For the parent as such the good of the child is identically his own, not that of another purely and simply, though it is his role to see that the good of his child develops into a good in its own right.

It follows, therefore, that though justice has to do with the external order of action and things, it remains ever a very personal affair. It has to do only with persons in proportion to their very capacity for action, whether actual or potential, whether manifest or presumed. Rights and duties, which can be predicated properly only of persons, are no more than particular instances of relations that constitute the order of justice. In this personal aspect of justice we shall find also its point of contact with friendship, its opening to love, which always presupposes equality or respect.

The equality which justice connotes, however, is not something already fully established. In fact, justice in our modern world does not presuppose equality, as did the Greek idea of politics; it aims at it, equality for all. Yet, without admitting that there have to be slaves as well as freemen, this does not mean that the ideal of justice is simply egalitarian. Egalitarianism is only a bad dream that overlooks both the rich diversity of persons — a diversity that is heightened, not toned down, in a properly understood common good — and the beneficial as well as necessary differences of role implied in any social structure — roles that intimately affect persons as they foster, or frustrate, genuinely human interaction. Egalitarianism does in fact contain a germ of truth which has to do with the internal aspect of persons and which even touches on personal liberty and the good of communion. At this level all men are indeed equal. But this equality is only an abstraction and can be falsified if we take it apart from the external structures in which communion has to find expression or apart from the real diversity which this expression entails. Genuine human equality exists only in diversity.

To determine concretely the specific shape that just equality is to take in history would, of course, take us far beyond fundamental social ethics. We cannot hope to do anything of the sort here, nor should we attempt it. What we can and must do, however, is see how such a task is to be approached in terms of justice. This we can do by a reflection on the division of justice itself and the tension that exists between its different poles.

The first and most basic division is that between general justice and particular justice. This division dates from antiquity and roughly corresponds to a division between social justice and individual justice. But it has been largely overlooked or misinterpreted in recent discussions of justice. For example, in a collection of essays published under the title *Social Justice,* the idea of social justice is taken only in the sense of distributive justice[9] or of a more particular form of political justice,[10] but never in the full dynamic sense that includes every aspect of the good. It is seen as distinct from the justice owed by individuals to other individuals (commutative justice), but still only as the justice owed by a group or society to individuals (distributive justice), never as the justice proper to the whole as such, which includes both of the other forms of justice, which are only particular forms, and not general, since they aim at the good of individual parts, and not the whole.

The distinction to be made here is more than just verbal. It goes right to the very historical essence of justice. One way of stating the distinction is in terms of law or government which has always been understood to have a special role to play in providing for the common good.[11] In this context general justice was called legal justice. This is the way it was presented by Aristotle, for example, in the fifth book of the *Nichomachean Ethics*, because, as Hegel saw very well,[12] in Greek society there was a sort of immediate identification between the ethical order and the political order.[13]

But a word of caution is called for in this approach. The key term is not the law so much as the common good — which is irreducible to the law, as we saw in the preceding chapter. Given Aristotle's organic understanding of law and its essential orientation to the common good, one can well see that he would transfer the name of law to justice itself as leading to that good. But the transfer is not without its snares and possible delusions, which Aristotle himself and the Greeks may not have escaped completely. It tends to give precedence to a legal system, a *politeia*, and not to the good it is supposed to serve. It can, in fact, betray the very radical nature of the common good by restricting it to the particularities and the limitations of an all too established order. It sounds almost too natural and not historical enough. It can be too immediate, calling for a further mediation of historical reason, as Hegel also saw.[14]

The advantage of the term "legal justice," however, lies in its bringing the focus of justice concretely where it should be to begin with, on the whole as exemplified in a particular system, though never exhausted by such an example. The other (*ad alterum*) of justice has to be viewed not just singly or individually, but also in common; individuals have to be seen as constituting a whole together and justice cannot be real unless it takes this whole into account as well as each individual. Indeed, the same thing applies to justice as we saw applied to the good: the universal, or rather the common, takes precedence over the particular — without prejudice, however, to the particular, since the latter is not opposed to, but a participation in, the common good. Hence the essential connection between justice and the common good: the order of justice is identically the order of the common good, though the good as such includes friendship, the good of communion, over and above the equality which justice strives for.

Perhaps the better term for general justice today would be "social justice" rather than "legal justice." But we would have to be careful not to confuse it with "distributive justice," which is not universal but only a particular form of justice. What is, in point of fact, the good sought in distributive justice? It is not precisely the good of society as a whole, though that good is served by it; it is rather the good of individuals as such. The benefits and the burdens of the social order as distributed for individuals to share. The fact that society as such or its representative appears as the subject of this virtue, rather than an individual as such, does not make it essentially different from commutative justice. Both distributive and commutative justice are the same in that they aim at the good of the part as such. This is what distinguishes both of them from general justice, which aims at the good of the whole as such. Needless to say, the two, particular justice and general justice, do not serve the good apart from one another; they are aspects of one and the same exercise of justice. But the historical dynamics of justice will not be understood without a clear understanding of the distinction between the two.

The distinction depends on where we start in sorting out the various aspects of justice. If we consider commutative justice, the one-to-one form of justice, alone as basic, then we may come to see distributive justice, the many-to-one form, as part of the same virtue of justice, but we will never see what can be the object of general justice or social justice as distinct from either of these two, since the object there is not "one," but the whole. Thus, according to one division of justice,[15] commutative justice is distinguished from the other kinds of justice on the basis of individuality and sociality: the first has to do with relations between individuals as such, the other two, with the relations between individuals and society as such, the one with the obligations of society as a whole to individuals, the other with the obligations of individuals to society as a whole.

The logic of this division is quite clear: it is a logic of obligations based on the subject of the virtue, not the object, the good to be sought. From an individualistic point of view it may seem plausible enough, but it does lead to a certain amount of confusion. To begin with, it forces us to think of society as a subject, as an individual person with rights and duties. While it may be a useful and important ploy in the courts to oppose individuals and the state, for example, as if both were individual persons, one real and one "moral," it can be misleading to stop at this sort of opposition in fundamental social ethics. In fact, it can get us hung up between individualism and totalitarianism because, strictly speaking, the latter is only the counterpart of the former, since it arises only when an individual or a sector of society wishes to annex the good of others as part of its own good, which itself can only be particular. Both individualism and totalitarianism suffer from the same defect, particularism, the reduction of the whole to a part. The only way out of the dilemma is to abandon the inadequate notion of justice on which they thrive by coming to a better understanding of social justice as the general virtue which includes two particular forms, distributive and commutative, in a dialectical relationship. This is the only way of overcoming the confusion of mere opposition between individual and social. It can be done by a return to the object, not the subject, as the ground for distinction — to the good which is at once common and particular.

The logic of social justice thus opens the way beyond any static opposition between individualism and totalitarianism. The tension between individuals, or between individuals and society as a whole as personified in particular individuals, is not an end, a limit situation, but a means toward a good to be realized through this tension. This good, a common good, is precisely and irreducibly an object of justice in its own right, not apart from but above and beyond particular goods, a good encompassing them in a relation of participation.

The proper division of justice, therefore, is to be found in terms of the good — the good as common to many and the good as particularized — and it gives rise not to different categories of justice than the ones proposed but to a different relation between them. In this division, as in the division of the good, not the individual but the whole is seen as more basic, so that social justice is represented first. But it is not represented apart from distributive and commutative justice, as separable from them, in the way that commutative justice can be separated from "social justice" in an individualistic perspective, since general justice is not real apart from particular justice. The priority of social justice is intentional; it has to be worked out by means of commutative and distributive justice. There exists the same kind of dialectical relationship between particular and general justice as we found between means and ends in the exercise of moral judgment.

This supposes, however, that we have an absolutely open understanding of social justice, open to the dimension of friendship in the common good, but, more precisely, open to any social structure that will be both means to and expression of a genuine communion among men. The proper focus of social justice is social structure, external actions and things. This is why justice requires a theory of good institutions and good social habits leading to the creation of better economic and political structures at the service of mankind as a whole. Indeed, if we understand "institution" as a community of action, social justice can best be defined only as a common habit to be found in good institutions.[16] No one can have social justice by himself. Others can also limit my own possesion of that virtue, because it is not real except in my involvement with them in a community of action. But on the other hand, every man should be a subject of this virtue according to his time and his place in history. It entails a positive obligation that is no less *pro semper* than any absolute negative command.

In conclusion, and to help bring a final clarification to the notion of social justice, we might ask what is the evil that is directly opposed to it. It would seem to be *exploitation,* not the exploitation of an individual or a class by another, nor the exploitation of society by an individual or a class, but the exploitation that is inherent to certain social structures as such, exploitation, for example, as Marx saw it in bourgeois society. Stealing from another or withholding a benefit that is due to another are surely forms of injustice but perhaps the ultimate form is exploitation as this has been built into the social structures we have known until now in history. All other forms of injustice may be evil only because they are forms of exploitation. If so, then *restitution,* the act of overcoming injustice, becomes not just a matter of restoring, of rendering each man his due as this was established in the past, but much more a matter of overcoming the limitations of any social system, so that all men may have all that is due them. Restitution is something which all of us owe, regardless of past responsibilities, as long as exploitation persists in our social institutions.[17]

The fact that we have become more aware of exploitation as a radical form of evil is a sign that we are becoming more aware of the radical good justice aims at, the common good as expressed in social structures, institutions, the community of action. For justice does not consist merely in the recognition of inequality; it consists much more in the promotion of an order that will enable each man to find his due in richness and diversity.

II — *Friendship*

Just as justice is concerned with the external aspects of the common good, friendship has to do more with its internal aspects, the good of communion rather than its expression in social structures. The two are of course inseparable, but before we consider them in their unity, let us pause to consider friendship for what it is or ought to be in itself, as distinct from justice.

This, in a sense, takes us beyond what is ordinarily considered the realm of ethics, which has always been more concerned with justice than friendship, with rights and duties rather than with love, and has always been reluctant to enter into this realm where planning and legislation seem so insufficient at best or obstructive at worst. At the beginning of his discussion on friendship in Book Eight of the *Nichomachean Ethics,* for example, Aristotle feels the need for justifying such a discussion in a context of moral philosophy, which, as we have already noted, he considered to be more political than anything else, but he argued for introducing such a discussion on the grounds that it had to do with the end of ethics and politics and therefore should not go unexamined in the science of ethics and politics.[18]

Later on when Aquinas took over the Aristotelian ethic in his theological perspective, the discussion of friendship was assumed into the treatise on divine charity, the theological virtue, while love was treated as a passion prior to any discussion of virtue.[19] Thus, friendship was not treated as a human virtue apart from the theological virtue, though its human dimension was not neglected in the treatment of divine friendship.

In fact, it is significant to note that friendship as we wish to talk about it here does not fit into either one of the two classical schemes of virtue, that of the cardinal virtues (prudence, justice, temperance, fortitude) or that of the theological virtues (faith, hope, charity). It seems to take us beyond the first without however taking us immediately into the second. What we wish to dwell on now is the human dimension of friendship, independently of or prior to its relation to the divine. The point of insertion for divine charity in human history can only be in the opening provided by the experience of human friendship.

It might be argued, as a justification for discussing friendship in fundamental social ethics, that there are in fact rights and duties, obligations in friendship as well as in justice. Though such obligations have never gotten the attention they should have, there are theologians today, like Fletcher, who insist on the "law of love."[20] But this is to take away from the understanding of friendship as we wish to think of it here. Many of those who insist on a "law of love" do not have a proper concept of social justice and so are forced to resort to such a "law" to ground the social dimension of rights and duties. With social justice already understood as grounding all rights and duties, both individual and social, not apart from friendship but as distinct from it, what we wish to do here is consider friendship as transcending the whole question of rights and obligations. It is only in this sense that friendship has a proper role to play, a proper light to shed, in the exercise of moral judgment.

Love is something real and actual here and now, though it is far from being universal, and as such it purports to be beyond obligation. People in love are always sensitive to the distinction between doing something out of love and doing it out of a sense of duty. To be sure, one can act out of both at the same time; in the concrete the two are inseparable, since friendship does not exist apart from social structures, the proper realm of justice. But lovers always feel that, as long as something is not done clearly out of love, it is never all that it is meant to be, no matter how just it may be. Thus friendship appears as a measure beyond all measures.

Love's measure, however, is an indispensable ingredient in all moral judgment because it is an essential part of the end, the essential part, for it is identically the good of communion which transcends and assumes, by informing, every other part of the common good.[21] To the extent that love is actual, that we have appreciation and feeling for friendship, we have an anticipation of the end and find ourselves in a better position to evaluate means toward human excellence. Thus actual friendship is a means in the present for judging *what* is to be done, and *how* — a necessary means, for without it we become victims of our own technology. Planning and calculation uninformed by friendship eventually becomes inhuman, as we are coming to realize more and more, no matter how well intentioned the planning may be in the abstract. Real love and affection for others is the ultimate ingredient we cannot do without in the concrete.

But how precisely does friendship enter the concrete exercise of judgment as a measure? It has to do directly with the highest human good; it is indeed that good with a certain immediacy, but with an immediacy that will have to be mediated historically by justice and the other virtues. Friendship has to do with the very end of human action. Hence, as we have seen, it goes beyond the cardinal virtues; it is the end sought in them; it informs them with its own universal dimension.

Friendship is a general virtue along with prudence and justice and like them. Its proper focus has to do with the internal and spiritual aspect of community, but nothing in human action is independent of that aspect. Everything in the realm of justice — external actions and things — has to be considered as part of the means of communication and communion among men, a means of friendship.

Aquinas spoke of a twofold rule for good acts: reason, which when rectified becomes prudence, and God, whose communication gives rise to charity.[22] In between the two and prior to any rule of divine charity, we must introduce a third rule, or rather a third and more historical aspect of the one rule in the concrete and a more immediate one, the *other* who is simply a man. However much divine love may be necessary to arrive at real human love, the other is always to be loved humanly and for himself; his good, he himself, not just my love, must become an operative norm in all moral judgment. There is a kind of death to self implied in friendship and this death is the passage into the concrete historical transcendence of the common good. We shall see how this passage begins in the dialogue that has to be part of all moral reasoning.

Before we come to that, however, it remains for us to say how we understand friendship. We have insisted on friendship rather than just love because, though the two are inseparable even conceptually, friendship entails an important dimension which may not be found in love alone. Friendship always entails love, but love does not always entail friendship. There can be unrequited love. Generous and noble as such love might be, it calls for recognition and response and it is always somehow incomplete if there is no reciprocation. Friendship, reciprocity in love, brings greater completion than one-way, one-dimensional love; it raises subjective love to a plane of life none of us can reach by himself.

Thus, when we say friendship must inform moral judgment, we do not mean just love alone. Like good intentions, love alone is not enough. There is an amplitude of judgment which only friendship can bring through the mutual recognition that becomes a sharing in understanding and a broadening of vision. There is a sad counterproof of this in those who never seem to have experienced any friendship: such people often seem to be deprived even of any moral sense whatsoever, let alone good moral judgment. The other never becomes real for them, except as an object of pleasure or use, and the idea of the good seems to be locked in the particularity of the self. Those who love others truly are not so locked in, because they have experienced friendship in one way or another, but to the extent that their love remains unrequited they do not receive the light they might receive through this love, a light that comes only from the other. The commitment in love does bring real light, but not the fullness of light that can come from a response to one's call.

A second aspect of friendship which should be emphasized is communication. This, it might be said, is the essential act of friendship in the concrete. The reciprocity of love has to be conscious and communicated. In a word, it has to be experienced. Without the experience it is not real and the experience of friendship consists precisely in the communication between friends. This aspect of friendship is undoubtedly what makes it

91

most crucial for the exercise of moral judgment, as can easily be seen from the example just referred to of those deprived of any moral sense because they have never experienced friendship. Communication is the way that light takes in friendship, for communication is not just an expression and an exchange of love; it is also dialogue and discussion.

Communication, however, supposes presence. This is also an important aspect of friendship in the concrete. It is not enough to have been friends. Prolonged absence or great distance can dissolve friendship and, to the extent that it is dissolved, it ceases to play a positive role in judgment. The point here is to see that friendship is not to be presumed upon even after it has been established. It has to be nurtured by real communication, if it is going to remain an actuality. Inasmuch as friendship is a habit that can exist only between two people or more, the constancy we associate with any virtue will endure only by the actual exercise of mutual love.

Finally, the third aspect of friendship to be brought out has to do with the kind of love it is based on. In its highest form, friendship consists in wanting the good of the other. But this level is not reached immediately, nor independently of lower forms, nor does it exist for man in history without the mediation of these lower forms. To look at all these forms, and the relations between them, therefore, will help us to understand friendship as a historical reality meant to inform moral judgment.

The classical division of love[23] speaks of two basic kinds of love, each determined by its own specific good, the love of concupiscence specified by the good that is either useful (*bonum utile*) or pleasurable (*bonum delectabile*) and the love of benevolence specified by what was called the honorable good (*bonum honestum*), the good of the other precisely as other — *ipsum habens bonitate,* the one having goodness *himself.* The quaint language suggests all sorts of biases to our ear, but underlying the division is a dynamics that is well worth retaining for a fundamental social ethic. The notion of love contained in this division is not univocal. "Love" is not a genus divided into species. It is analogous; it can be understood only through the relation that exists between the two kinds of love in their historical actuality. In short, it is a dialectical reality.

The relation becomes manifest according to an order of generation. Love appears first as satisfaction and *pleasure.* The child has needs, simple biological needs, and loves whatever satisfies these needs; genetically speaking, the first act of love is the act of taking pleasure in the satisfaction of one's vital needs. In this act there is no clear distinction between the feeling of satisfaction, the thing giving satisfaction, or the source itself of satisfaction; there is only absorption, absorption *in* and absorption *of* whatever gives satisfaction. The child is only a consumer of the mother's milk. One important thing to note, however, is that in this pleasurable absorption whatever gives satisfaction is consumed; the lover remains, sustained and enriched, but alone. The child consumes the milk of the mother without knowing her except as a source of milk or perhaps even without distinguishing her as a source or as a person distinct from himself.

In time needs become more complex. They become psychological and sociological as well as biological. But in all of these needs the structure of satisfaction remains the same: things are seen as good to the extent that they satisfy needs and in giving satisfaction they are consumed. On the psychological and sociological level this applies to persons as well as things, as can easily be seen when others become no more than means of immediate satisfaction, the mother for the child, or the child for the mother, for it is not only the child, but also the mother, that can keep the mother-child relationship from developing in a direction of authentic and mature human love. Clinging to immediacy can stand in the way, whether it comes from the child or the parent. Many subtleties and rationalizations can be used to cover up this immediacy of pleasure, even that of "self-sacrifice," but the destruction that ensues when only this kind of immediate love obtains between persons is a clear sign

93

of what it really is, love turned in upon itself. It goes out to the *other,* but is not yet prepared to take the other for all he really is; it accepts the other only as an object of immediate consumption.

Beyond this first moment of immediacy, however, there comes a moment of reflection, a realization that pleasure, if it is going to be as complete or as continuous as it might be, will have to be put off until a later time, it will have to be mediated by planning and labor. The "pleasure principle" gives way to the "reality principle." In a Freudian perspective this appears as a putting off of love: pleasure is put off until a later date, and so, love, which in its first moment is identified with pleasure, is set aside for the time being. Reason is seen as taking over, setting up the proper distances between things and people, beyond the immediacy of the pleasure principle, and opening the way to civilization through culture and technology. History thus appears as a consequence of reason, which breaks out of the immediate circle of needs and satisfaction. Supposedly this break will lead to a broader and higher circle of the pleasurable life, but reason can get lost on the way and become its own end. The plan, not to say the planning, absorbs all the energy and there is nothing left for life afterwards.[24]

Despite the appearances, however, this second moment is not an absence of love; it is a passage to another form of love, a love of things as *useful,* over and above a love of things as immediately pleasurable. This second form of love can be opposed to the first: there is a pleasure of reason itself, the pleasure of knowing how things work and of making them work as we want them to, the pleasure of calculation and successful manipulation that becomes ever greater in proportion to the complexity of achievement. But this second form is not essentially different from the first. In this the ancient distinction was quite perceptive when it put both forms under one category, the "love of concupiscence," distinct from another category, radically different from it. In a way, the Freudian outlook is only renewing this ancient insight when it ties together the "pleasure principle" and the "reality principle," the pleasurable and the useful, without however giving sufficient attention to a further category, what we might call the "benevolent principle," the love of benevolence based on the good of the other in himself, over and above his satisfaction or his needs. This connection between pleasure and use can be seen clearly if we reflect on the pleasure we can take in reason itself and in the form which this pleasure takes.

The second form of love, based on the *bonum utile,* does indeed recognize the reality of the other as such, more than the first. It knows that the other cannot be simply consumed for one's immediate pleasure. It acquires what we call a healthy respect for the otherness of things and people, their irreducible reality. But it does not depart from the original self-centeredness of the first moment with its focus on *needs.* Enlightened self-interest is still self-interest. It starts with the self and its needs, and goes out to others as to other selves also with needs of their own. While it sees these as real, it sees them only according to the model of its own needs, so that the question of satisfaction becomes more complex, including the needs of others as well as the needs of self, but it remains within the same circle of needs and satisfaction. The circle is only amplified and magnified. It does not open into a new order of love. The golden rule may come into play: do unto others as you would have them do unto you; but as long as this remains only a question of needs and calculation, the good of the other is not yet seen for all that it is. Beyond the immediate good of the self, the only good that is recognized is still only the pleasurable or the useful, the good that can serve the self or the group of selves, but not the good of a self or a community of selves in all its actual fullness. This comes only in a third moment of love.

This third moment cannot be understood or realized apart from the first two, but it gives the whole movement of love a completely new meaning. First of all, it does not come apart from the love of concupiscence; it comes in and through that love. The passage from the first to the second moment in that love, from the moment of absorption to the moment of recognition of the other in his irreducible reality, was a beginning of the movement leading to this third moment. But the full meaning of that movement of love becomes manifest only in this last movement and it appears as a complete reversal of that first movement, starting no longer from the self but rather from the other, recognizing that other in his own goodness and going out to that goodness, not as useful for anything or anyone, but simply for its own sake, because the person is a good in itself — *ipsum habens bonitatem*. Such goodness is found only in persons, never in things, but the radical difference has to be noted carefully if we are going to enter into this third form of love. The temptation is always to think of others only as satisfying our needs, and not as beings desirable in and for themselves.

The key distinction here is between *need* and *desire*.[25] What characterizes the first two moments is the circle of needs and satisfaction; utility may expand the circle but does not break out of it. Desire does, desire for the other precisely as other in all and for all that he is. If the "reality principle" leads us to a greater sense of objectivity than the "pleasure principle," it stops short of reality taken in and for itself, the objectivity that can be found only in the love of another for what he is. Desire takes us into this realm of recognition, beyond self-absorption, into a higher form of "absorption," a sort of emptying of oneself.

It is not that desire takes us out of the world of needs and satisfaction. Desire penetrates to consciousness through needs: the child comes to discover its mother as really another, and in the same act discovers itself, through its need for milk. Without need there would be no desire, no discovery of real objectivity in a communion between persons. This remains an historical condition of all human desire even in its highest forms: the object of desire will always bring satisfaction and thereby satisfy a need, a need that has to be satisfied. That is why psychology, which operates more on the level of satisfaction and utility, will always have a good deal to say about love even in its highest form.

But the point here is to see how desire and love in its highest form transcend need. They suppose a level of fulfillment, but they take us beyond it. This is a level on which only the healthy person can operate; as long as we are concerned only with therapy, whether it be individual or social, on the couch or in a group, we are still not concerned with the proper realm of desire and love. We need the therapeutic moment, the moment of growth and satisfaction. The love of benevolence can never be immediate for us; it requires the mediation of "concupiscence," immediate pleasure and utility. But these are not enough. The love of benevolence calls for more.

We can make the distinction from a subjective viewpoint, with the difference between need and desire as seen from the viewpoint of the self, but the distinction cannot be fully appreciated without the presence of another. It is impossible to explain this distinction to one who has no experience of recognition of another through desire and love, the child absorbed in himself who is still using others only for his own purposes, or the sick person who is so tied up within himself that he cannot relate to another. Indeed, one cannot even come to the experience without the presence of another: the child does not first desire and then discover another who can be the object of such a desire; he discovers the desire in the presence of the other, in the love that is already present in the other and invites him to love in return. Love is discovered à deux or else it is not discovered at all.

This *presence* of the other is important to keep in mind for two reasons. First, it helps us to see the inadequacy of the Freudian analysis even as completed by the Marxist and hence more social outlook of Marcuse.[26] Without the presence of another recognized in his own being, we remain locked in the circle of needs and satisfaction. We oscillate between a "pleasure principle" and a "reality principle," without the possibilty of a real historical transcendence. The tension between the two fails to become truly dialectical because it lacks the necessary mediation of the other as such. Worse still, the circle of needs and satisfaction becomes vicious: pleasure is put off as an end to be sought through useful activity; but it continues to be conceived with the same immediacy as it was first conceived, with the same kind of absorption as we find in the first moment of love, so that we are tossed from one need to another, from pleasure to utility and from utility to pleasure in an endless, self-enclosed and frustrating cycle. History thus appears as little more than a struggle for resignation and acceptance of limitation which eventually turns into a sort of despair in the face of death, the last, brutal and insurmountable fact. Only the real presence of an other can draw us out of this cycle of perpetual oscillation toward a really new end, a radically different kind of "pleasure" which can never be immediate, as love is in its first moment, but which is all the more real because it transcends, as it assumes, the first two moments of love. Only the presence of an other can summon forth desire and give new meaning, real hope, to what is first experienced only as inescapable necessity, because the discovery of an other is really the discovery of a new dimension of life, the dimension of love which gives history a real meaning not overcome even by death. One never loses the experience of having loved and having been loved.

The second reason why the presence of the other is important has to do with the role of death in the experience of love. Death remains an inscrutable mystery as well as a brutal fact, but some sense can be made of it through this third moment of love. The passage from the first two moments to the third has to be, in a sense, an experience of death. While there is continuity, there is also radical discontinuity, a complete transformation, a reversal of perspective that has to take place. The center of my concern has to be transported, so to speak, from myself to the other. I must empty myself, mortify my love of pleasure and things, die to self, in order to live anew in and through the other. This, of course, does not take place in an instant. It takes time: mortification has its own pleasures and utility. But it is an experience of death in a real sense of the word, not death as observed externally and meaninglessly, but death as an act, the act that seals the meaning of a truly human life. True love has to be mediated by death: that is the condition for escaping from endless oscillation between pleasure and utility; but the mediation itself gives some meaning to death, a new light that comes from the exchange of love that takes place through this mediation.

Thus, it becomes apparent that the true meaning of love itself cannot be discovered except in this third moment, the moment of pure and simple benevolence. Though it does not come to be apart from the movement of the first two moments, it is only from the vantage point of this final moment that the whole movement of love can be judged. Love is ultimately based on the good of the other; pleasure and usefulness, real and irreducible moments of love as they are, find their ultimate meaning in this other. They are good because they are the way, the only way, to the other. The source of their goodness, however, we discover in the end, in transcending them. Communion is the source of all goodness in human intercourse.

The good of the other we speak of, however, should not be taken abstractly. It has to be something positive and real. With his keen sense for the concrete, Aristotle observes that base men cannot be friends; friendship supposes a certain amount of virtue.[27] There is more here than just a question of ontological goodness and abstract, though inalienable, rights. It is a matter of real and actual friendship, with constancy and permanence. Lower forms of friendship, based on just pleasure or usefulness, cease once the pleasure or the usefulness cease. Real friendship, however, based on desire and the love of benevolence, is not so volatile, even when virtue seems to have gone out from one of the friends. Friendship grows only on virtue, which it fosters, and it diminishes with any disappearance of virtue, but once it has come into being, because it transcends even the constancy of the other virtues, it can survive a loss of virtue or be revived more readily than any other virtue. In this way, once it has become real, it can be a source of virtue and be a real inspiration, in the enlightening sense of the term, for the exercise of moral judgment. Friendship has a way of cutting through impediments and obstacles and bringing us quickly to what is essential and crucial.

Finally, there remains a difficulty to be dealt with. In the concrete which we have insisted on throughout, friendship always seems a very particular affair. I cannot be real friends with everybody. How can friendship therefore serve as a basic norm in the exercise of all moral judgment, especially in view of the common good? How can friendship be a general virtue? This calls for a complex but very precise answer. Justice, it would seem, can more easily be understood as a general virtue; it has to do with the external management of man's world. But not so with friendship; it has to do with the very intimate relations between persons. Are we then to abandon the idea of friendship as a general virtue?

Part of the answer to this question will be given when we come to the dialectic between justice and friendship, but the beginning of an answer can be given already at this point from an historical understanding of friendship as such. There is a dialectic of friendship, a dialectic between the universal and the particular. The actual experience of friendship is always particular; if I think I can be friends with mankind as such I am deluding myself and most likely evading friendship of any kind. Moreover, that same experience always takes place in a context of particular needs to be satisfied immediately or provided for in the future; indeed, as we have seen, it comes to the fore only through such needs: human *desire* always assumes the form of needs. Yet in all this movement, friendship does not become closed on its particularity. As it breaks out of the vicious circle of needs and satisfaction, desire turns to another in particular, and another, and another, to each in a unique, particular way. But it is never exhausted in the way that needs can be sated. True desire is ever open to others, to all others, within the limits of historical possibility. As it breaks out of the circle of self-centeredness, it is the entrance into true universality. It has to express itself always in the particular; that is the condition for its reality. But of itself it is unlimited. It reaches farther than reason itself, whether it be in prudence or justice. Social structures may always entail a certain element of exclusivity. But the desire for communion, of itself, breaks through, and out of, these limitations.

It is not that any real human love is ever actually unlimited. Friendship remains always a very particular affair. But as a historical reality it is essentially open to what lies beyond the narrow confines of established structures, whether these be family enmities, as they were for a Romeo and Juliet, or the strictures imposed by society as a whole. It is open to the future. As an actuality in the present, friendship is an end in itself, never to be superseded, but as an actuality *only* in the present, it is a means, a way to deeper dimensions of love and a greater extension of friendship. Once the realm of recognition and communication has been opened, it can no longer be legitimately closed off.

The difficulty we encounter in regarding friendship as a general virtue stems from a still too static, unhistorical outlook. Real friendship is not something to be clung to, whether it be in two's or three's, in families or in nations.[28] To do so is to lose it or to betray its essential reality. It should never be abandoned or lost wherever it is real, but it should never be closed in upon itself. As a free spirit it calls for its own transcendence wherever it exists. It is the general virtue par excellence, since it can take many particular forms and remain free to follow the universal dimensions of reality.

We have tried to speak of justice and friendship as actualities, as actual dispositions found among men in the present, not just as ideals for the future. Indeed, to the extent that we have spoken of the future, we have done so on the basis of an actual experience of justice and friendship. Virtue, as we said at the outset, entails an element of sensitivity that is necessary to complete the element of reason in the exercise of moral judgment.

In the dialectic of justice and friendship it is this actuality of each that is of primary importance. In the strict sense of the term, dialectic is a relation between actualities. The passage from potency to act is not as such dialectical. Movement can be processional and evolutionary without being dialectical in the full sense of the term. Historical movement, where dialectic comes into its own, supposes the open potentiality of nature, rides on it, but at the same time constitutes a qualitative jump that can be represented only in terms of revolution, rather than evolution, or of resumption of an old order into a new order. Thus dialectic supposes the actuality of things given in nature, including of course man with all his potentialities, actualities given in a tension, but raises these to a higher order, as it assumes them.

The dialectic of justice and friendship thus supposes each of these virtues as given to a certain extent, as actualities caught within a certain tension between one another. This of course is not a simple relationship, just as neither justice nor friendship are simple virtues. There are many persons involved in the actuality of each and many relations coming into play between them. The actual communication that takes place in justice and friendship is as complex as man's social world. Our purpose here is to articulate the most basic aspect of the relation between the two as it affects the concrete exercise of judgment.

The relation can be seen, first of all, as one of means and

ends, a reciprocal relation where each one appears in turn as means and as end for the other. In our historical actuality, justice is a means for friendship, but friendship is also a means for justice. This is possible by reason of the open nature proper to each of these virtues in their actuality. Each of them *as given* is a means of fulfillment for the other as well as for itself, while each of them, as something still to be achieved in its universality, remains an end for both itself and the other. Thus the justice and the friendship we know mutually condition one another and mutually serve or reinforce one another in the historical tension that makes us move in the directions of the common good.

The hinge of the dialectic, as Aquinas saw quite clearly, is equality: the end in justice, but the beginning in friendship — *ultima in justitia, sed principium in amicitia.*[29] Ultimately the relation is irreversible: friendship supposes equality and hence comes only once justice is realized. But this can only appear as an abstraction in historical consciousness. Attempts to offer friendship before justice are often little more than a salve for a false conscience. At best such attempts are manifestations of pity, rather than love, but, in the absence of any real intention to right a prevailing injustice, they are exactly what Niebuhr termed "philanthropy," an expression of power and complacency.[30]

Yet to the extent that friendship is a reality now, not universally but in part, hence based on some equality, and to the extent that equality is still an ideal to be realized, friendship can serve justice, not by skipping over it as it were, that is, by offering friendship without justice, but rather by reinforcing the push toward justice itself. Justice supposes that I recognize the other as other, in his substantiality and his power to act, even in his ability to counteract what I would like to have done or the way I would like to have it done. Yet, recognition of the other goes much deeper in friendship than in justice alone. Friendship supposes a basic recognition of the other in his rightful existence, the equality of justice, but it goes further in the actual communication with the other. Hence, once I have come to know someone in genuine friendship, I can find greater reason for seeking justice for others with whom friendship is not even possible yet because of a prevailing injustice. I become all the more sensitive to injustice as I feel the alienation between myself and others, an alienation I would not feel if I did not already have an experience of friendship with some, an experience of non-alienation.

Thus, both justice and friendship literally revolve around a sense of equality with others, a recognition of the other in his own right; there they meet and run into one another without separation and without confusion. One aims at real recognition for all; the other starts from the same recognition as realized in part and confirms the movement of justice, as it seeks its own intensification and extension to all as well. There is a real tension between them which can be fruitful for the common good, but which can also degenerate into an opposition, where power is sought to the exclusion of friendship or "friendship" is imposed at the expense of justice.

There is perhaps no better way of characterizing the historical struggle for the common good than through this dialectical tension between justice and friendship, since the struggle is productive only through the tension, on the condition that it avoid exclusivity at any moment, whether it be the exclusivity of false friendship or that of hardened justice, and on the condition that it respect the irreducible exigencies of each moment, the moment of justice as well as the moment of friendship. In the terms of this dialectic the common good could be defined as wanting the other with me in the world, so that each has the recognition that is his due, with all the accoutrements that recognition presupposes, and so that each can freely enter into the friendships he chooses with others. Any attempt to describe the struggle of history only in terms of animosity between classes, races or any other sort of human grouping is not only an oversimplification, but it is a reduction of what is most internal in the struggle to what is purely external and it is an oversight of what is most essential, the desire for communion that is at the source of the struggle itself.

All of this is based upon a certain community between justice and friendship, a passage from one to the other.[31] In one sense friendship can be said to come under the category of justice inasmuch as it entails a certain proportionality, a certain *exchange* of love,[32] which can even be said to exist according to a form of communitative justice, the basic form of justice as it governs the relations between individuals. Friendship in the concrete, we said, consists essentially in an act of communication; such an act is a form commutation, of mutual change or exchange, which cannot go without the mediation of justice, since it has to be expressed in an external form. On the other hand, however, the communication proper to friendship takes us further than that found in justice. It consists in an equality, but an equality of love,[33] not just the equality of rights, which it presupposes. Thus actual communication binds justice and friendship together in history in a spiralling ascent toward the common good.

This dialectical bond between justice and friendship should serve as a warning to those who would speak too easily of "direct love" between persons based only on the good of the other.[34] Such an expression could be misleading. For though there is an aspect of direct communication between persons in the love of benevolence, such a communication does not take place without expression and interdependence. This ties the love of benevolence not only to the love of concupiscence, but also to justice itself, whose function it is, not love's, to rectify the order of expression, the system of social relations or institutions. Even in its highest and most intimate reality, friendship always has to be mediated by justice. There are always rights as well as rites to be observed, an order which is not separable from love. These are, in a real sense, constitutive of friendship. It is in this sense that we can speak of justice as the minimal content of love — *minimum caritatis*: below this limit and without its order real love does not exist.

Thus, to define the historical tension, the reciprocal priority, between justice and friendship, we shall say first of all that justice is the precondition for friendship. Friendship consists in an exercise of equality, but this equality has to be already constituted somehow.[35] Justice, on the other hand, seeks to bring what is unequal to equality, that is, to constitute justice in reality.

In justice we attend first to the *dignity* of person, in view of establishing real equality, so that recognition and exchange can take place on an equal footing. As long as inequality remains, as long, for example, as I have not paid or guaranteed payment for the pack of cigarettes handed over to me, I cannot claim to have recognized the other enough in his own right to start becoming friends with him. His real dignity has to be established first, before any friendship can come into being. As long as I have not assured anyone his due within a social context, I cannot make overtures of friendship to him. In friendship, however, we attend to the *equality* first, an equality already constituted, and then to the further requirements of dignity. This does not imply mere egalitarianism: there are various kinds of friendship according to various economic and political relationships.[36] But it does imply a concern of friendship for its own conditions in justice.

This brings us to the other side of the relation between justice and friendship: not only does friendship take us beyond justice; it also magnifies justice and injustice.[37] It is a motive, stronger than even justice itself, for seeking justice, and it makes the neglect of justice a worse evil. Injustice among friends is worse than among strangers; there is a special baseness connected with it, though from the viewpoint of justice alone there may be no difference. Treason, betrayal by a friend, is worse than just betrayal by an alien, though it may have the self-same general effects. In the same way one feels more bound to do justice to one's friends than to strangers, though it may cost neither more nor less in either case. Indeed, one is usually led to do justice to one's friends before others, even though others may be in more pressing needs of justice. If there were anything wrong in this, it would be for justice, not friendship, to rectify it.

Seen in terms of general or social justice this magnification of justice and injustice by friendship can have far-reaching consequences. It takes a real sense of justice, as well as an understanding of a particular social system, to perceive a social order as unjust or exploitative. Such a sense will be greatly heightened, if one has also had an experience of friendship and feels called somehow to make such an experience available for all men. There can be a sense of community with all men, based on a somewhat abstract ideal of identity and brotherhood and on the more concrete experience of actual friendship with some, along with the growing communication and close interaction between the various peoples of the world. Such a new sense will inevitably enhance the demand for a just social order to be established and a greater indignation at the injustice of the present system, even though such injustice may not be imputable to anyone in particular. Through the universal sense of friendship it is a whole new dimension of responsibility in strict justice that comes to the fore.

There are, of course, immense problems connected with passage toward a less unjust social order, problems magnified by the bigness and the inextricable complexity of our socio-economic systems. The solution to these problems, however, will not be helped if we think of the ideal of communion among men as impossible. There are some who think of love as an "impossible possibility," especially for larger groups.[38] They conceive of society as a coalescence and cohesion of natural forces impenetrable to reason and to love. They see no possibility of establishing a rational social force powerful enough to cope with the evil or the intractability of these natural social forces. Such a view, however, fails to see the possibilities than can emerge through an actual dialectic of justice and friendship.

107

Social reality is not a kind of impenetrable natural whole often supposed in such views. It exists already only on the basis of intentions that have transcended nature from the beginning. It is a moving reality and an important part of that movement comes from an actual sense of justice and friendship, to be found, with serious limitations and shortcomings, to be sure, and amid a great deal of perversion, but nevertheless real, among men, beginning with the critics themselves who allege the impossibility of dealing with society as it is. Much that may be in fact impossible in the present could become possible through the mediation of the real justice and the real friendships already underway in their mutual historical tension. The danger is to resign oneself too soon, because of a too static as well as a too massive view of social reality, to an impossibility that may be only provisional. The apparatus of justice may be falling far behind the technological and economic realities, but the sense of justice has not entirely disappeared and is being reenforced by the new capacities for communication made available by technology itself. If we feel the injustice more, it is because we know it better. Moreover, through the same new means of communication, the experience of friendship one finds in intimacy can lead to an awakening of universal aspiration for communion among men. Such an aspiration has long been found among certain men, but it has of necessity remained somewhat abstract and ideal. It has lacked the means of communication that would have been necessary to make it concrete and real. With the new means at our disposal who is to say what is altogether impossible? There is still too much to be done, and that can be done, for us to fall prematurely back on such a closed attitude.

This is not to say there are an infinite number of possibilities open to us, nor that the future will take care of itself. It is to say that, given the initiative of man, if he has a sense of justice and friendship, it is less logical, less in accordance with the dialectic of these two virtues, to define impossibilities, to set limits based on the present to what the common good will be, than it is to begin envisioning new and real possibilities. Of themselves, the experience of justice and of friendship are open to a future we have yet to see. The limitations are due to structures given in the present. Such structures are necessary by reason of the material and external reality in which we actually find, and can only find, ourselves. But that reality is not confined to its present limitations. Our experience is confined, but open. External reality can be transformed and made into a better expression of human communion, which calls for human friendship.

IV — *Dialogue and Labor*

How this is to be done concretely will be determined only in the exercise of moral judgment itself, not in a fundamental ethic. What we can do here, however, is lay down certain conditions on how to proceed in formulating the kind of judgment that is called for in accordance with these fundamental virtues of justice and friendship.

The first and most basic of these is *dialogue*. We have already seen how an ethic of responsibility opens the way to dialogue as the means of arriving at more adequate judgments on what is for the good.[39] There is such a rich diversity of talents, gifts, ideas, visions, within cultures as well as in the diversity of cultures, that no adequate view of the good can ever be achieved in isolation, no matter how firm and well grounded one's principles may be. The real value of the principles themselves can always be illuminated anew by the light that comes, and can only come, from another in history, whether that other be of the same culture or of an alien culture. We have a certain and undeniable knowledge of the end in the idea of the common good, but that knowledge remains open to enrichment from all sides.

Now it is possible for us to see the necessity of this openness in responsibility grounded in both justice and friendship. For if the *other* is truly a norm, as he must be in both justice and friendship, he must enter into any concrete exercise of moral judgment of mine. This he must do not only as an abstract object of consideration, as something or someone to be taken into account, but as an active participant in the formulation of the judgment itself. This is not to say that moral judgment ceases to be a personal affair, to be carried on by each individual with and in his own conscience. Nor does it mean that no moral judgment can be valid apart from consensus. On the contrary, moral judgment remains more than ever a matter of personal conscience. Only now it is clear that the other, who also has his conscience as well, must inform my conscience, and this takes place concretely only in dialogue, where there may be expressions of irreconcilable differences in the present as well as some agreement and hope for the future, but where there also takes place a real information, a mutual formation or transformation of conscience through confrontation and discussion, through listening and responding to one another. Anyone who is not prepared to enter into dialogue with another in the formation of his personal judgment cannot be said to be thinking in accordance with the exigencies of justice and friendship, to be acting fully in accordance with the good of history. Any private, exclusive determination of what these virtues and the good require will be suspect.

In this we see how justice and friendship come to complete the exercise of prudence. Dialogue brings both the dialectic of sensibility and the dialectic of reason into play in the unity of one and the same act. Recognition of the other is at the same time recognition of our own limitation and the beginning of transcendence toward a higher level of reason and prudence. Acceptance of the other by taking him seriously in our own judgment, by trying to see things from his viewpoint as well as our own, takes us further along in this way of transcendence. It becomes a veritable anticipation of the end itself. Real dialogue is always an act of communion, even when there is profound disagreement. It is the first concrete actualization on a personal level of the dialectic between justice and friendship: it initiates real recognition of the other both in himself and in his rights and power, as it opens the way to a more effective realization of the common good. Without such dialogue the dialectic is corrupted into a struggle unto death, without issue for the good of history; with it it becomes a loving struggle, with the possibility of real issue in the good.

Besides dialogue, two other conditions for the proper exercise of moral judgment have to be at least mentioned at this point, *planning* and *labor*, lest dialogue remain little more than endless chatter and lead nowhere. Planning and labor are, of course, complex realities — increasingly so in our technological world. Indeed, they call for dialogue themselves, by reason of their very complexity. But the dialogue grounded in justice and friendship itself needs discipline and orientation through planning and illumination through praxis, because justice still needs to be established for all men, so that greater friendship may become possible. The still ideal dialectic of justice and friendship must gain expression in a real dialectic of the struggle between man and nature and between man and man. It must overcome real obstacles and create means to real communication in a way that is not only fitting but also effective. Otherwise justice and friendship will remain merely ideal and fail to affect the course of history, their only *raison d'être*.

With planning and labor, and the discipline they presuppose, however, we complete the circle of the historical effort required for the common good. With dialogue as their context and as their center, they constitute a structure for the process by which men can strive for the good both effectively and fittingly. While dialogue assures a certain quality in the struggle, one that does not exclude reconciliation, planning and labor assure that the dialogue has real history as its subject and not just some utopic vision. In this way the real exigencies of the common good can emerge in the light of justice and friendship and can be met through a common, dialogical initiative of men.

CHAPTER 4

AUTHORITY AND LAW

The pursuit of the common good, radical as it may be, never starts from scratch, at least not in a society that has already been formed. Even in a society just being formed the situation is not essentially different: consciousness of the common good does not appear out of the blue; it rises with the development of social structures, whatever these may be, sometimes surging ahead of them, sometimes lagging behind, but always historically bound to them. In the growth of a person the idea of the common good as the primary good comes explicitly to the fore relatively late, only after a social system has had time to give it a definite shape. So too with a society: its idea of the common good gets shaped long before it begins to reflect upon it. The shape may eventually have to be broken, but in any event it will have to be reckoned with.

So too with justice and friendship: they do not appear in a vacuum, nor are they purely internal realities that govern the relations between people, apart from any external medium. Justice itself is concerned with the creation of a proper medium for communication, but it always arises out of a medium, before it begins to shape its own. Friendship seems to break through structures, but it always supposes some and uses them even in transcending them. The medium is not the message, but it does mediate the message.

We have skirted the subject of law in dealing both with the idea of the common good, which is often spoken of in terms of the law, and with justice, which gives rise to law inasmuch as it has to do itself with external actions and things. We have

113

avoided any discussion of law, however, in an effort to articulate notions that are more fundamental and that do in fact
give human meaning to law itself. This we have tried to do
independently of the law, since in a fundamental ethic the flow
of meaning logically has to go from the ideal good to the given
and from the intentional to the external, and not the other
way around. But we cannot go any further without considering law and all that goes with it in social structure.

The historical dimension of the good itself demands this as
well as our social context. Our good is not an immediate good;
it is a mediated good and law constitutes an important part
of that meditation. Law is, in a sense that will have to be understood quite precisely, a necessary means for the common good.
Beyond the dialectic of reason and the dialectic of sensibility,
fundamental social ethics thus has a special interest in certain
aspects of the social context that can be symbolized through
this polymorphous and all-embracing term — *law*.

What we wish to speak of, as closely as this can be defined
at this point, is the external domain of human action as this is
governed by set ways dictated by reason and past experience.
This is something quite distinct from the common good, at least
taken as the end of all human action, and from virtue, which
consists essentially of internal dispositions in persons. It is law,
but it is not to be equated to order, since order can be identified
with the end as well as the means while law cannot. Strictly
speaking, law is only a means and a particular law can be a
means of disorder as well as order.

The external aspect of the moral life represented by law is,
of course, not independent of the internal and dialectical aspects we have considered up to now. Presumably it is informed
by them and derives its ultimate meaning from them. But it
does have a consistency of its own which is at once an advantage
and a danger. Law is a constraint that brings direction and a
certain constancy in the development of persons without which
it is difficult to imagine how any of us could come to and per-
severe in a real moral consciousness. And yet the constraint can

114

take on a life of its own, so to speak, and so become an impediment to the internal, dialectical growth of the moral life. Law results from past action, more or less in view of the common good, with a tendency to become rigid and fixed with regard to the future. In its dynamic reality, as oriented to the common good, law carries us along even before we are fully aware of its intentionality, but it can stop short and become its own end or be turned to the particular end of a tyrant. Seen in its best light law represents a set of judgments already made based on experience and on a success already achieved, partial though it may be. This is what gives it its strength. But it always remains *still* to be seen what is to be done with that strength.

There is thus a certain necessity for law. The question is to determine what sort of necessity this is. Is it just a necessity *de facto,* a fact we have to contend with but could do without? Or is it a necessity *de jure,* not based on any claim of the law itself, since that is precisely what is in question, but based on the good — *ex suppositione finis.* If it is a necessary means for the common good, as we have already stated, it will be *de jure* but it will remain for us to understand this "juridical" necessity concretely and historically, starting from the end intended but coming down to the very concrete necessities of history in the here and now. Because of the inescapable connection between the institutional and the personal, law has a very definite, though by no means final, role to play in determining the exigencies of the common good in the here and now. It has to enter into the complex dialectic by which we come to judge what is to be done.

Yet, we cannot deal with this question fully without discussing the weight of this necessity, a weight that can be more burdensome than liberating, and without going into the efforts to overcome this burden of the law. This we shall do when we come to deal with totalitarianism and revolution. Before we do that, however, we shall look at law in its lighter aspects as a real means to promote the common good. This we shall do as we have proceeded up to now, following the order of historical genesis, starting from an intentionality and going on to its expression in an external order.

Law, authentic human law, does not come automatically. It comes from persons, from certain individuals who assume a special role in social relations and give these relations a special stamp of their own making. This is the way all important societies come into being. We shall, therefore, start with these persons and the role they play, with authority, therefore, which before all else is a personal relation between individuals. Then we shall consider the kind of institution that flows from this special kind of personal relation, that is, law as a historical reality. At the end we shall come back to the role of authority itself, as a personal factor, with regard to established law, for its role cannot be restricted merely to maintaing the law at all costs in its given state.

I — *Authority*

It is easy to define authority within a juridical context. A written constitution, for example, explicitly determines what authority there will be, how it will be established, and how exercised. When the constitution remains unwritten this is done more subtly, but no less stringently, through custom or precedent or, more generally, established tradition. Constitutionality serves to define authority and to judge whether it is being properly exercised. Thus, in an established society, the order of determination proceeds from law to authority.

This is the order usually followed in discussing these two subjects. From a discussion of law one proceeds to a discussion of authority, and then to justice, until one gets back to the principle of the whole order, the common good. This is not a false order to follow. It has a certain element of concreteness to recommend it, since it starts from the actual social structures in which we find ourselves. But it is not the order we have been following. Indeed, it is the reverse of it, for we started from the common good and then proceeded to justice. Now we approach the subject of law through authority, and not authority through law. This order is no less concrete than the other, since it deals with the whole phenomenon as much as the first. In fact, in one sense it is more concrete, since it tries to deal with the whole from the standpoint of the whole. But it does go counter to our spontaneous and natural attitude and this makes it more difficult to follow.

What we wish to do, therefore, is reflect upon the broader and more fundamental aspects of authority, prior to any particularization of it in this or that social system, to see whence and how the more juridical aspects and law itself emerge. This will not give us of itself a justification for law, since origins alone do not justify anything in human action, but it will give a better understanding of what human law is, or should be, and how it can be justified.

In its more general and basic understanding, authority always entails a capacity to influence or direct others in some sphere of human action, whether it be intellectual or moral, or both at the same time. Presuming they have what it takes, teachers and doctors, parents and rulers, all have such a capacity. The actual exercise of authority always entails at least one person communicating his will to another and the other accepting to follow that will.

This is authority in the most proper sense of the term. It is in this sense that it presents the greatest difficulty for man's free will and it is in this sense that we wish to discuss it here. Even the best and the most appropriated as well as appropriate set of laws will always have an element of heteronomy about them, an element that remains irreducibly external and even foreign to an individual's freedom, though not necessarily opposed to it, and the source of that heteronomy is in the heteronomy of authority itself.

In its historical genesis authority first appears through force or sheer domination.[1] Hegel's dialectic of the master and the slave was as much an account of the rise of authority as of self-consciousness, as can be seen from a reflection on the most

117

obvious forms of authority. Whatever else may be said of parental authority, parents surely have it because at least for a time, they are bigger and stronger than their children while these remain extremely dependent on them for sheer survival, let alone growth and development. When, with maturity, the time of emancipation comes for the children, parental authority may continue for other reasons, but there can be no doubt that it was first established on a basis of domination. This is not the sole ground of the parent/child relationship, nor ultimately its most important; love and affection are no doubt more important in many respects, especially to temper the force and make it humanly productive in the education of children. But force remains undeniably a principle of the relationship. It is as an extension of this same force that the other forms of authority akin to parenthood also rise, authority in the tribe, in the clan, and even in hereditary kingship, where the force appears less openly as overpowering strength but is no less real in custom and in the accepted ways of transferring power from one generation to the next.

Another way of gaining authority where the priority of force is most in evidence is, of course, mastery through conquest and war, armed force in a struggle unto death where one authority comes to replace another. But even in less violent situations where someone gains ascendency without use of physical force or any appeal to reason or customs, but only through a charism of his personality, there is still a real force that comes into play, a force perhaps stronger than any other, capable of overcoming the inertia of a social milieu and setting it in motion as it fashions it in its own image. The charismatic leader is surely not less forceful than an intruder from the outside who gains control; the influence he exerts is all the more penetrating because it answers the needs of the society it takes over. Let it last for only a time and it will reshape the entire social body and engender a new mode of existing for it, the structure of which will spontaneously find expression in new customs and a new style of life, in short, a new juridical situation, whether this be revolutionary or not.

Force alone, however, is not enough to constitute authority as a social bond. It is an element of nature and has to be completed by an element of reason. Force is only a beginning; the end must come into play before the process initiated by procreation and the struggle unto death can come to fruition. Might alone does not make right; it is incapable of creating a social bond by itself. The intentionality hidden in the life and death struggle must come to the fore before a *de facto* situation can become *de jure*.

This bridge from the fact to the right is easy enough to see in the case of the charismatic leader whose influence has given rise to a juridical power that surpasses his individuality. The ideal represented in the juridical situation continues to appeal to members of the social body even after he has disappeared and ensures their cohesion under the rule of an authority they accept more or less willingly. The common desire of well-being revealed by the embodied ideal in the institution effects the passage from *de facto* power to *de jure* power.[2]

But the passage from one to the other is also found where there is no such convergence of aspirations between adversaries locked together in a life and death struggle. It takes place through the same fundamental and universal desire of being which binds master and slave together and sets under way the same sort of transformation from fact to right. Only, in this instance the desire does not appear in its positive aspect for the slave; for him it appears on its negative side and becomes fear, flight from radical non-being, from the death threatened by the master. The terror of death draws from the slave a minimum of consent that ties him to his conqueror, with perhaps the need of an occasional reminder to keep him in line. But should that terror disappear there can only be revolution or suicide. As long as it is there, however, there does arise a social bond between master and slave.

119

Of course, it is a long way from that minimal bond to a full fledged juridical structure based on some degree of equality and respect, but already we see emerging in the master/slave relationship the essential act which effects the transformation from brute fact to right, the act of recognition which is given as grudgingly here as it was given willingly to the charismatic leader, who would himself remain only a taskmaster if he did not succeed in eliciting an act of real recognition from his followers. In fact it is not impossible for a proper juridical structure to come out of this first begining of a social bond in the master/slave relation, just as it is not impossible for a proper juridical structure to fail to emerge after the passing of a charismatic leader. We have seen any number of demagogues on the historical scene to prove the point. What the master/slave relation brings out, however, which no other relation does so clearly, is that the passage from fact to right does entail a profound commitment, a serious act on the part of man which somehow implies a risk of life and death.

This passage, of course, is not realized in the naïve way that the master would suppose in his triumphalistic attitude. The master remains a child of nature and knows only the language of brute fact. Nor does it follow immediately from the act of the slave as such, terror-stricken in the presence of the master. It has to be mediated by the slave's labor[3] with nature, his growing mastery over nature in behalf of his master, which leads him to reflection and eventual mastery, not only over his fear and nature itself, but also over the master, because the slave is the first to learn the language of reason through the discipline he is forced to undergo. He is the first to come to recognize himself and his power over nature in the product of his own hands. Thus, through the initial act of *recognition,* which is to be found no less in the relation with a charismatic leader, for there is also something of the master/slave in this relationship, the juridical order touches almost immediately, though only very obscurely, upon the good of communion and friendship, not to mention justice itself. Through the mediation of this act which we saw to be at the root of both justice and friendship[4] there develops a social body of law that serves as a means in the search for communion. In the act of recognition it is not only the other who comes into view, but also the common good, the end which alone can bring justification to any rule.

With the advent of recognition and a sense of the common good brute force can no longer be satisfied to rule just by might. In the act of recognition human force finds an exigency to transform itself into real authority. Thus even the conqueror will eventually argue that his rule is for the good of the conquered and he will seek recognition from them, for without recognition his rule is not only uncomfortable but incomplete. Similarly in a political society, if a party has real power it will seek to have that power recognized, by election, for example, in order to bring its power to completion. For elections not only bring added power; they bring legitimacy to power, a legitimacy based on the common aspiration to the good. No one is ever satisfied to rule only from the wings.

It is not for us to discuss here the many forms which this essential act of recognition can take, whether it be paying homage to a lord or electing a president. It is enough to have seen its priority to any juridical system. Force alone cannot constitute such an institution; only recognition can. Force remains an existential component for any juridical system. In fact, at times force may seem to be the only thing that holds a society together; but such a society could not be called truly a society nor would it last long as human institution. Beyond force, the bond of society requires the human act of recognition.

It should be noted, however, that this bond is not merely an internal act. It is an external act that takes the subject out of himself into the will of another or into a legal system where he seems to lose himself. Real authority, as transcending merely brute force, begins in an act of recognition, which is at once entrance into the realm of liberty as well as communion, but it

121

tends to become institutionalized, and hence alienating in many respects. The exercise of authority is never just a personal act, as we have seen already even in the case of the charismatic leader; it has its own external momentum that can escape the personal dimension and is in constant need of being re-assumed by persons. This is not just something incidental to authority. It is part of its historical necessity, for authority is both good and risky at the same time, like any other means required for the common good.

We should note also that authority will inevitably be a complex phenomenon in historical actuality. There will be the authority of experts in practical matters and of scientists in theoretical matters, though authority in science is of a special nature: it only supposes a better understanding of the truth and the ability to lead another on the way to truth, not an act of the will as such. In the more properly political sphere, there is legislative authority, executive authority, and judicial authority. These can be vested in one and the same man or in different men in a system of checks and balances, but they are inseparable and keep running into one another in the concrete.

What distinguishes one kind of authority from another is the precise end which each one is supposed to have in view. Just as the end justifies authority, so also it is the end that specifies it. The end of parental authority, for example, is the good of their children, their education and their eventual liberation. Political society supposes this end to be already realized, at least in part, though it also has its role to play in this education-for-liberty. But its end is communion between free persons, friendship, and its role is to overcome all the obstacles to this end as an "ordering power in society."[5] In view of this end the role of legislative authority will be to determine the order to be followed, the role of the executive will be to see that the order is implemented, and the role of the judicial will be to keep the order open to the end as much as possible whether it be the good of persons here and now or the good of communion in the future, beyond the alienation of the present, beyond the inevitable limitations of any given legal system.[6]

Paradoxically, however, and most importantly for a proper understanding of it, authority has to *will its own end* — a time when it would no longer be necessary, a time when there would no longer be any need for the heteronomy of authority and law. This is a limit situation, so to speak, which cannot be reached in history as we know it, but the thought of the limit sheds light on the nature of authority itself in our historical actuality.

The aim of authority in a true teacher is not to keep his disciples in tutelage but to bring them along at a faster pace than they would take if left to themselves, so that they may come to a communion of knowledge with him based on an equality of understanding and to a community of research where the one-time disciple becomes himself teacher in turn even for the one-time teacher. Such a dialectical harmony of teacher/ disciple relations should not be presumed to exist too easily, but it is the end of all genuine teaching, so that in the end the teacher is called to disappear as *the* teacher. The aim of parental authority is somewhat the same, especially as educational. Its purpose is to make full-fledged citizens of children so that they can operate freely on an equal footing with their elders. Bonds remain between parents and children once equality has been reached, just as bonds remain between teachers and former disciples, deeper bonds, bonds of piety as well as communion, but these bonds depend less and less on authority.

With political authority things are somewhat different. Equality there is not so much part of the end but more a presupposition at least in the ideal. Equality alone is not the end of the social order. Equality is the end of justice, but the beginning of friendship.[7] Thus, even supposing that a perfect equality and a liberty of persons were to be established in society, political authority would still have an end to look to, communion and friendship. But at the same time it would have to recognize that it cannot properly enter into this domain, because friendship transcends the competence of political power or authority of any kind. If authority were to suceed in establishing equality once and for all, it would have to will its own end as authority. Beyond that it can do nothing and would serve no purpose. It is a social bond only as long as there is inequality and alienation, in much the same way as teaching authority and parental authority are bonds only as long as there is inequality between master and disciple or between parent and child. Authority can only have historical necessity.

But is it possible to say that there will ever be a time of perfect equality, established once and for all, when authority will have to will its own end in fact? Such a view would be utopic. It would fail to take the liberty implied in human equality seriously enough. As long as man is free, that is, as long as history lasts, equality can never be established once and for all. The struggle of liberties will go on both as a loving struggle and as a struggle unto death and will have to be regulated. Yet it is not an idle statement to say that authority has to will its own end, since it serves to delimit precisely its function. The exercise of authority by someone will always be necessary as a social bond in history to overcome the alienation of individual liberties, but its role will always have very definite bounds. Instead of saying "as long as," we should rather say, to the extent that (and only to that extent) there is inequality and alienation, authority is required as a historical force. But to the extent that there is equality and wherever there is real communion there is no need for authority. Authority is thus a very essential part of the dialectic between justice and friendship, but its intrusion into the free realm of communion is a perversion of authority itself as well as a destruction of the deepest social bonds in the common good. Authority remains in constant tension with that realm, but can never enter into it. It is only a matter of justice, and not of friendship as such.

In every form of authority, then, there are two elements at

play, power and recognition. These are not found just at the origin but remain as the essential constituents. If might does not make right, neither is right real in a society without might. The passage from factual ascendency to rightful rule does not abandon all use of force. It transforms it into something human. Hobbes saw the reality of these two elements quite well, but he was unable to understand the dynamic relation between them. On the one hand he saw the violent chaos of infinite natural desires and on the other, the peaceful harmony that could come from contractual agreement.[8] But he did not see the historical unity between them. Society for him had to be unnatural and nature, antisocial. Force was all on one side, right all on the other, and the two never became one. Because of this Hobbes never came to a proper understanding of social reality; he could only have a social contract theory of political society.

Authority is a unity of power and right. It can be harsh or brutal, but it always entails an element of coercion guided and legitimized by a vision of the common good. That is why Weber's sociological definition of politics[9] as a way of using physical force is ethically quite correct; it only needs to be completed in terms of the end, the intentional element that transforms force, a thing of nature, into something properly historical. The element of power thus makes the acquisition and the exercise of authority a proper study of social science. But that is not the whole of authority; there is also the more personal element of recognition which takes it beyond the realm of mere observational science into that of more personal relations. This is why in this subject, as in so many others, like that of community, for example, social science has to be open to human action as a whole and a different kind of reflection than its own, something more "ethical."

Finally, it might be useful to distinguish between leadership and authority in an established society. At the origin of a particular society these roles are usually vested in one and the same person. This is especially clear for the charismatic leader whose action gives rise to a juridical structure stamped with his personality; he defines legitimate authority by the force of this personality. But this identification of leadership and authority is also true in terms of the master/slave dialectic. The master is not properly an authority because he rules only by brute force. It is the recognition of the slave that begins the process of legitimation. This legitimation may not come through a direct transformation of the master himself; it may come only through the slave as he gains ascendency over the master who rules by the force of nature alone; but however the legitimation may come, it will come by whoever is first to discover the language of reason and the primacy of the end in human action, whoever becomes the truly historical leader.[10]

In an established society, however, the roles of leadership and authority can be separated. The person in authority need not necessarily be the leader, nor does the person with leadership have to have juridical authority. To have the two vested in different persons will certainly give rise to tensions within a particular society, something that could lead to revolution, but the tension can be healthy and fruitful even without radical upheaval. This would require a certain recognition on the part of both leader and authority, a healthy respect for the role of the other, but it could lead to a high degree of social productiveness since it would free each one to do what he can do best without encumbering him with things another can do better. Perhaps the tension would become too great in time and the master/slave dialectic would take over once again, so that the leader would eventually become an authority as well, but we should not be too hasty in identifying the two roles. They are not necessarily the same, nor is the presence of real leadership in a person other than the one in authority a sign that the person in authority should immediately be dismissed. There is a function of management to be considered, especially in complex society, and this does not necessarily go with leadership, not any more than with authority for that matter, but it could be a reason for keeping the roles of leadership and authority separate, without presumption on either side. The distinction is something we shall have to come back to in discussing revolution.

II — *Human Law as Interpretation*

The law, as we have to think of it here, is something which emanates from reason and is meant to direct human action concretely toward an end. It is therefore with reference to action that we have to discuss law, and not as something in itself. Reason is not only a principle of human action, but also the principal agent of direction for it. This is what we call practical reason, the originator and the director of action. Reason intervenes in every human action, assumes it in its own intentionality, and leads it to its own end. It does this quite particularly in each instance, but at the same time it also comes to formulate some general norms for action which seem useful in many or most cases, if not absolutely in all cases. Thus, along with the concrete exercise of practical reason, there emerge from experience certain rules which reason stores up, so to speak, to help it in judging future instances so that it will not have to start *ex nihilo* at every moment. This is what we call law, essentially a rule of action that becomes a measure for action, a norm for judgment on what is to be done. It comes with experience and grows with it.

The origin of law, therefore, is reason itself which commands and governs human action. Ontologically or theologically one might argue that the origin of law is in nature or the author of nature. But that would not be to the point here. We do not deny that God is ultimate ground of being, nor that nature enjoys a certain priority over human reason. Even in his historical initiative man is never purely creative; nature is always something he has to contend with no less than his past. But the question is whether anything can appear as a rule for human action apart from human reason, without the mediation of practical reason

127

in concrete experience. Historically and phenomenologically speaking we have to answer *no*. Whatever else may be said about the origin of law for human action, reason remains the key to it.

This is not to deny the validity of so-called "natural law" in ethics. It is only to say that such "natural law" always remains something to be discovered and acknowledged by man before it becomes effectively a rule for his action. Nor is it to say that we have learned nothing of that "law." This writer would be prepared to argue that a good deal of that "law" has been discovered historically and is well grounded in a number of traditions and cultures. But even so, knowledge of that "law" is not something that can be closed off in history nor is the "law" itself something static and hermetically sealed off from man's own free initiative. It gives rise to it and, within limits that are increasingly difficult to determine a priori, remains responsive to it. Man is coming to fashion nature to his own image, for better and for worse, to an astounding degree, so resort to "natural law" alone is becoming increasingly difficult and futile. Man's most pressing concerns arise quite beyond mere nature, though they remain very much implicated in it.

Even when we admit the reality and the irreducible priority of "natural law," we are still not entitled to refer to it as the moral law purely and simply without the historical mediation of reason. Reason, with nature, to be sure, but never nature alone, is the source of moral law. In a sense, reason, the moving force of human action, much more than nature, is the creator of moral law. Fear of historicism and relativism should not blind us to this very positive function of reason, which is not arbitrary but rather has to be strictly rigorous in its procedure, since that is the condition for its very creativity.

The problem for man is to determine the modality of this rigorous procedure in reason as it proceeds from the given of nature and experience. Here Aquinas' understanding of the relation between reason and nature can be of some help. In this, as in so many other things in ethics, he is following Aristotle, but he brings a focus of his own that sheds more light on a properly historical consciousness. As a theologian Aquinas thinks of the natural law in man as a participation in the eternal law of divine Providence itself.[11] The idea of nature connotes direct dependence on the Creator, but does not preclude a special form of providence for rational beings. The latter are to *provide* for their own good in the light of their own reason. Thus, natural law in a rational creature is the light of natural reason which in turn is nothing else than an impression of divine light in us. From this light understood as the principle of reasoning, man is to proceed — *per industriam rationis,* by the toil of his reason — to specify more particularly what is to be done.[12] This gives rise to what Aquinas calls human law. It is, however, the passage from natural law to human law which interests us more precisely here.

How does this passage take place? First of all it is not something automatic, based on nature alone. It supposes the initiative of reason itself seeking what is more useful for man's well-being, an inquiry which takes it beyond anything merely given in nature.[13] This is why natural law itself can be said to be different in different men — since circumstances differ and it has to be applied differently[14] — and changeable — since something can be added to it, though nothing can be taken from it.[15] Of itself, therefore, nature is open to the work of reason in its quest for what is better for man. Reason starts from nature and proceeds in two different ways, one by way of conclusion from principles and the other by way of determination for things that remain common and indeterminate.[16]

The first of these two ways is a strictly rigorous process. It is akin to the process of demonstration in speculative science, but it does not give rise to the same kind of necessity in the conclusions. While drawing the analogy Aquinas is careful to make a differentiation between speculative reasoning and practical reasoning. In the former, whoever knows the principles

and how to proceed from them correctly arrives at the conclusion of necessity. He may err on the way or fail to go to
the end of the reasoning, but if he does go to the end without
erring, he will necessarily draw the same conclusion as anyone
else. In practical reasoning, however, it is not so. The common principles are the same for all, but as for the proper
conclusions to be drawn from them, these are neither the same
for all nor are they known the same way by all even where
they are the same.[17]

Everyone should act reasonably. From this principle there
follows the *quasi* proper conclusion that borrowed property
should be returned to its owner. This is true for the most part,
that is, it should be done, but not in every case necessarily.
To return a gun to someone with homicidal intentions would
not be according to the exigencies of the good here and now.

This does not mean that practical reasoning has to be any
less rigorous than speculative reasoning. Rather it means that
the rigor of practical reasoning has to be different; it has to
respect the exigencies of its subject, human action in view
of an end, no less than speculative reasoning; and this will
demand greater diligence of inquiry since its subject is impossible to nail down abstractly once and for all as is often
the case in speculative science.

This distinction concerning practical reasoning could be interpreted as applying only to concrete judgments made in the
here and now, and not to law as such, which always has a
certain generality about it. But Aquinas makes the same distinction between the two ways of proceeding from nature for practical reason with reference to bodies of law as well as to
particular decisions. This is how he interprets the distinction
between the "law of nations" — *jus gentium* — and civil or
positive law:[18] the first has to do with what is derived from
natural law by way of *conclusion,* as for example just buying
and selling and things of that nature without which men cannot live with one another; the second has to do with what is

130

derived by way of particular *determination* according to whatever a civil society may decide is for its advantage.

The idea of a *jus gentium* presents some difficulty to anyone accustomed to divide law only according to natural law and positive law. The "law of nations" seems to belong to positive law on the one hand, since it seems to be proper only to man, but on the other hand it seems to belong more on the side of nature, since it seems to be less open to man's decision than positive law. Aquinas hovered between the two poles: he did speak of *jus gentium* as part of natural law, not without some confusion since this tends to reduce reason to nature, but he also more consistently spoke of it as human law, a category in which he included both positive law and the "law of nations" and which in the treatise on law he was careful to distinguish from natural law. Yet even when he allowed the "law of nations" as part of natural law, he did maintain a distinction that becomes doubly interesting to us since it touches on the distinction between history and nature which we have found so important and have tried to maintain throughout our discussion.

What is according to natural right or justice (*jus sive justum naturale*) is what is adequate or commensurate to another.[19] Now, Aquinas says, this happens in two ways: one way, according to an absolute consideration of the thing itself, the other way, not according to an absolute consideration of the thing itself, but according to something that follows from it. The examples are especially interesting: for the first Aquinas mentions the male who of himself (*ex sui ratione*) has a commensurate relation (*commensurationem*) to the female in the order of procreation, and the parent who has a like relation to his son in the order of education; for the second he alludes to the propriety of possessions (*proprietas possessionum* — not exactly "private property," though that comes into play), and he illustrates as follows. If I consider any particular field absolutely, there is no reason why it should belong more to one

131

man than to another. But if I consider it with regard to the likelihood of its being tilled and used peacefully or amicably, then it has some commensurate relation for belonging to one and not to the other.

The argument goes on that man has natural law in the first sense in common with other animals, but natural law in the second sense is the proper area of reason, since to consider something according to what *follows* from it is something only reason can do. This second mode of law is natural for man in the sense that it flows from natural reason, which dictates it — *quae hoc dictat* — and not in the sense that it exists in his natural constitution as such.

The thing to note, however, is how precisely the passage is made from mere nature to reason. The illustration is taken from Aristotle's argument against common ownership of fields in the *Politics*.[20] Significantly enough it has to do with justice, like other illustrations of *jus gentium* we saw earlier, such as buying and selling and whatever else is conducive to social well-being. Aristotle's argument supposes that all things should serve the common good. The question is whether this purpose can be served better by individual ownership or common ownership. It is decided on the basis of experience and rational interpretation: individual ownership is the right thing, what is *justum,* because it proves to be what makes for a better development of things and a more peaceful use of them for the common good. In any case the use should be common, never strictly private, as Aquinas, following Aristotle still, is careful to point out,[21] so that a man should readily communicate his goods to others in their necessity. The argument, it should be noted, is not necessarily in favor of capitalism, as most interpreters often suppose. Capitalism is something else than individual ownership of a field in a Greek city-state. For capitalism as such one would have to argue from other historical circumstances and show a similar usefulness and peacefulness, not to mention a just distribution of benefits, in the private ownership of means of production. But that is not our point here. Our point has more to do with precisely how reason comes to this sort of conclusion starting from nature.

Reason has to follow a strictly rational process. But now we see that it starts from nature in two senses of the term, from nature taken as a thing given absolutely, though open to man's use-full appropriation, and from the natural light of reason itself. Through the interplay of these two forces in experience, human reason, that is, the reason actually exercised by persons concerned for the common good in justice and friendship, comes to its own conclusion concerning the historical use of things. It cannot do this arbitrarily, without taking nature itself into consideration, as well as the end of human action, but in doing so it arrives at a level of law which is no longer merely natural, nor is it yet properly "positive," but has to be termed *historical,* a law proper to human existence as such, the law of nations or of people as such.

III — *Human Law as Creation*

But that is not the last word on human law. There is still to be considered what has been referred to as positive law, the law which is constituted according to the second way of proceeding from nature by reason, the way of particular determination. This way is quite distinct, though historically inseparable, from the way of conclusion from principles; it has its own exigencies and requires a special kind of genius, that of a true leader as distinct from a mere teacher. It is in the nature of genuine artistic creation, where man is called to express himself in external forms, in social structures, that will more adequately manifest and serve his universal aspiration to the good. It is the realm in which man most properly exercises his historical initiative since it takes him beyond interpretation into a creativity based on his own vision of what is for the best. It gives rise to the art of politics, the historical art par excellence since it makes history while at the same time flowing

133

from it. The true leader always appears in answer to the aspirations of his time.

We cannot, of course, here go into the dynamics of this art with its infinite variations. This would require a long study of political systems in history, present as well as past. While such knowledge is important for the concrete exercise of moral judgment, it is not the task of fundamental ethics to elaborate it; that is more the task of political science and other social sciences. For our task it is enough to see this art and what it produces in its relation to the other ingredients of moral judgment.

We could ask where natural law, including the law of people as such, leaves off and where positive law begins. What in human law is arrived at strictly by way of conclusion from principles, and what by way of free determination? The question, however, would presuppose that we can separate a number of things that cannot easily be separated in the concrete, only distinguished in a dialectical process. It would presuppose that we can separate the "positive" from the "natural" in our experience when in fact we see that our very decisions affect experience itself and hence the knowledge we derive from experience by way of conclusion. Our own decisions can and do in fact lead us to new conclusions that were not clear in our first awareness of the principles, not directly as decisions, for that would make conclusion an arbitrary and not a rational process, but indirectly, by way of a new interpretation in the light of results and consequences of decisions. The question would also presuppose that we can know the end apart from the means, the principle apart from actual experience, or that we have arrived at a final knowledge of all that can be concluded from principles, in other words, that we have arrived at the end of history, and that experience can bring no new knowledge.

It is difficult to draw sharp lines between principles and conclusions when the principle is the end and the conclusions have to do with the means to the end. But it is all the more difficult when those means have been devised by human initiative as well as by nature. In any given culture, let alone the multiplicity of cultures, it is impossible to draw the line between what is natural and what is the product of human creativity or perversity. There is simply no state of pure nature to start from for historical being. Everything we find is a product of both nature and man. It is the attempt to separate the two abstractly that leads to skepticism and cultural relativism. Because we cannot find nature in isolation, we say that all is arbitrary. In doing so, however, we lose sight not only of nature but of the rational aspect of liberty itself. Social reality is indeed open to man's free initiative, but that initiative is not without a positive orientation, an orientation to the good that reflects back on what the initiative is to be. This is what enables us to judge between good and evil precisely in the realm of initiative beyond nature.

Thus, nature is not closed in upon itself nor is liberty independent of nature, but the two together constitute historical reality. For purposes of analysis it is better to think of law in history in terms of a continuum extending from nature at one end to liberty at the other, from natural law to positive law, with the law of people as such in the middle. Some laws can be seen as belonging clearly in one category or the other, at least according to some of their aspects, while others are not so clear. Lack of clarity in all respects, however, does not infirm the distinction of categories in the law nor the historical importance of this distinction. It is reason that makes the distinction in its twofold relation to nature, that of concluding and that of deciding, and that holds the categories together in their distinction as it passes from one end of the continuum to the other, and back, in its historical task of learning and inventing the good at one and the same time or in alternating phases. The distinction is important because it clarifies the various aspects of reason's task in history, while the continuum represents the horizontal dimension of law which reason totalizes, as it introduces the vertical dimension that comes from the end.

It is for each society, then, to work out its own law, both rigorously and freely, through a rational interplay of liberty and nature, starting from nature and going toward the end it shares with all other societies, the good of history itself. It would be insufficient to rely on nature alone, apart from the free initiative of men, just as it would be imprudent and irresponsible to fly in the face of nature. We have to maintain the distinction, therefore, while seeking the unity of man and nature, of liberty and law. Positive law does lead to a certain extension of the necessity that comes from nature, a necessity created by man, so to speak, but hopefully it will make that necessity a better means of liberation.

But how, concretely, does positive law come into being? It is a work of art, as we have already suggested. But who is the artist? We have spoken of law as an expression in social structures of a universal aspiration to the good. Does that aspiration express itself directly as such in certain structures or is it mediated by certain individuals, those who assume a role of leadership in a society? The question of positive law brings us back to the question of authority, for even if there is a universal spirit of mankind, that spirit does not express itself directly without the mediation of individuals who function as leaders. That is why the classical definition of law usually included a note concerning promulgation by whoever is responsible for the common good of society. The determination of a particular law comes as a result of a decision by an individual or a group of individuals and the fact of this determination has to be communicated to others, since such a determination is beyond the realm of nature or what could be concluded from natural reason alone.

We find here an important distinction to be made about political leadership. Just as there are two ways of proceeding from nature for reason, so there can be two kinds of authority, one that consists in authentic interpretation of what can be concluded from natural law, which gives rise to clarification of the *jus gentium*, and one that consists in a simple declaration of what has been decided will be the just thing for a particular society. Once again we see how impossible it is to separate the "natural" from the "positive" in law, for legal documents often spend as much time interpreting what is required by natural law or the universal rights of man as they do declaring the particular determinations that will obtain in a society. This is by no means a shortcoming since the interplay leads not only to a better understanding of natural rights but also to the formulation of a more appropriate and effective positive law. The thing to note, however, is that here we are concerned primarily with the second form of authority which is more properly that of the political leader who is more than just a teacher but rather a shaper of institutions.

The question of positive law, however, is not reducible to the question of authority. Only authority can make law, but authority is not free to make or not to make law. There is a certain necessity about positive law; it comes whether we want it or not. Even the leader wishing to steer clear of institutions inevitably ends up affecting some, if not creating them outright. This is a necessity of fact, of brute force. Yet the question is somewhat different, since it has to do directly, not with relations between persons as such, as authority does, but rather with external structures that are in a sense independent of persons. Can this fact, the necessity of external social structures, be transformed into a matter of right? Is the decision of legitimate authority sufficient of itself to make this passage from the factual to rightful? If not what more is needed?

Once again the act of recognition must come into play, along with the exercise of authority, to effect this passage. This is the same recognition which appeared as the first social bond in the master/slave relationship and which gives rise to justice and friendship in more advanced forms of communication. But it is now extended to include, besides the persons themselves, the external structures in which the relations between persons find expression. Law is such a structure or, more precisely, it is a human organization of such structures, and it comes into play for moral judgment as a means to the common good. Thus it flows from prudence for the common good, a prudence that is not found equally in all, and it becomes law in the full sense of the term when it is recognized as such by the members of a society. This does not mean that members as such become authors of the law. Recognition of the law does not eliminate the role of personal authority in society. It presupposes it. But it does take the law beyond the realm of mere individual authority, out of the hands of its authors so to speak. Recognition confers upon law a certain universality and objectivity that is independent of individuals, for once a law has been recognized as such it becomes binding for its authors as well as for other members of society. It becomes an objective social bond that ties members together.

This objectivity, though it is by no means the last word about law, is very important for it as a means to the good. It provides a certain stability that allows us to escape mere whimsicality or the fluctuations of subjective dispositions. Man needs a kind of assurance from day to day in his social relations, since we are not all equally constant nor do we all fluctuate according to the same rhythm. Law provides this assurance, at least externally, inasmuch as everyone, including authority itself, recognizes it as a norm to go by and to judge by. Moreover, even though it has the partiality of a particular society, it can also serve as a means to universality for the members of that society, since it forces everyone to go beyond his own individual viewpoint. The good law is the one that helps persons transcend their partiality.

We should carefully note, however, the kind of universality in question here. Human action is always something in particular that becomes universal with reference to the common good. The universality of the law is derived from the end of that action. Hence law is universal not by a community of genus or species, but by a community of the final cause, inasmuch as the common good is a common end.[22] It is not the abstract consideration of man's species-being that founds the universality of law, but the fact that it is meant to lead us out of our partiality into the universality of the common good.

Recognition also lends a degree of seriousness to positive law that has not always received its due in so-called liberal or laissez-faire society, where law is often regarded as little more than a necessary evil to be kept at a minimum. Its positive role as a means to the good is often overlooked, so that a penal approach to the law comes to the fore: one is not really bound to obey the law unless one gets caught disobeying; then one is bound to accept the consequences, the penalties of the law — as if the law itself had nothing to do with the proper exercise of moral judgment. Law is seen as purely external, as having nothing to do with conscience. Such a view is impossible to maintain in an ethic where recognition of the law plays its proper mediating role and transforms the dictate of authority into the positive means to human betterment it should be. This does not imply that we should have as much law as possible. As we shall see, law, like authority, has to will its own end. But it does imply that we do not a priori try to reduce law to a strict minimum. We must devise as much law as will be useful for the common good. This will vary according to times and places.

On the other hand, however, recognition allows us to maintain the unity between law and conscience without collapsing the one into the other. This sort of collapsing can take place in either one of two ways, either by accepting external law as the sole norm of conscience — "my country right or wrong" — or by making a law out of conscience, accepting conscience as the only law. These two attitudes are direct opposites of one another and they feed on one another in their opposition. But they both flow from a common confusion about the relation between law and conscience which they share. The one empties conscience, which can only be an internal reality, into the law, while the other betrays the nature of law, which inevitably entails an external reality, by trying to absorb it in conscience.

Law, however, is a product of reason as reason tries to work out the necessary and useful means to the common good. It is a special kind of means. Unlike virtue which is an internal disposition — including justice, though it is concerned with external actions and things and therefore with law — law is external to conscience and conscience must come to terms with it as external, especially in an ethic of responsibility. Recognition, along with the prudence of the lawmaker, is what makes this external reality into a human instrument for social betterment, but in doing so it does not make it something internal like conscience or virtue. Law remains no less external and objective, irreducible to conscience as such, and to be reckoned with in moral judgment positively as well as negatively, in its recommendations as well as in its sanctions. Recognition mediates between the external and the internal, the objective and subjective, as it mediates the social bond between persons, but it keeps the two dimensions in a dynamic tension. They converge, but only in the future, that is, in the end; in the present we have to face up to heteronomy in law as well as in authority.

Does this commit us to a static and immutable view of the law? Not at all. It commits us only to taking the law in its objectivity seriously as a necessary means of moral betterment. This is something even the revolutionary leader does as he risks life and limb to change or overthrow a system of law he judges to stand in the way of man's good. The classical notion of positive law must be watched carefully here. It does suggest something external to any individual conscience, even as informed by natural law, something irreducible to the autonomy of individual reason. Yet it does not allow a separation of conscience from the external nor a divorce of law from reason. Positivism, along with Kantian formalism, has played strange tricks with law in this regard. By keeping the two apart in nominalistic fashion it has forced us into a view of the law that cannot transcend a given or established society as such. Law thus becomes reduced to establishment and nothing more. Divorced fom actual reason, or reduced to the so-called positive idea of reason which is concerned only with clarifying the given,[23] law does imprison us in the *status quo;* it does not provide the means of getting beyond the limitations of a given society in any real sense. But law does not have to be so. Reason, which is the author of positive law, is in fact much more creative than positivists have imagined and positive law has to be one of its most imaginative creations.

Admitting, then, the tension between the internal and the external, the subjective and the objective, in human law, we have to say that law will be a very dynamic reality in history. The law cannot directly attain the internal aspect of human excellence; it cannot of itself produce virtue, an internal disposition. But it will have to serve in the development of virtue and excellence, in the formation of conscience. It will have to prevent certain acts, vicious acts, that stand in the way of such development, and command other acts for common service and usefulness. This is the ancient idea of law as discipline, as providing the means to develop virtuous citizens, and it presupposes great flexibility and openness to change in the law for two rather obvious reasons.[24]

First of all, as a product of human reason the law shares not only in its creativity but also in its historical limitations. Reason proceeds from principles to conclusions only gradually; it grows only little by little. So also do the positive determinations it makes in law: brilliant and genial as these may be in the beginning, they can come to practical fruition only gradually. In fact, the really creative innovations, not to mention destructive ones, are hardly ever recognized as such at the outset: it is only in time that we come to realize all that they meant. Thus what the first lawmakers wanted or intended in a society was not always clear, even to themselves. Nor could they be in complete possession of the situation in which they found themselves with all its ramifications. They had vision enough and understanding enough to set something important in motion, if they were truly founding fathers, but they could not anticipate in every way and in every detail what their innovation would lead to or call for in the future. Things which they did and said, therefore, were deficient and would have to be changed, hopefully improved upon, as time and experience brought these deficiences out in the clear. In this way deficiencies of the early law were corrected.

This takes away nothing from the genius of original lawmakers. Indeed the improvement of law is part of the exercise of piety which descendents owe their forefathers. But it does make clear the need for constant revision of law, not just because of changing circumstances but because of the imperfection of reason which is tied to these circumstances in experience. Reason itself is changing, hopefully improving with experience. This is why there is always both room for improvement in the law and the real possibility of making innovation.

The first reason for flexibility and openness to change in the law came from the part of reason which creates it. The second comes from the part of man at whom the law is aimed, for whom it is intended. If law is meant as a discipline for men and if the dispositions of men differ at different times, then it is clear that, if law is really going to achieve its purpose, it will have to change and be adapted to the different dispositions of men in different places and at different times. Law for its own sake is a monstrosity; it serves no purpose. Law has to provide a certain stability in human relations, but it can do so only if it takes the real dispositions of men into account.

142

Otherwise it will not really lead anyone to virtue or keep him from vice; it will not lead anyone anywhere; it will only cause stagnation and turmoil. Children need to be led differently from adults, quiet people differently from tempestuous people, conservatives differently from liberals, vicious people differently from virtuous people, and so on. Law must deal with people as they are and must therefore change as they change to lead them effectively to the good. Different societies also differ; some are more advanced in certain respects than others. Each must find its law, suited to its needs, and the law must change as the needs change. Any static system of law can only be a perversion of law.

This brings us to our final consideration on law as such, a point that parallels one we made in connection with authority: just as authority has to will its own end, so also it has to will the end of law. We have spoken of the purpose of law diversely, as either the formation of virtue in those under the law or as orientation to the common good purely and simply. On both scores law has to will its own end.

First of all, as a means of discipline, law has the same kind of finality as any form of teaching. It aims at creating a certain equality and, to the extent that such equality is established, its function ceases. This is especially evident in the case of justice. Ideally speaking, the lawmaker has achieved in himself dispositions of justice toward the common good and is in a better position to form others in the same kind of dispositions. Nothing can take the place of positive leadership, personal influence, in this regard, but the leader also makes use of external rules of action to orient his followers in the right direction. Such rules cannot directly create dispositions in others, as personal influence might, but they can remove obstacles and open the way to their emergence. In fact, this way of looking at the matter is still too dualistic: the personal influence of the leader himself, as well as his creative genius, is mediated by the external rules he devises and proposes. The rules can have their proper effect only if they communicate the leader's personal ideal, his vision of and concern for the good. In any event, the aim of the law is to bring about an equality of disposition in the members of society and, to the extent that such equality exists, the law ceases to be necessary as an instrument of discipline. If that equality did not at the same time imply personal liberty for each individual, we could say that it ceases to be necessary absolutely, but such a hypothesis would take us beyond history. In history the disciplined man may choose to go against the exigencies of the common good.

But even while admitting the close interconnection between an internal ideal as personified in a leader and the external regulation by law in its disciplinary function, we still have to recognize a further limitation of law within our historical perspective. Not only should the law recognize that in the end it should be useless, unnecessary and therefore no longer any good, but even in the meantime, in historical actuality, its usefulness has very definite limitations. There are aspects of human action that simply cannot be touched by law, beginning with the very internal dispositions of justice and friendship from which law derives its own ultimate value. Moreover, even in its own external sphere, there are always things that are best left to take care of themselves to avoid greater harm. Human reason simply is not up to controlling every facet of external action a priori. Without falling into the error of *laissez-faire,* which has never accepted the positive value of law as a means of real moral discipline and which always seeks to minimize the law as much as possible, to "liberalize" the law as it is often said, not seeing how the moral awareness of a society is very seriously affected by and implicated in its laws, we still have to say that law can never directly inject itself in the internal forum. It can provide, and should provide, an environment conducive to the proper development of a social spirit, but it cannot provide the spirit itself. This depends on something else besides the law as such, not something apart but something more internal.

This brings us to the second score on which law must will its own end, its orientation to the common good. This good, as we have seen time and again, is composed of two basic dimensions intimately bound to one another, an internal and an external dimension which we have characterized as communal and structural, respectively. We have maintained a necessary relation between the two, the basic historical tension of our moral life, but at the same time we have viewed communion primarily as the end and structure primarily as means to the end, though there always remains a two-way communication between the two in our historical situation.[25] Law is a means for managing the structure so that it will serve communion among men.

It is not a necessary evil, though there are aspects of the law that are necessary because of evil. It is a necessary good. Indeed, it is good precisely because it is necessary. Its necessity, however, is not an absolute necessity like that of the end; it is only a necessity of means, a necessity that supposes willing the end — *necessitas ex suppositione finis.* Absolutely speaking, the end is good of itself, whether it is necessary or not. But the means as means is both necessary and good with reference to the end. Necessity is truly a measure of its goodness. Hence if the law ceases to be necessary and useful it ceases to be good. If it tries to transgress beyond the bounds of its usefulness, either by prolonging itself when or where it is no longer necessary or by trying to pass the limit of justice into the realm of friendship, it becomes an intruder in a realm where it can only do harm, that is, where it can only stand in the way of communion.

This is an argument we have already seen in connection with authority.[26] Here, however, in connection with the common good, it brings new light on the idea of the end of history. Marx shared the same idea of civil society as nineteenth century liberalism. In fact, he identified civil society with bourgeois society and he could not see how such a society could continue once communist society came into being. Marx thought it possible for man to come to an end of antagonism in history and to enter into

145

a completely new form of social existence. That was for him the communist ideal.[27] Law, the State, was only a way of organizing the struggle in favor of a certain class. Where liberals saw only an absence or a minimum of control, Marx saw an organized domination of all classes or, more precisely, the reduction of all classes to one class, the proletariat, by another class, the bourgeoisie, under the protection of the State. Law, civil society and the State thus came to be identified in his mind with only a particular stage of the historical development leading to the end. Its necessity was not the sort of necessity we have tried to define, but the necessity of just a stage in the process.[28] Beyond that stage, law, or at least law as determined in civil society or the State, would cease to be necessary.

Marx was able to separate the law from the end in this way, however, only because his view of law was too particularized. When he tried to represent for himself what the ideal communist society would be, he could not see how law could enter that picture, since it was law only as envisioned in *laissez-faire* society, which, in the absence of any real equality or justice, was more a form of *laissez-dominer*. This separation was no doubt an important part of the reason why he could think of the coming of communism as the end of pre-history and the beginning of real history: a society beyond all law as well as beyond all strife is surely *toto caelo* different from ours. It would be heaven on earth. It would not be properly historical. In maintaining a more universal concept of law, one not restricted to any particular form of civil society or state, one founded on the universal aspiration for the common good as seen in the tension between communion and structure, we do not have to abandon all concept of law in our ideal society. Furthermore the ideal itself becomes all the more credible for historical man since it has a real correspondence to his actual experience. Law is not the last word of history. But neither is communion by itself. For us here and now that remains an abstraction. History is rather the struggle to establish and maintain real hu-

146

man equality among men, with a certain amount of real communion already informing the struggle from the beginning; it is a loving struggle as well as a struggle unto death, a struggle where the end is already present. Law is itself an expression of the equality struggling to emerge, an essential ingredient of historical planning and labor.

IV — *Law and Judgment*

We have sought to deal with authority and law in a positive fashion, without however overlooking the intrinsic limitations of this external aspect of human relations. Perhaps a history of law and of the exercise of authority in the past would incline us to be more sanguine as to man's ability to use authority and law only for the common good. Perhaps it would reveal that they have been means of domination more often than means of the common good. This is the way many see them today at any rate. Yet that would not be precisely to the point here. We have been concerned not so much with the role authority and law have in fact played in the past, but rather with how they enter as ingredients of moral judgment in the present.

As such they have more to do with the future than with the past. In the exercise of their function lawmakers have to think of the future above all else; they legislate for the future, and even in passing judgment on the past they must think more of improvement or rehabilitation than just punishment or reward, for the ultimate justification of either one is still only in the future. In the exercise of his own moral judgment each man must also be concerned primarily with the future. This is how law and authority come into view, in the mutual concern of all for the future. To be sure, knowledge of the past will give a better appreciation of what authority and law can really do, and of what they cannot do, but that will not be the last word. The necessity remains: authority and law are something we have to deal with in human *praxis*. This is not just a necessity of fact to be taken into account; as we have tried to show, it is a matter of moral necessity, a necessity rooted in our common aspiration to the good. Law is a necessary means for the common good, a good we cannot do without.

Besides, a history of authority and law would not necessarily reveal only shortcomings and perversions of human intentionality. There are many ways of reading the past. Even while admitting the inadequacies and the shortsightedness of legal institutions in the past, including the real evil purposes which they have served, one can still see that without such institutions to open a way we would never have been in a position to recognize their defects and limitations, let alone do something about them. In law, as in science, we see better and farther than our predecessors because we stand on their shoulders. Even a revolutionary spirit can only be a function of the system against which it is revolting.

In any event, whether we are optimistic or pessimistic with regard to any particular system, the law must enter into our planning for the future, both as part of the plan itself and as a condition for proper planning. The planning we speak of is not to be done in isolation, as we saw in connection with justice and friendship; it must be carried on in dialogue.[29] One of the basic conditions for dialogue, however, is an equality of sorts, a respect for rights as well as a readiness to hear and listen that cannot be assured without law. Law is not necessarily a leveller of persons, but it does give individuals an equal opportunity to know where they stand and what they can expect to come from what they say and do. It may even give them an equal opportunity to be heard, though this degree of equality is more difficult to attain and has yet to be reached in most societies. With law dialogue can proceed confidently; it can become heated without fear of recrimination. Without law insecurity is inevitable and voices are muted, if not completely silent.

What we mean by law here, of course, is not just a set of rules and regulations duly set down in documents or customs to be applied rigidly without consideration of circumstances. Law, as we have seen, emanates from leadership and authority. It also cannot function properly without leadership and authority to apply it and to adapt it according to changing circumstances. Law is an expression of judgment as to what is to be the appropriate way of proceeding in the future. Such judgment is always open to a revision, something that cannot be merely automatic, written into the law, so to speak; it will always require the mediation of further judgment. A truly open legal system is not one that tries to take care of every eventuality a priori, but one that actively calls for new judgment from persons with the learning that takes place from the experience that has been shaped by the law itself. Law not only has to will its own end. It also has to will its own obsolescence as society changes. This is the only way in which a legal system can transcend itself, as it must.

Thus the established law can never be rightly invoked against a better judgment. Authorities have a way of shirking their responsibility in this regard by hiding behind the law, by invoking the law when their own judgment is at issue. But such behavior cannot be justified in a genuine social ethic aiming at the common good. Law cannot be used to close off dialogue, that is, the communal exercise of judgment; it can only be used to make it more honest and measured, so that what is proposed as new will truly be better than what is already established. The presumption in favor of the law is by no means absolute, especially if we keep in mind the perversions of the law. This presumption can itself only be historical, based on experience but open to the future.

Moreover, law is also the expression of a spirit. As expression, it concretizes the spirit, makes it historical, and so adds a dimension of reality to the spirit. As such it is ahead of the spirit: it brings the spirit to a certain completion. On the other hand, however, any concretization in history is always a particularization, a limitation in space and time. No law can adequately

149

express an authentically human spirit. Thus we first learn the meaning of a spirit only in its expression, but through this expression we come to understand the broader and more universal intentionality of the spirit itself and so we are led to seek a new expression of that spirit, not just by reason of changing circumstances, but by reason of the universal exigency of the spirit itself. It is this dialectic of intention and expression that gives rise to cultural change and a diversity of political constitutions, but the dialectic does not take place independently of persons. It takes place in the dialogue that goes on between people and leaders as they try to face together their historical task. As an expression of past experience, as a sedimentation from past judgment, the law shapes this dialogue, gives it direction, keeps it from disintegrating or going around in circles, by bringing people together on the basis of their common experience, but it does this only in the hands of persons who always have still to exercise their own judgment, because the spirit transcends the law, the intention of social existence always goes beyond any of its particular expressions.

We insisted at the outset on treating authority before law, since the first is truly the source of the second. Now, as we think more in terms of the future, it is important to reverse that order, for law is no guarantee for the future except in the hands of people concerned for the future. Just as authority cannot hide its authorship of the law, if the law is going to be duly constituted, so also it cannot hide from its responsibility to use the law prudently in view of the common good. Authorities of the past are not authorities for the present in the full sense of the term; it is the living authorities that count, those that are living literally today, and not just symbolically. These are the ones that are called to interpret and to exercise judgment, inevitably their own, and these are the ones people are called to face up to here and now, not some authority abstractly remembered from the past.

This is what makes the difficulty and the continuing importance of authority over and above the law. People are more ready to submit to a spirit, a cause, and even to a law as an embodiment of that spirit, than to an individual who can impose his will, not arbitrarily if he is a true authority, but still unmistakably, so that others have to do as he chooses. No man, it seems, should have this kind of power over another. Nor does any man have the kind of wisdom such power would seem to presuppose. Who has enough wisdom to manage his own affairs adequately, let alone those of others as well? We are more prepared to trust a system than the judgment of any individual.

Yet this greater difficulty with personal authority is also a sign of its greater usefulness in the pursuit of the common good. Keeping in mind the limitation we spoke of earlier, a limitation that applies to authority as well as to law, the role of authority remains more personal and hence more productive, if the person in authority assumes his responsibility personally and if he truly has the prerequisite of any good authority, a higher degree of prudence in view of the common good. This may seem too much to expect of any individual in the abstract, but it is not impossible nor unheard of if we keep in mind that such responsibility and prudence are not acquired in isolation but in communication with others. Is not the true leader, the man of real authority, the one in closest correspondence with the aspirations and the judgment of his followers? Is he not formed by them in the very act of forming them? If he draws ahead of them, it is not by separating himself from them, but by expressing in a new and better way the wisdom they share in common. Recognizing this his followers can obey him even as an individual, because they accept his will as an expression of their own freedom and liberation.

The mechanisms for this exchange between leaders and followers are extremely diverse and complex. They also get increasingly so with the complexification of society. We have placed these mechanisms here under the basic symbol of dialogue. But it must not be supposed that the only dialogue we have in mind is a simple form of one to one communication. Such a form is no guarantee for an extensive legal system. Also required, and more importantly, is a modicum of good will on the part of those involved. In speaking of dialogue we wished to include all forms of communication that constitute the bond of our large societies, the election process, the various ways of exerting influence in a democratic society, the formation of public opinion and so on.

In view of the fact that we are more often concerned with propagandizing than with real communication, it may seem naïve or overly idealistic to speak of dialogue in this regard. But even propaganda can be a beginning of dialogue if it doesn't stop at that. Moreover, it remains that without the kind of real communication which we associate with authentic dialogue, a personal exchange, a give and take on a rational basis, starting from the diversity of experiences, there can be no lasting social bond of any significance for the good of history. Man is reduced to a brute life and death struggle for mere survival in a new jungle of technology. Instruments of communication serve only to alienate people from one another. Is not this fragmentation the most fundamental aspect of the crisis in modern society?

Finally, it should be noted that the model we have had primarily in mind in this discussion has been that of political authority and civil law. This model of society, whether it have a monarchic, oligarchic, democratic or any other form of government, supposes liberty on the part of its members and rests more on explicit recognition than any other model. This is why, even after distinguishing between the role of leadership and the role of authority in established society, we have continued to combine them in our reflection on the relation between law and authority. This model, with its infinite historical variations, remains the prototype, a sort of perfect example, in the sense that the ancients spoke of the polis as a perfect society, for seeing what is involved in the exercise of authority and the use of law in creating the bond of society, communication.

But authority and law are found at both lower and higher levels than political society in the social order. At the familial level there is parental authority which has special responsibility not for the common good in the full sense of the term, but for that of the family. This does not suppose liberty on the part of all; rather part of the good toward which it aims is the liberation of those who are not yet free. Nor does familial "law" as dictated by parental authority require the same kind of explicit recognition as political society does, which supposes a degree of real liberty. Normally, however, parental authority should be able to count more on immediate communication and affection, trust and confidence. This is why parents should beware of ruling only from a distance or "objectively." What may be proper for civil authority is not so for parental authority. On the other hand, familial society is not self-sufficient, it is not a "perfect society." It has its own proper and irreducible exigencies as a nucleus and social incubator, but it is essentially open to political society. It leads into it and is influenced by it. It cannot be replaced, but neither can it remain closed in upon itself.

To think of a higher level of authority and law than political society is to be forced to accept the analogous meaning of the terms. The analogy already begins to appear in the distinction between political and parental authority, but when one tries to think beyond political society as we represent it today for ourselves in the nation-state, one can only wonder what such terms will mean. Do we have a model for thinking such authority and law? We do speak of international law and international courts, and we have an Organization of United Nations. But no one will say that we have anything like an adequate model yet. Even if the United Nations had real police powers, would we be any closer to an effective international society? Is not the idea of a "police force" still too much of a national form to be of real service to supra-national society? Indeed, are we not still thinking of the requirements of international society in general too much in terms of national societies?

Yet international society can presume good will on the part of all involved even less than national society. The problems it has to deal with are also infinitely more complex than those of any national society. What, then, can we do, besides wait and hope for the leaders we need at this level, the people who will be able to do the creative planning and work required to bring all nations into a real society based on communication instead of the present antagonisms based on war and the struggle for survival?

We can at least recognize that authority and law have to remain radically open even on the level of "perfect society" as represented in the national-state. The Greeks thought the city was sufficient. The nineteenth century thought the state was. We can no longer entertain such thoughts of sufficiency for anything short of a universal society of all men. At this level we find ourselves caught in a purely master/slave dialectic between nations and races, but we are coming to realize that we shall have to go beyond into a different kind of struggle. War is becoming less and less a viable, not to say morally acceptable, form of international relation. But what are we to do without war on this level? Who will be our leaders if they are not the warriors, or the diplomats — those social engineers of our warlike society? Perhaps if we have a radically open concept of authority and law we will be able to recognize these leaders when and if they come on the scene. The point is not to do away with the nation-state, which also has its own proper and irreducible exigencies and which has a necessary role of mediation to play for universal society itself, but to discover a new mode of authority and law which will effectively assume the lower modes into a higher order. Our next revolution will have to be truly a world revolution.

CHAPTER V

TOTALITARIANISM AND
REVOLUTION

We have tried to think of authority and law according to its positive aspects as instruments of liberation for man in view of the common good. Our experience of authority and law, however, is not always liberating. Often it can, and does, become oppressive. This is due not just to the will to power and domination in men, but also to a certain ponderance in institutions as such. Human institutions have their origin in active communication between people. They serve the good by providing a framework of stability that is both necessary and useful for a continuing communication. Yet these same institutions have a way of developing their own life, so to speak, apart from the purpose they are supposed to serve, apart from the life of communion they are supposed to express and make possible. They become calcified: stability becomes resistance to change even when change is necessary for the sake of communion; or else they become fixed on a set course of action even when that course no longer serves the common good.

Pushed to its extreme in a technological society this tendency of institutions gives rise to totalitarianism, a phenomenon that has reached terrifying proportions in our day and one which no social ethic can fail to confront. The possibility of totalitarianism has always been there in human society by reason of the distance there exists between intention and expression, between communion and the structures of communication. It has been actuated in part in primitive societies or by despots and tyrants in the past, but never in the total fashion we have seen in the

155

twentieth century. If this were just a question of historical circumstances, it would be of no special concern for a fundamental social ethic, since such an ethic has more to do with a basic perspective than with particular historical facts. But when it comes to totalitarianism this does not seem to be the case: the fact here touches on a relation that is of supreme importance for the proper exercise of moral judgment, the relation between social structure and the common good, our first principle of judgment.

Totalitarianism has indeed been like a ghost haunting our discussion from the beginning, in our reflection on social reality as a human existential, in our atttempt to show the primacy of the common good in moral judgment, and throughout our presentation of authority and law. This is due not only to the proportions which the problem has taken for us, but also to the very nature of a social ethic as such, especially one based on the primacy of the common good. Totalitarianism is the ultimate temptation of such an ethic: it is the most radical and most pernicious perversion of the common good under the guise of the common good itself.

Along with totalitarianism, however, there is also another characteristically modern phenomenon that calls for special attention in a social ethic, the revolutionary movement. To be sure, there were revolutions long before the American and the French Revolutions gave this movement a new impetus, but they have never been as pervasive and as radical as what we have seen in the last two hundred years. The revolutionary spirit in our time has reached down deep into the masses and far across the face of the globe. The poverty and misery which man used to take for granted no longer seems as necessary and inevitable as it did formerly, given the new means placed at our disposal by technological developments. Only the will to power and domination seem to stand in the way of a universal well-being. The few, relatively, seem bent on protecting vested interests, while the masses labor and strive to overcome the social structures that keep them in their destitution.

Thus, revolution too becomes a matter of intimate concern for a social ethic. It has become a sort of universal fact that we not only have to take into account but that enters as a dimension in the very exercise of moral judgment. It calls into question the structure of our social reality and, understood properly, it does so in the name of our basic norm of judgment, the common good. We spoke of a distance, a tension, between the good of communion and social structures which allows for the possibility of short-circuiting the historical process by totalitarianism. The same distance and tension, however, also gives rise to revolution as a possibility and even at times as a necessity. Just as man can turn his institutions into means for a particular good or into ends in themselves, so also he can turn against established institutions for the sake of the good for which they are supposed to exist.

This does not mean that an authentic social ethic has to be revolutionary, though the question might well be raised in our day. The intimate connection between the modern revolutionary movement and "the social question" has been clearly established.[1] This question is identically that of the common good as the good of history. We have insisted repeatedly upon the historical tension between the internal intention of communion and external structures in society. It may be that there is only one word to speak properly of that tension in its extreme states — revolution. Does this mean that history will have to be a revolutionary process? It may be. One thing is certain: the question of revolution is intimately connected with that of the common good. Even if it were not to demand such radical steps, it is clear that only this good could justify revolutionary action.

But this revolutionary movement also brings us back to our concrete starting point in historical consciousness,[2] except that now the question of the good, of right and wrong, comes explicitly into play. Revolutionary action presupposes some sort of moral judgment which takes the good of history into account. If the democratic spirit and a more generalized sense of responsibility are relatively modern social phenomena, so too is the revolutionary spirit. All of these seem to have been correlated historically since the recognition of the *Rights of Man* as absolutely universal. This recognition has remained abstract and will remain so, only an ideal still to be realized, as long as it is not actualized in history. *As such* it may have opened the way to totalitarianism as well as revolution, since it can give rise to all sorts of confusion and aberration. The question is to learn to distinguish clearly between the true exigencies of the good in history and the tendencies that might lead us to a complete perversion of these exigencies, in short, between what might be called a true revolutionary spirit and totalitarianism.

This, however, cannot be done by separating the two, for both have a common focus in social structure. It can be done only by examining closely the attitude of each toward these same structures, and how the one inevitably betrays or perverts the role of these structures in the communication between men, while the other can serve to open up these structures to new dimensions of communion.

I — *Totalitarianism*

It would be difficult — not to say mindless — to speak of totalitarianism without reference to two of the most perfect examples of it known in this century, Hitlerism and Stalinism. Other régimes have also been rightly characterized as totalitarian, but none has been as completely so as the two we shall use as primary analogates.[3] Though the term totalitarian was first given prominence on the political scene by Mussolini, Italian fascism never fully articulated nor forced its totalitarian implications until the very end of its time in power, under pressure from the Nazis and in the face of advancing Allied armies.[4] Until this last moment when it began to show its true nature, Italian fascism had temporized with other political ideologies, the monarchy and the Catholic Church, allowing each of these in untotalitarian fashion a sphere of activity officially recognized by law or concordat. In Spain and Portugal also, where the dictatorships have been termed totalitarian by some, more observers and analysts recognize that totalitarianism has never become as absolute as in Nazi Germany or Stalinist Russia.[5] There have been self-admitted limits to the power of rulers, even if only in the internal forum of conscience or in man's personal relation to God. There have been attempts to control and manipulate all aspects of life, but never to subordinate them purely and simply to the state. Only under Hitler and Stalin do we find the radical intention of taking over every aspect of life and eliminating anything that could not be brought into line — an intention that was accompanied by a no less radical will of execution. This is why German Nazism and Russian Communism have been rightly recognized as régimes that were *toto genere* different from anything previously seen in history, beyond every form of tyranny, despotism or dictatorship ever known before as well as beyond any form of legitimate government.[6] In these two instances, and possibly in others that have arisen since then, totalitarianism has gone so far that it has transcended the very category of government (and its abuses) into a realm hitherto unknown to purely political man. Hannah Arendt has rightly seen it as the abolition of the political as such.

Our point, however, is not to study the phenomenon as such. While this would be very instructive for the concrete exercise of moral judgment in our day, it is not the task of a fundamental ethic to do so. That is more the task of history and social science. Besides, there are already a number of such studies for us to fall back on in our reflection. Our task here is to reflect on the implications of totalitarianism, not just to pass judgment on its manifestations in the past, but more to help us to formulate a better course for the future. Totalitarianism is much more than an aberration of our recent past. Since its appearance, it has become the chief threat and temptation of modern society, not just from the outside, as from a foreign power, but from the inside, as a worm that can consume the very fabric of our social order. The real trouble with one-dimensional man is that he is totalitarian and cannot come to an authentically common good based on liberty and diversification. Totalitarianism is inevitably reductionist, just as every form of reductionism tends to become totalitarian.

Totalitarianism is itself such a total phenomenon in fact as well as in intention that it is impossible to deal with it piecemeal. If one is going to pick up the subject, one ends up having to handle a vast array of interlocking facts and ideas. To facilitate our own task we shall reflect upon the phenomenon from the viewpoint of the different themes we have dealt with earlier starting with law and then moving back through authority and equality, the hinge of justice and friendship, to the common good itself. What we shall see, in effect, is that totalitarianism leads to a radical corruption of each of these ingredients in the good of history. It is the systematic corruption of all that we have seen to be necessary for a genuine social ethic.

It is on the level of law that totalitarianism is easiest to recognize. There the temptation first appears, even when there is no explicit totalitarian intention, and there also it has its most obvious manifestation. Five common and basic traits of totalitarianism have been distinguished:[7] an official ideology, a single mass party, a monopoly of control over all means of effective armed combat, a monopoly of control over all means of effective mass communication, and a system of terroristic police control. Except for the first, which touches on the way of conceiving the common good, all of these traits have to do with some aspect of law, whether it be in its constitution or in its implementation and enforcement.

Whatever may be the ideology, the rhetoric or the propaganda under which a totalitarian régime presents itself, it always insists on occupying the whole scene. In contrast to the liberal society which it is coming to replace, but still in the terms of that same society, it allows for only one ideology and one party as spokesman for that ideology. According to totalitarianism, there is only one way of conceiving the common good and the party represents that way adequately. There is no room for other ways and hence no need for other parties. In fact, there is no room for opinions other than those of the party. Within the party itself there may be room for differences of opinion at times, but in time these differences have to disappear. Once a line has been established, everything and everyone has to fall into line. Whatever or whoever fails to do so, is either suppressed outright or cast into outer darkness, which from the viewpoint of the party is the same as suppression. The one-party system is only the external face of an internal monolith of opinion with· in the party.

Though the liberal mentality, which still ties the pluralism of ideas to a plurality of political parties, might balk at this, one could possibly conceive a one-party system in which a rich diversity of the common good might be preserved and fostered. Indeed, it would not take much adjustment to think of our so-called liberal societies as one-party systems when we see how closely all parties share the same ideology and how united they are in opposing any criticism of the common ideology, whether it be from the right or the left. It is no wonder that liberal society has itself been accused of totalitarianism. But the one-party system in a totalitarian régime can never preserve, let alone foster, the necessary diversity of the common good. A state, whether it be city or nation, can harbor many differences of opinion as to what would be for the good; it can hold these in a healthy and fruitful tension, or at least keep them from simply eliminating one another, along with the good that might come from each. But this cannot be if it has fallen into the hands of a totalitarian party, where only the party knows and it alone can decide.

When this total identification between state and monolithic

party takes place, the very notion of state becomes merely equivocal and the situation of people, totally confused. The party never takes in the whole population; most of the time it hardly includes ten percent, if that. But those who are not members of the party are still ruled by the state no less totally than if they were members, for power resides not in the state but in the party.[8] The state becomes only a tool of the party. In fact, more often than not the officials of the state are not the officials of the party, so that they do not even have the power of decision they should have. Needless to say, this kind of equivocation and confusion exists not just in totalitarian one-party systems, but wherever the real power of decision making with regard to public policy is exercised by people behind the scene who are not public officials. Again instances of this could be cited in our own liberal societies as well as in the avowedly totalitarian states.

But this is only the beginning of equivocation and confusion. It gets worse as we look more closely into the ways and means of totalitarian government and the sort of activity it engages in.

Radical totalitarianism could only have been a modern phenomenon. It is not that men could not have had the idea before Hitler or Stalin; it is just that the means for implementing the idea were not available. Intentions wait upon means for development. Totalitarianism demands complete control over large masses of men. Before the advent of modern technology this sort of thing was simply impossible. Neither the ancient oriental despotisms, nor the tyrannies of the ancient Greek cities, nor the imperial establishment of Rome, nor the absolute monarchies of modern Europe ever reached the heights or the depths of twentieth century totalitarianism, with its capacity to control every aspect of life, including thought, through intimidation and invasion of privacy, a capacity it has shown itself more than willing to exercise to the full. The instruments of intimidation are bigger and more terrifying than ever before and the means of surveillance, as well as communication, are so refined that it is impossible to escape the probing eye of the party. And if anything should escape that watchful eye, it is absorbed or rendered innocuous by the constant flow of propaganda that fills the air at all times and the terror instilled against anything and everything that might seem to be not of the party, by the party or for the party. Only a technological society such as ours could reach the kind of control and terror that totalitarianism has come to exert.

But, besides technological refinement, there seems to have been another pre-condition for the rise of totalitarianism in our time, that is, a new insistence on the economic and the need for planning. Responsibility for this turn is often placed at the feet of Marx, who certainly had a great deal to do with giving it formal recognition. In his early political struggles he came to realize that what mattered most was not the ideals or the principles for which people stood but the economic structure, which may or may not have been in harmony with the ideals and principles, but which in any case was the ultimate determining factor of social life.[9] Though this realization became the guiding thread of his thought, however, Marx did not invent the principle; he merely discovered it in the bourgeois society in which he found himself and in which we still find ourselves.

The ancients had always been careful to distinguish between the economic and the political, between social life as based on the market place and social life as based on communication between citizens. Citizens were thought of primarily as men of dignity and virtue, not just economic agents, and the need for the state was based on a need to develop and educate men to virtue, much more than on the need to control the exchange of goods.[10] In fact, as the name itself indicates, economics was seen more as a household activity, while politics took over where the economic left off, where it proved insufficient to bring men into a common life based on freedom.

With bourgeois society this distinction has more or less collapsed, in spite of Hegel's attempt to maintain a distinction between "civil society" and "the State." Economics has become such a complicated business that it can no longer be considered merely a household activity, as the name implies in its etymology. It became "political economics" and is becoming more and more international economics. By reason of its complexification, economics has become more and more a fact we have to contend with at every level of the social order. More importantly still, as Marx saw, because it has to do with *man's relation to nature,* economics has become the concrete means for the effective internationalization, the universalization of social life.[11] In this sense economics goes beyond political life as it used to be understood either in the city-state or the nation-state, but at the same time it tends to reduce political life to only one of the dimensions it used to have, that of production and the exchange of goods, leaving out the higher dimensions of communication, which economic planning on even a national or an international plane cannot provide for.

This universalization of economics, which technology has only served to reinforce, is not of course an evil in itself. If accompanied with a parallel universalization of politics, with an appropriate development of political institutions, it could in fact enhance the possibility of reaching a truly universal common good. But in the absence of such political development it can only open the way to totalitarianism, as it has done in fact.[12] This is not to be blamed just on socialism, because the socialism we have known is only the logical outcome of bourgeois liberalism. Both socialism and liberalism have suffered from the reduction of the political to the economic which goes back to *laissez-faire* and belief in some invisible hand guiding the economy[13] — an abdication of prudence and responsibility in human affairs. Now that we have seen that the economy will not take care of itself, we have forgotten that taking care of human life entails much more than economic planning and control. Totalitarianism is only showing us to what lengths our forgetfulness can take us.

164

With these two pre-conditions, a propensity for strictly controlled planning according to a preconceived model of the economy reinforced by the technological know-how to elaborate and implement overwhelmingly complex plans, totalitarianism can take hold and run its inhuman course. With the technological means at its disposal, it can have exclusive control of all violent forces against which there can be no possibility of self-defense. It can also have such control over the means of communication, *mass* media,[14] that there is no possibility of withdrawing or hiding from its overbearing presence. And to assure this effective control it develops a system of police control based on terror such as has never been seen before.[15] According to totalitarian logic, the individual has no identity apart from the collectivity, and in practice it tries to make sure that there will be no hidden identity, no difference between the public and the private, because such hidden identity might not only constitute a threat to the régime: it would be a living contradiction of totalitarianism itself. The logic of totalitarianism is one of total identity or total opposition, with no possibility of an intermediate political participation for different opinions and different forces.

When we come to the question of authority, totalitarianism proves to be no less equivocal and confusing than it is for law. It might seem that, though law becomes totally arbitrary in totalitarian rule, at least authority reigns supreme, for there is no totalitarian movement without its *Fuehrer*, its Leader, whose sole will is law. In such a movement all "responsibility" is presumably vested only in the Leader, he is personally responsible for everything done by the movement.[16] Yet, with all of this concentration of power in the leader, if we look more closely, we find that there is in fact precious little authority in a totalitarian régime.

For one thing there is no communication of authority, for in a totalitarian movement only the leader has the power of real decision. He may be no less caught in the movement than anyone else, but still the movement does not decide anything except through him. There are no set channels of authority, no real hierarchies of command. The leader deals directly with everything from the broadest general policy down to the last details, because everything is totally one. The leader maintains his absolute control by using several tracks of communication at once, the party echelons and various services of secret police, for example, each isolated from the other and living in fear of the other. Only the leader knows and can know what is going on at all times and he may send conflicting commands down the different tracks in order to keep things confused and prevent them from coalescing into any sort of stable pattern. His commands may also be deliberately vague at times, but this is not to allow his subordinates some exercise of freedom and responsibility. Rather it is only presupposed that simple adherence to the movement will dictate what action is called for, while leaving the leader free to reverse himself at any time and keeping all subordinates guessing at all times as to what will come next. In a normal society authority is meant to limit freedom, to establish bounds for it, not to abolish it purely and simply, but not so in totalitarianism. There the Leadership principle aims at nothing less than complete abolition of freedom. That is why, as Hannah Arendt has shown, there can be no real hierarchy in a totalitarian régime.[17] The Leadership principle is in direct contradiction to any authority principle.

Indeed, it is so much so, that what is meant to open up into a genuine social relationship is frustrated at its very roots. In totalitarianism the struggle unto death fails to reach even a master/slave relationship; it leads only to death. There is no possibility for any passage from might to right such as we saw was necessary for the genesis of authority as a social bond.[18] The leader is interested only in exerting force, not authority, and does all in his power to keep anyone or anything from taking root in nature, the first condition of real liberty for the slave. With the technological means at his disposal he can succeed in preventing men from taking any distance from nature in reflection, from discovering themselves in their labor with nature. He does, in fact, reduce them to brute animals, and when he does not kill them physically he does manage to kill them spiritually.

This is so not just for the victims of concentration camps, for example, but even for those who manage such camps. All, including the most fanatic followers, become incapable of the slightest act of recognition, the beginning of reason and liberty, or else, looking at it from the other end, the last vestige of human consciousness. All is absorbed in a never-ending massive movement where death can come even while the body is still alive somehow. The active participants in the movement as well as its victims are not even slaves; they are reduced into robots. For some transformation is bound to take place — if it is not to new life it will be to a new death.

The idea of a mass movement brings us to the third ingredient of social reality which totalitarianism contaminates, equality. This, we saw,[19] is the end of justice and the beginning of friendship. But in the concrete, equality is not realized except by communication, the act which both justice and friendship have in common. Totalitarianism, however, is a mass movement of men taken only in isolation. It takes hold only where there are large masses of men who feel left out and it maintains itself by carefully nurturing this sense of isolation.[20] The totalitarian mass man is kept from identifying with anything except the movement, and this he has to do directly only as an individual, without mediation from natural or established social structures. Though the movement may be nationalist or racist or identified with a class, these are only temporary modalities. The intention of totalitarianism is to absorb all men into its leveling process or else eliminate them from the face of the earth. It harbors most universal social ambitions, yet it cannot accept any of the socializing agencies that have developed historically, whether it be the family, the nation or any other association. Loyalty has to be to the movement and its Leader and to nothing else, because loyalty to anything else undermines totalitarianism at its roots.

Totalitarianism is sometimes identified with state control, but that is to underestimate the full scope of the movement, which always goes far beyond any particular state. Not every excess in state control is totalitarian, though any such excess is a step in that direction, only that kind of control which recognizes no limits within or without the state. Whenever a totalitarian movement succeeds in taking over the government of a state it can never be satisfied with keeping it as it is or stopping at that one particular society. It comes as an intruder bent on destroying the constitutional identity of that state, but only as a step toward the destruction of all constitutional identities. It will use its entrenchment in one place as a means for world domination and rule, even in the nation where it has taken hold, as a foreign power.[21] This may be a form of egalitarianism, but it is egalitarianism at its lowest common denominator — so low that only quantity counts and nothing else. Judgment becomes only a matter of calculation and computation while human life turns into sheer barbarism, not to say animality.

Genuine human equality supposes two things: real identities and real diversity among identities. What makes for equality is not just the diversity of identities, and hence a certain inequality, but the communication and mutual enrichment that takes place through dialogue. Totalitarianism, however, not only keeps mass man in isolation from his fellow man, but it vitiates the means of communication at their very root in language. We have seen how it equivocates and causes confusion on law and authority, how it turns every social institution away from its proper end, but now we must see how the very basic institution of language itself, the ground as well as the expression of every other institution, becomes vitiated. In totalitarianism nothing means anything clearly any more, much less consistently. The only thing that is clear is that everything is subject to

168

change according to the whim of the movement, even the simplest and most basic meaning of the simplest and most basic
words. Nothing means anything any more because everything
can mean anything. Totalitarianism is the radical corruption of
all language, the father of the total lie.

Our contemporary obsession with language and its apparent
lack of clarity or consistency is a sign of how close we feel
we are to the brink of totalitarianism. Many use or, worse still,
encourage the general confusion of language for their own
economic or political ends.[22] Others are satisfied to analyze
the confusion of language in an effort to clarify the accepted
meanings of our society.[23] But others still, with a perverse sense
of rhetoric, only yell and shout obscenities to scramble meanings
further and exacerbate the general confusion of language.[24] All
of these, whether advertisers and propagandists, or philosophers
and social scientists, or just plain rebels, witness to the radical
importance of language in social life, and how close we are to
losing this first and most basic instrument of rational communication. But totalitarianism, like the father of the total lie
that it is, would have us go over the deep end.

Beyond language, however, and every other given institution,
there remains the more substantive issue of the common good
itself. It is here that totalitarianism reaches the height, or the
depth, of its equivocation and confusion. Here it is that we
find the reason and the ultimate explanation for every perversion we have noted up to now. For, even if it presents itself
as its first proponent, totalitarianism is the most radical betrayal
of the common good.

In totalitarianism there can be no substantive dialogue about
the end of man because there is no idea of the common good
as a historical reality. The totalitarian view of the common good,
if it can be called a view, is totally utopic, totally detached and
separated from historical actuality. That is why it can be so
ruthless in its day to day activity. In historical consciousness
and responsibility there is need for a certain amount of uto-

pianism, even if it be only to open the way toward transcendence over the limitations of an established order. Man must be able to conceive new and better ways of being if he is going to labor toward an ideal of justice and friendship. But totalitarianism does little or nothing to conceive *realistically* what that ideal will be or can be. It devises and elaborates far-reaching means of exerting total control, but these means are never rationally tied to an end. An end, some vague idea of a good, is sometimes proposed, but this is left so nebulous and remote or abstract that it can never affect the choice or the quality of the means chosen. Totalitarianism's sole concern is with means and cares not a bit about how its means might affect the end. All it wants is to assure continuation of the movement and the progressive radicalization of its hold on people. Perpetuation of the movement itself is really its sole end.

Every political movement has its ideology, its basic framework of justification, its social philosophy, and its doctrines about man, as well as its practical recommendations for action.[25] Totalitarianism is not an exception in this regard, but it is important to note how radically different ideology has become in its case. Of itself ideology can be fairly neutral, or open, and it can lend itself to any number of régimes within a political spectrum like that starting from the Greeks down to modern times. It is not necessarily absolute, but in modern times, once again, the tendency has been more and more to absolutize.

The process began to take shape with the rise of the modern European monarchies as they began to affirm their own authority in the face of the Church. This they did for a time by an appeal to the divine right of kings, but little by little, as so-called secularization set in, the reference to God became less and less pronounced. With totalitarianism the reference is totally excluded, since totalitarianism cannot allow even a domain of conscience that escapes its control, let alone a God who would be a point of reference for itself as well as for individual consciences. It has to be atheistic. Totalitarianism recognizes only

170

itself as the ultimate point of reference. Yet it is not any less absolute than the absolute monarchies were. Indeed, its claims are even more absolute.

This follows from two of its essential ideological traits. First its essential atheism precludes the possibility of any reference to an ulterior reality beyond itself. Hence the impossibility of relativizing its claims. One could debate whether this is a cause or a consequence of its claim to encompass absolutely the totality of reality, but it is clear that the two, totalitarianism and atheism, go hand in hand. What is more interesting from the viewpoint of a fundamental social ethic, however, is its view of the end of history. This is its second ideological trait which, supposedly, grounds a kind of absoluteness that has never been seen before.

In speaking of the meaning of history we distinguished three views of history, one cyclical, one linear, and the third cycloïdal or a combination of the first two.[26] The first, we saw, tends to be rather relativistic, especially if a sense of liberty in the political sphere is maintained. The third does not entirely abandon circularity, but it does introduce an element of direction. Hence it is not as relativistic as the first, though it remains open to a future that is at once directional and yet open to many possibilities. The second view, however, allows for none of this flexibility. It is linear presumably in function of an end that is determinate. And inasmuch as, *ex hypothesi,* there can be no end outside of the process itself, the process is itself determined. Hence it is that every form of totalitarianism belongs to this second view of history — another reason why totalitarianism appears only as a modern phenomenon, since such a view emerged clearly as a worldview only in the nineteenth century.

But totalitarianism always adds a special aura to the view of history that it adopts. This has often been noted by most of those who have studied the phenomenon. Far from being satisfied with suppressing religion, totalitarianism replaces and supersedes religion with new formulas, new rites, a secularized religion.[27] It appears not less but more exhaustive and infallible than any theology it wishes to eliminate. In fact, by reason of its atheism, it becomes false theology par excellence, with all the faults of a worldly theology but none of its saving features.[28] It becomes intransigent with a vengeance, even before there is any reason to doubt the total adherence of the partisans. Some have even gone so far as to characterize totalitarianism as essentially mystical,[29] either by reason of the special cult that comes to surround the leader or by reason of the fervor or fanaticism which it generates in its followers — as if they were at the service of a transcendent cause. This mystical element is so pronounced that it seems a special characteristic of totalitarianism, beyond both socio-economic planning and mere ideology. It is the totalitarian leader's distinctive approach to social organization, so that everything, including the arts,[30] is placed at the immediate service of the movement, the only thing that counts.

Besides this false mysticism, however, totalitarianism entails the most radical contradiction in its conception of the end of history. This contradiction can be brought out in two different ways.

First, though totalitarianism seems to reason from a knowledge of the end, its vision is so abstract that the end has, for all practical purposes, no influence on the choice of the means. Totalitarianism claims to be in sole possession of the end, to know it perfectly, and all that follows from it for practical reason. Thus, it alone can dictate what is to be done at any moment in history. What it knows in fact, however, is not the end at all, but only the process, its own *praxis* which has evolved in complete ignorance of the end. The end it speaks of is only an abstract community of species, the species-being of man, as Feuerbach and Marx would have said, without any real historical content other than its own perverse *praxis* — which is precisely what has to come into question. What is left out of consideration is the concrete community of men in the making, the community which totalitarianism itself can only

172

undermine. This community is far from having reached its end, but it is far more real than the "community" invoked by totalitarianism to justify its attack on the present community. It is a real beginning of the end in the present which totalitarianism totally ignores. Thus, in the last analysis, it is not from the end that totalitarianism argues in its reasoning, but rather from the forces which it has set in motion itself. It turns in an absolutely vicious circle, both theoretically and practically. Not only is there no influence of the end on the choice of means. There is not even any real consideration of the end, except to deny its validity in moral reasoning. Totalitarianism is locked in in its own infernal machine.

The second way of bringing out the same contradiction, one that hopefully will appear less abstract, is more in accordance with our understanding of the common good in the concrete. This good, as we have seen,[31] has two aspects, an internal aspect and an external aspect. It consists in a communion which finds expression in social structures which serve that communion. This good is the ultimate good, the universal good, for all men as well as for each man, on the condition that it be considered as a whole in all its aspects. As such it is the good without qualification and it is the object of the highest form of love, the love of benevolence. But taken only in its external or useful aspect it ceases to be universal; it becomes only partial and can no longer serve as the primary norm of moral judgment.[32] But this is precisely what totalitarianism has done: it has reduced the common good to the merely useful and functional. Whatever its intentions may be, totalitarianism is concerned only with the manipulation of men, with the external and useful aspect of social reality, leaving aside all internal and communal aspects. Thus it treats as universal what can only be partial and in the process destroys all possibility of preserving, let alone achieving, a genuine common good. It is not therefore just an incidental error when totalitarianism decides to set aside the actual good of communion, seemingly in view of a greater good

173

in the future; it is the radical error of totalitarianism itself from which there is no return, except by starting once again from the good of communion actually given in historical reality, limited as that might be, along with the structures in which it has found expression, which is tantamount to repudiating totalitarianism as such.

The temptation to totalitarianism is one that will not be easily overcome in our post-industrial society. Not only are technological developments furnishing new instruments for totalitarian domination, but the very complexification of our society will induce us to make greater and greater use of these instruments, at the risk of by-passing the internal and communal aspect of human reality, the only thing that can save us from totalitarianism. Sheer bigness is a weight which pulls us down in the direction of totalitarianism, always a phenomenon of masses. Institutions become humanly unwieldly and individuals feel increasingly overwhelmed both by their new social consciousness and the new weight society itself adds to their individual burdens. Totalitarianism is a modern version of tyranny, but it is a tyranny of the social process itself. Along with an added burden, technology also offers new means for alleviating this and other burdens of human life, new and more efficient ways of organizing the world for the benefit of all men. But it cannot realize this common good by itself. With it there is also need of a new humanism, a new "means" of genuine communication between men. Perhaps the revolutionary spirit can provide some of this complement for technology, but we will have to see first of all how well it succeeds in escaping the contradictions of totalitarianism itself.

II — Revolution

The term "revolution" seems to have been taken over by modern political language from ancient astronomy where the

174

movement of the heavenly bodies was represented as a revolution of spheres around the earth. The passage from one form of government to another thus seems to have been thought of, at first, as a kind of cycle going from one form to another within a limited orbit of possibilities such as monarchy, oligarchy and democracy, with each one bound to prevail in the course of time according to the interplay of political forces. Today, with our linear view of time, we think more in terms of a pendulum swinging from one extreme to another. The association of revolution with an image of the cycle in political thought has disappeared. But other elements borrowed from the realm of nature, such as force and necessity, have remained. We still speak of revolutionary forces and many see a certain necessity of revolutionary process. But in spite of this, revolution does seem to have become a properly historical category, transcending any merely natural necessity and rooted in human consciousness as such.[33] Modern man now sees it as a matter of human initiative more than anything else, though conditioned by the necessities of nature.

The term, however, has been coopted in many different ways, to characterize almost any change, whether it be in politics or some other realm of human activity. Thus, for example, we speak of the industrial revolution, scientific revolutions, cultural revolutions, revolutions in art, in education, and last but not least the technological revolution. In the political sphere itself the term has become so fashionable that almost anyone proposing even the slightest change, or even no change at all sometimes, will adopt it to gain attention. The general corruption of language induced by the totalitarian propensity of our society has not left the language of revolution untouched.

Hence it becomes important to say as exactly as possible what we mean by revolution and in what sense we wish to speak of it here. It is not enough to call oneself revolutionary to be one and very often those who are most truly such speak of it least. Some revolutions have been proclaimed beforehand, but most of them, and often the most important ones, were recognized for all that they were only *post factum.*

What, then, is meant by "revolution"? Here we shall speak of it only with reference to politics, leaving aside the question of whether and when it applies in other spheres. Seen in its best light revolution has to be understood as something quite positive, as aiming at a higher form of the common good. It is a way of transcending social structures as merely given. But this is not enough to specify revolution as such. There are other ways of transcending social structures, of aiming at higher forms of the good — including even the exercise of legitimate authority, if it is properly understood. Something more is needed to specify revolution as such and distinguish it from other ways of seeking the common good. It has to be defined in terms of both form and content.

Its form is that of negation. This is the way that it takes to transcend a given situation. But as pure negation alone it has no content. It takes its content from the historical situation to which it is responding. It is a *negation of established social structures.* The motivation or the intention that underlies a certain revolution may add a certain quality to this negation, affect its style, but it is the content that makes revolution what it is as a historical reality. Thus, revolution is always a function of its times, of the system to which it is opposed. It cannot be understood as a thing in itself, apart from its concrete, historical situation.

As a negation, however, it can be seen as transcending this situation. But this calls for close attention to precisely what is meant by transcendence. A good deal of rhetoric concerning revolution can be deceiving in this regard. In the absence of any positive doctrine of transcendence, of the common good and its content, revolution, as pure negation, remains fixed on the given system. It may wish to be quite radical, but it will only reflect established categories without any means of going beyond them. It will get caught in a vicious circle of pure opposition determined by the very system it is opposed to. It will be totally frustrated in its effort to go beyond, locked in deadly embrace with its enemy. This is why, even from the viewpoint of revolution, a positive doctrine of the common good as the end of history is necessary. Without it revolution can only be, in the literal sense of the term, a *dead* end, and its rhetoric nothing more than self-flattery and self-righteousness.

Yet, this does not mean that revolution can be reduced to a natural sort of process. As negation it is something that is properly rational and human. It denies the natural evolution of history and sets a properly human course in motion. It should be clearly distinguished, as a historical category, from mere evolution, which is more a category of nature. Evolution entails change, even radical change in the long run, but this change could be running toward entropy as well as toward living diversification. It is open to a number of possibilities, but left to itself it would follow a path programmed into the preponderance of its determinisms. Thus, any intervention of human initiative in this process is in a sense revolutionary. It brings new force and new direction. This is why revolution has to be seen as more properly a historical category than evolution. But this supposes that revolution really transcends the system against which it insurges itself. If it is not an *insurgence* to something new, it falls back into the natural process and becomes coopted into the normal, that is, programmed, evolution of the system.

Revolution, of course, cannot separate itself from the evolutionary process. It exists only in a tension with it — as negation. This tension is at once its strength and its weakness. The question is to see how it can remain faithful to its best intentions in its grappling with the forces it is trying to overcome, for revolution itself has to be a real force in history, without however being satisfied with being just a force.

As a basic form of political consciousness, revolution is a relatively modern phenomenon. It was by no means unknown

177

in earlier times. The rapid overthrow of governments was such a prominent feature of Greek political life that Aristotle had to include the subject as an important section of his *Politics*.[34] He even spoke of "revolution," along with birth, as one of the basic ways to obtain citizenship in a *polis*.[35] Later on, in the 16th century, Machiavelli also dealt with the subject in the context of of the Italian city-state.

What is peculiarly modern, however, about the revolutionary consciousness is the universal proportions it has taken and the depths to which it has penetrated the different strata of society. Earlier revolutions seem to have been the business largely of higher echelons in society. The masses were hardly, if ever, directly involved nor much affected. Now it seems that the masses themselves are the chief movers of revolution.[36] The modern revolutionary spirit has to be closely associated with the spread of the democratic spirit since the American and French Revolutions and the proportionate rise in the sense of responsibility which we saw at the beginning of this fundamental reflection.[37]

Along with this universalization, there is also another feature of modern revolution which is perhaps even more significant, what could be called its radicalization. Earlier revolutions seem to have affected only the suprastructures of political life, not its infrastructures. Even though there might have been slave revolutions or peasant revolutions in the past, we do not hear that they were aimed at the institution of slavery or the institution of feudalism as such. Behind the people in power modern revolution tends to see a whole economic system which has to be overthrown along with the mighty. It cannot be satisfied with merely changing people at the top. That can only be a first step, a means to the radical transformation of social structures from the bottom to the top.

To be sure, this is the socialist conception of revolution, and more particularly that of Marx, but it has come to characterize the whole of modern social consciousness. Any treatise on revolution today, whether *pro* or *contra,* would have to take it into account. It could not be relevant to our times to stay at the level of Aristotle or Machiavelli. Every significant social movement of our times, whether it be socialist or not, revolutionary or counterrevolutionary, manifests this awareness that our social system as such has come into question. Every movement develops its strategies accordingly. It is the given social existence as a whole that is in the balance, not just a few individuals or a particular class, and those who are defending vested interests have to see the struggle in this light no less than those who are attacking the system. It is little wonder that radical totalitarianism can so quickly corrupt any political movement, whether left or right. The temptation is built into modern consciousness itself and surfaces the moment attention becomes focused exclusively on the question of structures without consideration for the internal aspect of liberation and communion.

Such universal and radical bringing into question of the social system raises the problem of violence very acutely, both by reason of its proportions and the depths to which it can touch persons. Taken in isolation, doing violence to an individual is problem enough, but when one thinks of it in terms of millions and the extent to which they can be abused of, spiritually as well as physically, one can only be overwhelmed by the enormity of the problem. Without doubt, for a revolutionary spirit concerned with the betterment of men, not just humanity in the abstract or the acquisition and maintenance of power, this is the most serious question it has to face in practice. What light can a fundamental social ethic shed on it?

First of all, it should be noted precisely what the question is. It is not whether or not there will be violence. Violence is a fact of history we have to contend with. Nor is it a question of putting an end to it by simple fiat. No one can decide this in the abstract. He must take action in the concrete. Nor is it a question of contributing or not contributing to the level of violence already existing. Violence seems woven into the fabric of history. To take action against a given society, as every true revolutionary must, means inevitably to raise the level of violence in that society in one way or another. Strictly speaking, there can be no such thing as a non-violent revolution.

When people speak of non-violence in revolution we must carefully examine what is meant. There can be "non-violent" revolutionaries, but they are not an exception to the rule of violence. Apart from the fact that they often suffer violence, without wanting it, it must also be recognized that they are responsible for provoking it. This the nonviolent revolutionary leaders themselves have acknowledged and have always taken into account. Theirs is a real power of negation which goes not only to the external conditions, but also to the internal roots of injustice, that is, the will to domination and pleasure, the readiness to accept an unjust state of affairs as incorrigible, the smugness that makes such a state acceptable. When a revolutionary touches upon these limitations of human consciousness, he is bound to get a reaction and the reaction is bound to be violent. He is doing violence to violence itself. The only way of avoiding violence is to do nothing altogether, but then that becomes a way of condoning violence, because violence will be done.

The question, therefore, is not one of whether but one of how violence is to be dealt with. The revolutionary must accept responsibility for the violence which will come as a result of his action. He may not want it as such and he may not be the principal cause of it, but he is a real cause. As a responsible agent, when he decides to intervene in the historical process, he must reckon with the reaction. This is where the difference between non-violence and other forms of revolution comes into play.

The non-violent revolutionary provokes a crisis within a social system, raises the level of tension and hence also the risk of violence, but he has his own way of dealing with this violence he has provoked. His aim is to bring it out in the open and disarm it, so that, hopefully, society can pass on to a new form of organization, a higher level of humanity. In the means that he chooses he is already banking on an anticipation of the end sought; he is presupposing a certain community of concern for the good and trying to make this prevail over the violence that stands in the way.[38] For this he must estimate the probable reaction to his own action, make every effort to keep it within certain bounds, and plan ways of meeting this new violence concretely. He must not only be in control of himself and the situation, but he must also be prepared to sacrifice himself rather than others, as other revolutionaries might be more prepared to do. In this way the non-violent revolutionary can be, not less, but more radical than another because, not only is he touching an established society where it hurts most, in its conscience, but he is also bringing into play, as a means in the present, the good of communion which is the end sought.[39] Other forms of revolution may not reach as far into the depths of historical consciousness.

Yet for these other forms violence is no less a problem than it is for proponents of non-violence. It should be noted that the use of force can be justified in revolution no less — and, of course, no more — than in the exercise of authority. If the revolutionary accepts to use violence against violence, so to speak, he must recognize very definite limits both as to what can be justified and as to the relative efficacy of the means he chooses. Both of these considerations eventually run into one another, since justification of a means depends, in part at least, upon its real efficacy. A totally useless means, especially one that did violence to persons, could never be justified.

But the first and most fundamental limitation to be considered is that of what might be called *radical violence*. This is not the same as radical revolution, which can be called for when a social system needs radical transformation. Radical violence can, in fact, stand in the way of radical revolution, that is, prevent it from attaining its radical aim. The point, however, is that such violence, in the way that it destroys persons or the actual

181

good of persons, can never serve the common good. It cannot serve the liberation of man because it destroys the very being to be liberated. Terrorism, for example, cannot serve to bring men to any form of communication. It can only force them to withdraw deeper into isolation and alienation. Revolution turned to terror is the same as totalitarianism: it can only be a total perversion of any means to the common good. Almost any use of violence, in the exercise of authority as well as in revolution, entails an element of terror, or of fear, that can serve in the development of a proper social consciousness. It is difficult to draw lines a priori as to what can and cannot serve the good in the concrete, just how far one can go in the use of force; but it is important to have this principle clearly in mind in exercising judgment: radical violence, affecting man in the very dispositions necessary for the constitution of the good, violating his conscience, his sense of dignity, his desire for friendship as well as for justice, cannot serve any good whatsoever.

Even with this clearly understood, however, there remain important questions regarding the use of violence. Violence tends to generate violence. Here the revolutionary, even with the noblest of intentions, cannot afford to be self-righteous. He is dealing in a realm that has been rightly defined as the organization and the management of political forces and he must learn to respect the laws that govern these forces. The admonition of Weber applies to him as much as to anyone else.[40] He must learn to anticipate the consequences of his actions and avoid unleashing forces that cannot be controlled, especially in a mass society such as ours. The revolutionary cannot fall back upon the subterfuge of blaming the ineptitude or the malice of others for the disasters that may occur, as if he were not himself part of them. He must accept his share of the responsibility for the situation in which he finds himself and learn to deal with the evil in it such as it is, in himself as well as in others. The revolutionary can be the most dangerous of those who live only by an ethic of absolute ends because he is appealing to the most vital forces that can determine man's destinies. He must therefore learn to deal realistically with the evil he encounters and recognize his own limitations as well as those of others in his striving for the good. This will be the true mark of his sense of responsibility.

This problem of responsibility and genuine prudence in the exercise of revolutionary action has come to be very complicated in modern technological society. If the revolutionary has any hope of being successful, he will have to mount a force proportionate to that of the system he wishes to transform. In the larger developed countries it becomes almost impossible to see how an effective revolutionary force could be built up in the face of the established power structure; and if such a revolutionary force could be successfully maintained, it becomes even more difficult to conceive how it would be an improvement over the existing force. If it were capable only of opposing the force entrenched in power, force against force, something difficult enough in itself, would it lead to anything more than a confrontation of giants with a crush of individuals in between? In smaller developing countries the problem might seem less complicated, and armed revolution more plausible, but even there, given the involution of international relations, a revolutionary action could not be isolated from the larger socio-economic system. These are complications which the responsible revolutionary cannot fail to take into consideration. What kind of force will be needed to provide even a chance of success? What is such a force likely to become? Which way is it likely to go? Can it be controlled and directed toward the good?

But the question of violence, decisive as it may be, is only a beginning for the revolutionary. Supposing that a revolutionary movement has been set in motion, it remains to be seen what sort of society this movement is aiming at and what concrete means it is using to lay the foundations for that society. If a revolutionary movement is to be clearly distinguished from mere anarchy, as it should, opposition to an established system is not enough. At best opposition could serve to create an initial unity in the movement, but it could never provide the kind of consistence required to bring the movement to a term in a better social order.

This is where the Marxist idea of revolution ultimately breaks down as a means to the good of history. It is rooted in a very high ideal of society, but it has failed to show the way in the concrete to that idea. It has only presumed that the ideal would come spontaneously about, once the prevailing system of social relations collapsed. In this regard it has rightly been assimilated to anarchy.[41] In the meantime, however, the Marxist revolution has concentrated only on opposing the system of capitalism to hasten its demise. Marx himself passed from the sort of reflection that had characterized his early writings on alienation and other such subjects to a systematic study of *Capital,* the enemy to be overcome in *praxis.* He thought he had found in capitalism itself the contradictions that would cause its downfall and his tactic was to accelerate this dialectical process by exacerbating the conflict as much as possible, thus bringing the antagonism to its logical and hence historical end. This is why he ruthlessly opposed all forms of compromise with the system coming from those he called utopian socialists or from trade unions. But in the end the movement which has come from him has only succeeded in spawning a different, and worse, kind of capitalism — state capitalism. Locked in combat with the system it was opposed to, and concentrating only upon the structure of that system, it has been trapped in this deadly embrace. It has failed to develop a positive orientation for the new society which was supposed to emerge. In the meantime capitalism itself has changed and the established communist society is still only trying to keep up or catch up with the changes. If there is to be a really new direction for society as a whole it will not come from Marxism as we know it now.

Perhaps the basic mistake came when Marx decided that the revolution had to become purely practical. In this he may have been, not less, but more utopian than the utopian socialists, especially with regard to the movement that was to come from him. Perhaps he would not himself have lost sight of the vision of society he had and which was at the origin of his systematic revolutionary spirit, but *the movement* has. Perhaps he would eventually have developed a positive doctine of social orientation beyond the conflict with capitalism, but his successors or his followers have not. Most of them are still thinking only in terms of conflict, pure negation where the content is defined by the opposition. The time has come to break out of this vicious circle of a stationary master/slave dialectic, but the Party goes on rehearsing the old battle. Revolution has to break out of the lines set down for it by the established system. This means that it has to think more actively, more positively, of the end it is seeking, the good it is striving for and the kind of society it wants. In short, it has to develop a more positive doctrine of the common good than capitalist or liberal society have given us. Marxism has not done this yet. One wonders whether it can ever do so.

What is more, revolution has to become even more practical than Marxism has been. It is not enough to understand the structure of the system to which it is opposed so as to become more efficacious in its action. It must also provide the means of developing both a new social consciousness and the social structures that will go with it. It is not enough just to exacerbate the conflict in a given social situation. The conflict must be overcome, something which cannot come automatically. It presupposes some creative thinking and planning on the part of man.

Thus the revolutionary leader cannot be satisfied just with creating a mass movement that would be successful in "overthrowing a given structure." To do so may well achieve nothing more than change the individuals at the top and leave the structure more or less in place. The revolutionary movement must not remain merely a mass movement; it must develop a real political consciousness in those who participate in the movement. Indeed, the revolutionary leader may have to create such a consciousness from nothing. He certainly should not fail to see to it that something positive develops along these lines. In other words, every revolutionary leader has to somehow bring his vision of the end effectively into the present. He has to educate the masses, create a diversified social consciousness that will become co-creative with him. Man becomes free and enters into human communication with others only by the actual exercise of such activities.[42] He develops a sense of initiative only by the exercise of initiative, rather than by just passively following others.

The position of the revolutionary leader is in many ways analogous to that of a person in authority. He is in fact an authority for an emerging social order. We saw how the "leadership principle" in totalitarianism corrupts the exercise of authority on the part of the leader and prevents anyone else from exercising any authority, let alone initiative, in the movement. The revolutionary leader has to guard against this temptation even more than any established authority because he is appealing generally to more basic drives and aspirations in his followers and, if he be a charismatic type, he is more likely to have an overpowering effect on them. He has to make his followers revolutionaries themselves, even while requiring the discipline necessary in the movement. Indeed, any proper exercise of authority should be willing to see such a spirit develop in the members even of an established society, but that is beside the point here. The revolutionary leader has to work at developing it directly. Only in this way can the revolutionary movement become a truly human movement, where the participants contribute of themselves to the common good. For revolution, as much as for anything else, if not more, what we said earlier[43] about dialogue in the context of the dialectic of justice and friendship holds true: dialogue has to be the concrete norm of morality.

In connection with authority as means for the common good,[44] we also envisaged the possibility, in an established society, of having leadership and authority roles separated, that is, exercised by different persons who would respect one another's role while each would contribute differently to the common good. In a revolutionary movement such a separation of roles is unthinkable. The leader has to be the one in authority as well. Not only is he the principal mover, so to speak, but in the emerging social structure he has to impose himself as the authority, not as the sole authority, since the delegation of authority is part of the means to encourage initiative at different levels of society, part of the means of liberation, but as the real head that gives the body of the movement consistence and unity.

This "imposition," of course, should not be dictatorial, like something external to the movement. It could take place in the best democratic fashion. But it will be based on the fundamental act of recognition which constitutes members as participants in the movement as well as the leader at its head. The revolutionary movement does not leave behind this essential dialectic of social structures. It only transforms old structures into new ones.

In a sense, then, every revolutionary has something to learn from the non-violent activist. The point is not just to overthrow governments or destroy structures, but to overcome them in view of a better society. This supposes a certain growth in social consciousness in those opposed to change, for one reason or another, as well as in others. It would be much more important and beneficial to bring such people around, since they too could contribute to the good, to convert them, so to speak, rather than to simply eliminate them. This is what the non-violent revolutionary tries to do. He wants every possible good to be brought into play.

But, on the other hand, the non-violent revolutionary also has something to learn from those who attack structures directly.

187

In fact, without this direct concern for social structures as such, the efficacy of the non-violent approach would be greatly limited, if not reduced to nothing. Revolution is essentially a matter of transforming social structures. The highest of intentions based on the good of communion may and should be brought into play in this struggle, but it should be recognized that what defines a revolution as a historical actuality, as a means to be used for the common good, is this opposition to a given system. The non-violent approach by itself could lead to a transformation of society, but such a transformation might be only gradual and stay within the normal evolutionary process of that society. That might be enough by itself in the long run, but it could not give rise to revolution here and now even if that were what is needed. It might be radical enough in intention, but it would not satisfy an immediate need. Revolution implies a sudden surge away from the normal curve of evolution, a break with a given social system, something that cuts more sharply into the established structure.

The question therefore arises as to whether revolution is really necessary if the transformation of society can take place without it. We saw how, even in their own right, authority and law are not meant to be static and repressive. They are meant to foster liberty as well as to channel activity toward the greater good, and in doing so they are meant to evolve of themselves, to keep pace with the real developments of society. We might think of the non-violent activists as essentially calling society to task in this regard, forcing it to be faithful to its better nature, so to speak. Given the enormous risks involved in inciting revolution, the proportions it almost inevitably has to take to be successful, and the kind of extraordinary leadership it requires to make of it a truly human and humanizing movement, might it not be more prudent and responsible to stay within an evolutionary and more gradual framework?

Of course, having to decide whether a particular political movement is really revolutionary or only evolutionary could be a purely academic exercise. Nor should such a question preoccupy anyone too much in practice. The important thing is that whatever has to be done be done, whether it be evolutionary or revolutionary. Evolution itself can be painful enough for a society. Yet it is important to recognize the *right* to revolution in the strict sense of the term. This right ultimately rests on the primacy of the common good and the obligation to pursue that good socially. But more immediately, this right would stem from an established disproportion between a particular social system or structure and the good it is supposed to serve, a disproportion that has become a positive impediment.

A social order in the concrete is always something particular. As such it is not adequate to the universal good. A particular good is always partial with regard to that good. Hence the possibility is always there for a revolution. It flows from the essential limitation of any legal or political system. But possibility alone does not constitute a right, especially if revolution itself can only give rise to another legal and political system which will also have its limitations. There is no getting away from a certain disproportion between an external structure and the total good it is supposed to serve. What constitutes the right of revolution is a limitation or an inadequacy that makes it impossible for a particular structure to serve the good any more. This, of course, is what essentially constitutes the injustice of a social system and, if the injustice is endemic to the system, then the system itself must be overcome. Revolution is the negation of this negation. The right of revolution arises out of social justice. It is ever an historical possibility and in some circumstances it can become an historical, that is, a moral necessity. In the concrete of historical actuality, under the exigencies of social justice, right and necessity become one and the same thing.

What makes revolution an important question for a fundamental social ethic is the essential role which social structures play in the pursuit of the common good. Still influenced by a longstanding *laissez-faire* attitude, liberals tend to minimize this importance, to let structures take care of themselves, as it were, while they work at redressing individual wrongs and developing the potential of society. Liberals do not tend to become revolutionaries, except in very particular respects. The real modern revolutionary is born out of the consciousness that individual wrongs are only incidental to a more basic wrong, a structural wrong. He wants to get to the roots of the wrong in the social system itself, to what occasions the individual wrong and, in fact, makes it inevitable. What he sees is not just one man exploiting another, or one part of the world exploiting the other, but the basic structure of society as essentially exploitative. What he sees also is the ferocious intent of this exploitative system to maintain itself at all costs, even while making genuine and good-willed attempts to rectify some wrongs and ignoring the basic wrong. Thus it is that he sets out to overthrow the system as such.

What he must not fail to realize as well, however, is the danger that threatens him, not in the sense that he might be suppressed, but in the sense that, even in whatever success he might have, he may only be playing the game of the system, in reverse. Not only is he himself a child of the system, but even in his attempts to transcend that system, if he knows only how to play force against force, violence against violence, structure against structure, without at the same time working at developing a new social consciousness, a new concern for justice and friendship, he can only perpetuate the injustice he is presumably fighting. He will be caught in the circle of pure negation, causing untold harm to persons and their good without hope of a really new day. He must be sure to develop what is really new in his outlook, the only thing that can ultimately justify the sacrifices that will inevitably be called for. In other words, revolution has to be more socially *minded* than the system it opposes.

This ultimately, and not the power of mere negation, is what will prove the true value of revolution. It may be that, at least in advanced technological society, we have gone beyond the position where revolution by confrontation can be of any real use. The technostructure of such a society can either resist or co-opt such a movement all too easily.[45] Revolution cannot be satisfied with being just a noble gesture that leaves us nowhere. Nor is violent agitation of itself a measure of true radicalness. It may be that revolution will have to attack the structure from another angle, not by opposition from the outside, but by infiltration from the inside. This would be the work of men who know the technostructure not only from a distance but, having worked with it in practice and resisted the temptation of simply going along with it, also know it from the inside. In keeping with the best revolutionary tradition, such men will know more exactly what they are up against, how the system works, and will be able to find ways of turning or overturning it in the service of universal justice. They will also know how to make better use of the new possibilities for human betterment available in technology itself.

III — *The New Consciousness*

What then is to be done? Whether it be revolutionary or not, this is not something for a fundamental social ethic to answer alone. This calls for a much more immediately practical consideration than what we have done here. A fundamental ethic is only a beginning, not the end of the reflection required for a proper exercise of moral judgment. Revolution brings us to the end of our fundamental reflection as such and calls for a passage beyond into actual practice, the actual exercise of moral judgment.

At the same time, however, revolution brings us back to our concrete starting point in historical consciousness, to the question of our concrete responsibility in the actual historical, social order. What remains for us here is to understand clearly the nature of the tension in which we find ourselves.

We have spoken of this tension as the historical tension between the internal dimension of communication and the external dimension of social structures, and we have tried to maintain a distinction between this tension and the more external tension between different forms of social structure such as "community" or "society," which are more properly the subject of analysis in social science.[46] This historical tension, which is part of the common good itself, appeared in the dialectic of justice and friendship and then gave rise to the question of a need for authority and law in society. Through this same tension we were able to understand the true nature of legal systems as something dynamic and the possible justification of revolution when a particular system could no longer serve the common good. In totalitarianism we found a total perversion of everything that comes from this tension, but at the same time we tried to distinguish from it the kind of approach to social structure that keeps it from becoming totalitarian, whether it be in the exercise of authority or in revolution. It would be a serious mistake to think of the exercise of authority or any form of legal system as inevitably oppressive or totalitarian just as much as it would be a mistake to think of revolution only as a liberation from all authority and law. Authority and law are not only necessary for the good of history. They are positive instruments of liberation as well, or at least they should be. The historical function of revolution is to make them such when they are not, not to eliminate them as such, as if man could do without them.

To understand this polarity which runs through every particular social system in history it might be useful to go back to the basic dialectic of the master and the slave. Just as this dialectic helped us to understand the origins of authority and law, so also it can help us to understand the relation between an established legal and political system, on the one hand,

192

and revolution, on the other, for the latter, understood properly, can only be the beginning of what will be a new form of authority and law.[47]

The development or the transformation of society could be viewed as a sort of struggle unto death which could lead only to death or to a new start in social relations. The idea is not to eliminate, but to create new conditions for man's appropriation of nature and his satisfaction of his needs. This entails not just the development of technology, the means of naturalizing man as well as of humanizing nature, but also a continuing tension in relations of domination. This may mean some kind of slavery for different people at different times, but such a relation is never stable or final. Through recognition, as we saw, the beginning of reason, it contains the seeds of its own reversal. Labor, the shaping of nature to man's needs, and reflection, a certain distantiation from the immediacy of mere nature, give rise to a new form of culture where former slaves become masters. This may come through gradual, almost unnoticed evolution, or through sudden revolution, but it does not mean merely a reversal of positions between former slaves and former masters. Such a case would give rise only to a static dialectic, or rather to no dialectic at all but a pendular movement in one and the same system of social relations. Rather the reversal takes place in the passage to new relations of domination within a society in movement. At first these may be just a matter of fact, mere force in one form or another, but eventually, through recognition again, they come to be seen and accepted as legitimate, as means to the common good. What first appeared as mere might and force, through a process of rationalization, becomes legitimate authority.

Thus, through a struggle of masters and slaves, or more exactly through a shifting struggle for domination, since history has long ceased to be a simple struggle between a few individuals, society passes from one stage to another. Marxism has conceived this struggle in terms of classes and has seen

193

the struggle of the proletariat against capitalism as the final struggle of history. But this classification of the struggle for domination is an over-simplification, not without its obvious dangers when someone begins to speak in the name of a class which is as much a fiction of his imagination as a historical reality; and there is no reason to think there can be a cessation of this struggle, an end of history or of pre-history as the Marxist sometimes speak of it, not without some ambiguity.[48]

But this passage from one stage to another takes place through another struggle besides that of life and death, the loving struggle of a man/woman dialectic. This is what Marxists and others who think of the historical struggle only in terms of domination have failed to notice. As a result they have left out of consideration some of the most fundamental aspects of humanization in the historical process. The dialectic of man and woman is even more basic than that of master and slave even as it places man in an immediate relation with nature. As Marx himself wrote, "In this *natural* species-relationship man's relation to nature is directly his relation to man, and his relation to man is directly his relation to nature, to his *natural function.*"[49] But perhaps Marx was too intent on the natural side of this relationship to give sufficient attention to its human side. "The relation of man to woman is the *most natural* relation of human being to human being." As a relation of *human* beings, however, it cannot be reduced to nature. It can indicate, as Marx concludes, "how far man's *natural* behaviour has become *human,* and how far his *human* essence has become a *natural* essence for him, how far his *human nature* has become *nature* for him." But it can also show how man can escape from the struggle of merely natural relationships. Reduced to a relation of nature, the man and woman dialectic is nothing more than a master and slave dialectic, a relation of domination through seduction. But taken more properly as a human relationship, it adds the necessary complement to the struggle for domination. It makes history something truly human, not just in some imagined future beyond, "the *definitive* resolution of the antagonism between man and nature, and between man and man," but in the present here and now.

As human beings, man and woman have equality, the aim of justice and the beginning of friendship. As equals, man and woman have language, along with nature, in which to give their relation expression. Most of the development in technology, man's relation with nature, is unthinkable without language, but language does not begin there. It begins in the relation between man and woman based on equality. This equality can be betrayed by seduction or by brutalization, so that one becomes a thing for the other, a plaything or a beast of burden. But it is given with man's very being and it is exercised in the act of love which, thanks to language, transcends mere nature.[50]

The man and woman relationship neither eliminates nor replaces the master and slave relationship, the struggle for domination. It is itself a loving struggle. Properly understood as based on equality, however, it does open the way to a better and more open understanding of the historical struggle which, in the master and slave relation, tends to stay closed in a vicious circle.

For this, language itself, the first sign of human equality, can serve as the model. Dialogue represents a higher form of recognition than the one we saw in the struggle for domination. It supposes at least a basic form of equality, a mutual respect between participants. This does not exclude inequality in other respects. In fact, because slaves were capable of speech, Aristotle, without abandoning the idea of slavery, saw a possibility of friendship between master and slave, admittedly quite limited, inasmuch as the relation seemed to entail a basic inequality, and he saw a certain obligation, on the part of the master, to care for the development of virtue, the ground of freedom, in the slave.[51] But the recognition of dialogue based on equality and mutual respect does qualify all these inequal-

195

ities in a basic way. If some of them entail anything less than human for some, it leads to efforts to overcome this inhumanity. If they entail special talents on the part of others, it means drawing these out for the service of men. For dialogue means listening as well as speaking, listening for the needs and listening to the good of others, and in this way being enriched oneself. In dialogue, the whole of society achieves a certain equality and is enriched by its very diversity. First sign, dialogue is also a means of creating equality and a realization in the present of the end sought in the historical struggle.[52]

Thus we see how inadequate the language of calculation alone or the language of power are for the historical struggle of man, and how this inadequacy can be overcome. Technological developments alone, whether it be in natural science or social science, in engineering or management and planning, cannot serve the fullness of man. Neither can the mere calculation of chances for success in the struggle for power or of the sacrifices that will be required in a sort of theory of the just revolution. We need still more advanced technology to meet the needs of men today. We need better ideas of government, yes, even revolutionary ideas on economic, social and political structures. But above all we need a new language to establish communication between all these developments so that they will enrich one another and serve men better. Just as totalitarianism has as its ultimate result the corruption of language, the breakdown of all communication, what we need most in this society, sorely threatened with totalitarianism of every sort, is a new language, a revolutionary language, not just rhetoric, that will enable, not just a communication between men, but, through dialogue, the actual discovery, the creation, of the social forms we need for the era to which we are called by technological developments and the actual historical tension in which we find ourselves, a language to fit the means and match the need of communication in our society. Without such a language no proposal, no revolution, can truly serve the good in the future.

It has been argued that the next revolution will have to be a world revolution, that the conditions for this revolution exist only in America, and that it has already begun there.[53] It has been further argued that this revolution can only be a revolution by consciousness, a revolution epitomized in the concept of choosing a life style here and now, in the present, not at some future point.[54] Much could be said in favor of such a revolution: the priority given to cultural change, the concern for recovering the self and recapturing our humanity, the broadening of the political to include more than what is susceptible to government administration, its sense of a need for transcendence in history and for a new kind of human community, one based upon love and trust much more than on law and organization. Yet one begins to hesitate when one sees how little is made of social structures in this revolution. The complexity of real liberation in our complex society is recognized,[55] but it is thought that this liberation can be achieved by a mere choice. The hard questions are alluded to, but relegated to a realm of insignificance and irrelevance. "All that is necessary to describe the new society is to describe a new way of life. When we have outlined a different way of life, we have said all that we can meaningfully say about the future."[56]

Would that revolution could be as simple as all that! But would we then still be talking about human existence? In history we cannot afford to be so angelic. To be sure, activists and leftists may tend to over-emphasize structure and in this way they may be playing into the hands of the "machine" or those who give primacy to structure over community.[57] But the solution, even if we affirm the primacy of community, is not to ignore or minimize the importance of structure. Social structure is an essential part of man's being as we have seen time and again; it is one of the poles in the historical tension that defines our social being concretely. Not only is structure not irrelevant, inasmuch as it can influence thinking,[58] but just as it has been constitutive of thought in the past and the present,

197

it will also be constitutive of thought in the future. Though consciousness is prior to structure,[59] it is not real apart from structure. If we want to change consciousness, we will have to change structure; and this cannot be done by the simple *fiat* of anyone, young or old.

The new consciousness, it might be said, is not unaware of the need for struggle in history, but it wants to see this struggle only in terms of a dialectic of man and woman — a loving struggle. It would like to do as if the struggle of domination could be done away with in history once and for all. Thus it tries to ignore the dialectic of the master and the slave that is also constitutive of our historical struggle. To do so will not solve the question of history. It may seem to open the way to a better human community, but inasmuch as it neglects the question of structures it remains an abstraction, a betrayal of its ideal in the real world. Just as Marxism insists too exclusively on the dialectic of the master and the slave in its concern for structures, so also the new consciousness insists too exclusively on the dialectic of man and woman in its concern for community in the present. Structural or institutional solutions are not enough, but neither are those of instant community. We must not freeze the future in our present image.[60] but neither must we freeze our community in its present form. There is still too much structural injustice to be overcome and that injustice affects our very present view of community. Both dialectics, the loving struggle and the struggle unto death, must complement one another in the interpretation of our historical task. This is why dialogue continues to be the concrete norm of morality for us today and tomorrow.

Moreover, the content of the dialogue is not a matter of indifference to it. If our problems already bring us together, our solutions will have to do so even more. It is around the solution of our historical problems that our truly creative communities are formed. Such has always been the case with our best revolutionary practice. Dialogue is a unity of form and content: wherever it exists truly, it already constitutes a community in action, but at the same time it calls for a development of that community, a development that hinges on the content of the dialogue. Given the complexity of our society, it is clear that the dialogue must bring in all the forms of competence available, experts as well as ordinary people. It must be an interdisciplinary dialogue. But it must not cease to be a dialogue at any cost. Otherwise it will revert to a mere struggle for domination. Dialogue must create the conditions for its own existence, a language that will sustain it and keep it open, since that is always the first structure for any new society, and a language that will enable it to cope with the complexities of its problems. Only in this way will a really new consciousness, one that transcends established society beyond mere opposition to it, emerge and maintain itself in history.

BIBLIOGRAPHY OF THE WORKS REFERRED TO

I. Books

Aquinas, St. Thomas. *Commentary on the Nicomachean Ethics.* Tr. C. I. Litzinger. Chicago: Regnery, 1963.
———. *Summa of Theology.* 3 vols. New York: Benziger, 1947.
Arendt, Hannah. *On Revolution.* New York: The Viking Press. 1963.
———. *The Origins of Totalitarianism.* New Edition. New York: Harcourt, Brace, Inc., 1966.
Aristotle. *The Nicomachean Ethics.* Tr. H. Rackham. "The Loeb Classical Library"; New York: G. P. Putnam's Sons, 1926.
———. *Politics.* Tr. H. Rackham. "The Loeb Classical Library"; Cambridge, Mass.: Harvard University Press, 1950.
Bendix, Reinhard. *Social Science and the Distrust of Reason.* "University of California Publications in Sociology and Social Institutions" Vol. 1, No. 1, pp. 1-42; Berkeley and Los Angeles: University of California Press, 1951.
Blondel, Maurice. *L'Action (1893): Essai d'une critique de la vie et d'une science de la pratique.* "Bibliothèque de Philosophie Contemporaine"; Paris: Presses Universitaires de France, 1950. (Reprint of the original edition).
Bonhoeffer, Dietrich. *Ethics.* Ed. Eberhard Bethge; tr. Neville Horton Smith. "The Library of Philosophy and Theology"; New York: The Macmillan Co., 1955.

Brandt, Richard B. (ed.) *Social Justice.* Englewood Cliffs: Prentice-Hall, 1962.

Brown, Norman O. *Life Against Death: The Psychoanalyitcal Meaning of History.* "Vintage Books"; New York: Random House, 1959.

———. *Love's Body.* New York: Random House, 1966.

Buchheim, Hans. *Totalitarian Rule: Its Nature and Characteristics.* Tr. Ruth Hein. Middletown: Wesleyan University Press, 1968.

De Koninck, Charles. *De la primauté du bien commun contre les personalistes.* Québec: Editions de l'Université Laval, 1943.

Drummond, William, S. J. *Social Justice.* Milwaukee: The Bruce Publishing Co., 1955.

Durkheim, Emile. *The Division of Labor.* Tr. George Simpson. New York: The Free Press, 1964.

Ferree, William, S. M. *The Act of Social Justice.* "Phlosophical Studies" 72; Washington, D.C.: Catholic University of America, 1943.
(Multilithed by Marianist Publications, Mount Saint John, Dayton, Ohio, 1951).

Fessard, Gaston. *Autorité et bien commun,* 2e edition. "Recherces Economiques et Sociales"; Paris: Aubier-Montaigne. 1969.

———. *De l'actualité historique.* Tome I: *A la recherche d'une méthode.* "Recherches de Philosophie" V; Desclée de Brouwer, 1960.

Fletcher, Joseph. *Situation Ethics: The New Morality.* Philadelphia: The Westminster Press, 1966.

Freire, Paulo. *The Pedagogy of the Oppressed.* Tr. M. Marcos. New York: Herder and Herder, 1970.

Friedrich, Carl J. (ed.). *Revolution.* "Nomos" VIII; New York: Atherton Press, 1966.

———. *Totalitarianism.* New York: The Universal Library, 1964. (Orig. Harvard University Press, 1954).

Galbraith, John K. *The New Industrial State.* "Signet Book"; New York: New American Library, 1967.

Gilleman, Gérard, S. J. *The Primacy of Charity in Moral Theology.* Tr. William F. Ryan, S. J., and André Vachon, S. J. Westminster, Md.: The Newman Press, 1959.

Gregor, A. James. *The Ideology of Fascism: The Rationale of Totalitarianism.* New York: The Free Press, 1969.

Hegel, G. W. F. *The Phenomenology of Mind.* Tr. J. B. Baillie. "Harper Torchbook"; New York: Harper & Row, 1967.

Hegel, G. W. F. *The Philosophy of Right.* Tr. T. M. Knox. New York: Oxford University Press, 1967.

———. *Realphilosophie I.* Ed. J. Hoffmeister. Leipzig: Meiner, 1932.

———. *Werke: Jubilaumsausgabe in 20 Banden.* Ed. Glockner. Stuttgart, 1949ff.

Hobbes, Thomas. *Leviathan (Part I and II).* "The Library of Liberal Arts"; New York: Bobbs-Merrill, 1958.

Jack, Homer A. (ed.). *The Gandhi Reader: a Source Book of his Life and Writings.* Bloomington: Indiana University Press, 1956.

Johann, Robert. *The Meaning of Love: An Essay towards a Metaphysics of Intersubjectivity.* "Deus Books"; New York: Paulist Press, 1966.

Kerner, George C. *The Revolution in Ethical Theory.* New York: Oxford University Press, 1966.

Klubertanz, George P., S. J. *Habits and Virtues.* New York: Appleton-Century-Crofts, 1965.

Kojève, Alexandre. *Introduction to the Reading of Hegel: Lectures on the "Phenomenology of Spirit."* Tr. James H. Nichols, Jr. New York/London: Basic Books, Inc., 1969.

Lobkowicz, Nicholas (ed.). *Marx and the Western World.* Notre Dame and London: University of Notre Dame Press, 1967.

Marcuse, Herbert. *Eros and Civilization: A Philosophical Inquiry into Freud.* Boston: Beacon Press, 1955.

———. *One-Dimensional Man*: *Studies in the Ideology of Advanced Industrial Society*. Boston: Beacon Press, 1964.

———. *Reason and Revolution*: *Hegel and the Rise of Social Theory*. New York: Oxford University Press, 1941. Paperback edition, Boston: Beacon Press, 1960. (With a new preface: "A Note on Dialectic," by the Author.)

Maritain, Jacques. *The Person and the Common Good*. Tr. John J. Fitzgerald. New York: Charles Scribner's Sons, 1947.

Marx, Karl. *A Contribution to the Critique of Political Economy*. Tr. N. I. Stone, New York: Kerr, 1904.

———. *Early Writings*. Ed. & tr. T. B. Bottomore. New York: McGraw-Hill, 1964.

———. *The German Ideology*. Ed. & tr. R. Pascal. New York: International Publishers, 1947.

Messner, Johannes. *Social Ethics*: *Natural Law in the Western World*. Tr. J. J. Doherty. Revised ed. St. Louis & London: B. Herder Co., 1965.

Mills, C. Wright. *The Sociological Imagination*. New York: Oxford University Press, 1959.

Moltmann, Jürgen & Jürgen Weissbach. *Two Studies in the Theology of Bonhoeffer*. Tr. Reginald H. & Ilse Fuller. New York: Charles Scribner's Sons, 1967.

Niebuhr, H. Richard. *The Responsible Self*: *An Essay in Christian Moral Philosophy*. New York: Harper & Row, 1963.

Niebuhr, Reinhold. *Love and Justice*: *Selections from the Shorter Writings*. Ed. D. B. Robertson. "Meridian Books"; Cleveland & New York: The World Publishing Co., 1967.

———. *Moral Man and Immoral Society. An Essay in Ethics and Politics.* "The Scribner Library"; New York: Charles Scribner's Sons, 1932. Paperback, 1960.

Parsons, Talcott. *Essays in Sociological Theory*. Revised Edition. New York: The Free Press, 1964.

———. *The Social System*. New York: The Free Press, 1964.

Pieper, Josef. *The Four Cardinal Virtues*: *Prudence, Justice,*

Fortitude, Temperance. New York: Harcourt, Brace & World, Inc., 1965.

———. *Justice.* Tr. Lawrence E. Lynch. New York: Pantheon Books, 1955.

———. *Leisure, the Basis of Culture.* Tr. Alexander Dru. New York: Pantheon Books, 1964.

———. *Prudence.* Tr. Richard & Clara Winston. New York: Pantheon Books, 1959.

Reich, Charles A. *The Greening of America.* "A Bantam Book"; New York: Random House, 1971.

Revel, Jean-François. *Without Marx or Jesus: The New American Revolution.* Tr. J. F. Bernard. New York: Doubleday, 1971.

Ritter, Joachim. *Hegel und die Französische Revolution,* Köln: Opladen, 1957.

Sartre, Jean-Paul. *Critique de la raison dialectique.* Tome I: *Théorie des ensembles pratiques.* "Bibliothèque des Idées"; Paris: Gallimard, 1960.

Tönnies, Ferdinand. *Community and Society (Gemeinschaft und Gesellschaft).* Tr. & ed. Charles P. Loomis. "Harper Torchbooks/The Academy Library"; New York: Harper & Row, 1963.

Vasse, Denis. *Le Temps du désir.* Paris: Seuil, 1969.

Weber, Max. *From Max Weber: Essays in Sociology.* Ed. & tr. H. H. Gerth & C. Wright Mills. "A Galaxy Book"; New York: Oxford University Press, 1958.

Winter, Gibson. *Elements for a Social Ethic: Scientific and Ethical Perspectives on Social Process.* New York: The Macmillan Co., 1966.

II. *Articles*

Blanchette, Oliva, S. J. "History and Nature in Karl Marx." *The Philosophical Forum,* II (1970), 24-35.

Brown, Norman O. "Reply to Marcuse." *Commentary,* XL (1967), 83-84.

De Koninck, Charles. "In Defense of Saint Thomas: a Reply to Father Eschmann's Attack on the Primacy of the Common Good." *Laval Théologique et Philosophique,* I (1945), No. 2, 9-109.

Dupré, Louis. "Situation Ethics and Objective Morality." *Theological Studies,* XXVIII (1967), 245-257.

Eschmann, I. Th., O. P. "In Defense of Jacques Maritain." *The Modern Schoolman,* XXII (1945), 183-208.

Frankena, William K. "Ethical Theory." In "The Princeton Studies: Humanistic Studies in America," *Philosophy.* Englewood Cliffs: Prentice-Hall, 1964, 345-463.

Gustafson, James F. "Context versus Principles: A Misplaced Debate in Christian Ethics." *Harvard Theological Review,* LVIII (1965), 171-202.

Hayen, André, S. J. "Note sur la dialectique de la justice et de l'amour selon saint Thomas." *Archives de Philosophie,* XXI (1958), 76-91.

Marcuse, Herbert. "Love Mystified: A Critique of Norman O. Brown." *Commentary,* XL (1967), 71-74.

McKeon, Richard. "The Development and Significance of the Concept of Responsibility." *Revue Internationale de Philosophie.* XI (1957), 3-32.

Milhaven, John G., S. J. "Towards an Epistemology of Ethics." *Theological Studies,* XXVII (1966), 228-241.

Milhaven, John G., S. J. & David J. Casey, S. J. "Introduction to the Theological Background of the New Morality." *Theological Studies,* XXVIIII (1967), 312-344.

FOOTNOTES

FOOTNOTES TO INTRODUCTION

1. William K. Frankena, "Ethical Theory," in *Philosophy* ("The Princeton Studies: Humanistic Studies in America;" Prentice-Hall, 1964), pp. 438 ff.
2. Cf. George C. Kerner, *The Revolution in Ethical Theory*, (Oxford University Press, 1966).
3. Cf. *One-Dimensional Man*, (Beacon, 1964).
4. Cf. Joseph Fletcher, *Situation Ethics: The New Morality*, (Westminster Press, 1960), pp. 29, 52, 55, 146 ff.
5. Cf. Dietrich Bonhoeffer, *Ethics*, Tr. N. H. Smith, (Macmillan, 1955), p. 23.
6. Cf. James F. Gustafson, "Context versus Principles: A Misplaced Debate in Christian Ethics," *Harvard Theological Review*, LVIII (1965), 171-202.
7. Compare, for example, John G. Milhaven and David J. Casey, "Introduction to the Theological Background of the New Morality," *Theological Studies*, XXVIII (1967), 312-344, with the article by Gustafson just cited. With Milhaven and Casey, Reinhold Niebuhr appears on the other side of the fence than he did with Gustafson. Gustafson himself ends up being labeled a contextualist by another author, Louis Dupré, in "Situation Ethics and Objective Morality," *Theological Studies*, XVIII (1967), 246-257.
8. One example of such epistemological confusion can be found in John G. Milhaven, "Towards an Epistemology of Ethics," *Theological Studies*, XXVII (1966), 228-241.
9. No ethic of principle, to be sure, is satisfied with leaving conscience in error. Indeed the slightest suspicion of error is for it reason enough to make subjective certainty suspect and calls for an effort to learn what would be "objectively" right. But the time to act often comes long before one has had time to solve all doubts. It is

to take care of this "doubtful" conscience that theories such as that of probabilism have been developed.

10. Cf. *Social Science and the Distrust of Reason*, (University of California Press, 1951).

11. Cf. *From Max Weber: Essays in Sociology*, Ed. H. H. Gerth and C. W. Mills, (Galaxy, 1958), pp. 120 ff.

12. Cf. the companion essay, "Science as a Vocation," to the one just cited, "Politics as a Vocation," *op. cit.*, 129-156.

13. Cf. L. Dupré, *art. cit.*

14. *Op. cit.*, pp. 22ff.

15. *Op. cit.*, p. 49.

16. Cf. *op. cit.*, p. 31.

17. *Op. cit.*, p. 93.

18. *Op. cit.*, p. 95.

19. Cf. *Elements for a Social Ethic: Scientific and Ethical Perspectives on Social Process*, (Macmillan, 1966).

20. Cf. "A note on Dialectic," Preface to the new edition of *Reason and Revolution: Hegel and the Rise of Social Theory*, (Beacon, 1960).

FOOTNOTES TO CHAPTER ONE

1. The point was made at some length and brilliantly in terms precisely of determinism already some time ago by Maurice Blondel in *L'Action* (1893).

2. Josef Pieper, *Prudence*, Tr. R. and C. Winston, (Pantheon Books, 1959), p. 26.

3. Dietrich Bonhoeffer, *Ethics*, Tr. N. H. Smith, (Macmillan, 1955), p. 226.

4. For this review we depend largely on Richard McKeon, "The Development and Significance of the Concept of Responsibility." *Rev. Internat. de Philosophie*, XI (1957), 3-32.

5. *From Max Weber: Essays in Sociology*, Ed. Gerth and Mills, (Galaxy, 1958), p. 119.

6. *Op. cit.*, pp. 126-127.

7. *Ibid.*

8. Gibson Winter, *Elements for a Social Ethic*, (Macmillan, 1966), p. 244.

9. *Op. cit.*, p. 225.

10. *Art. cit.*, pp. 29-30.

11. *The Responsible Self*, (Harper & Row, 1963), p. 65.

12. *Op. Cit.*, p. 71.

13. Cf., *Ethics,* pp. 218 ff., on the relation between responsibility and obedience to God, and pp. 222 ff., on the relation between responsibility and vocation. In the latter context Bonhoeffer quite rightly distinguishes himself from Weber's secularized concept of "calling" defined as a "limited field of accomplishment." He is concerned with life as a whole and not just a slice of it.

14. Unlike Bonhoeffer and other theologians, including Barth, for example, who treat the social order primarily as a part of God's command or "mandates," here we approach it as a reality open to the critical examination of reason. We do not oppose these two viewpoints, nor do we claim that created reality is anything apart from God. We simply insist on examining what is given fundamentally from our point of view, recognizing that even with revelation we can never get to God's point of view to talk down, so to speak, at the world, and recognizing that this fundamental human approach is the only way open for us to be truly open to God's own action and command. However, for a discussion of how Bonhoeffer actually used categories taken from the social sciences in his ecclesiology, see Jürgen Moltmann, "The Lordship of Christ and Human Society," in *Two Studies in the Theology of Bonhoeffer,* Tr. R. and I. Fuller, (Scribner, 1967), pp. 23 ff.

15. It is on this point of human action, and interaction, that ethics intersects with social science. Talcott Parsons, for example, speaks of an "action frame of reference" for his general theory of sociology in *The Social System,* (Free Press, 1964), pp. 3ff. and *Essays in Sociological Theory,* (Free Press, 1964) pp. 228 ff. C. Wright Mills, one of Parson's severest critics, focuses no less on action in his criticism of "grand theory." Indeed, he is for a social science that will be more relevant to problems of recognizable significance for human action and interaction. Cf. *The Sociological Imagination,* (Oxford University Press, 1959), pp. 25-49, 184, 194.

16. The point has been made systematically by Maurice Blondel in a work already referred to in note 1 above, *L'Action* (1893.) Cf. the part entitled "Le phénomène de l'action," which constitutes the longest and the central section of the work.

17. We refer here to the well-known classic of sociological analysis by Ferdinand Tönnies, *Community and Society* (Gemeinschaft und Gesellschaft), Tr. Charles P. Loomis, (Harper Torchbook, 1963).

18. Cf. Emile Durkheim, *The Division of Labor in Society,* Tr. George Simpson, (Free Press, 1951). See also note 27 to Introduction of the work by Tönnies cited in the foregoing note.

19. Note that historical tension, as we wish to speak of it here, entails a clear distinction between revolution and evolution and that this distinction depends upon the introduction of a vertical dimension into the continuum of horizontal dimension. History says more than mere process.

20. Cf. *Karl Marx: Early Writings,* Tr. T. B. Bottomore, (McGraw-Hill, 1964), pp. 127-128.

21. Cf. *Politics,* Bk. I, cc. 3-6.

22. We refer here mainly to Section B of the *Phenomenology of Mind,* which presents the emergence of self-consciousness and thought (*Denken*) as essentially a social event through a dialectic of recognition (*Anerkennen*). Cf. also Hegel's earlier Jena writings, especially what has been called *Realphilosophie* I, Alexandre Kojève, *Introduction to the Reading of Hegel: Lectures on the "Phenomenology of Spirit,"* Tr. James H. Nichols, (Basic Books, 1969), and Gaston Fessard, *De l'actualité historique,* Vol. I, "Esquisse du mystère de la société et de l'histoire," (Desclée de Brouwer, 1960), pp. 121-211. The last mentioned essay shows how the two modern totalitarian ideologies, Nazism and Communism, flow from a breakdown of this dialectic of the master and the slave. Here we are interested in it only as a way of thinking the relation between history and nature, between man as an animal and man as a social being. The relation is present in Hobbes' *Leviathan,* in the passage from natural to political man, but it has not been thought out dialectically.

23. Cf. G. Fessard, *art. cit.,* where the author traces the aberrations of Nazism and Communism both back to Hegel's dialectic of the master and the slave and argues that it needs to be complemented by a still more basic dialectic, that between man and woman. We shall return to this more basic dialectic below, in connection with the common good. Cf. ch. 2, section II.

24. This last manner of speaking is in keeping with J.-P. Sartre's approach to Society and History. Cf. *Critique de la Raison dialectique* (Gallimard, 1960), especially the idea of *project,* pp. 63 ff.

FOOTNOTES TO CHAPTER TWO

1. Though our notion of "spirit" here resembles that of Hegel, it does not go as far identifying this "spirit" of humanity with the Absolute Spirit. We prefer to leave the question open at this point because it does not directly concern a fundamental social ethic. Be it said

in passing, however, that the idea of the common good as the good of history could well be the best approach to the question of Absolute Spirit, which could be seen as giving a fuller content to the idea of the Concrete Universal Good of history.

2. This criticism of personalism was made some time ago in a little book that never attained wide circulation due to the time and circumstances under which it was published: Charles de Koninck, *De la primauté du bien commun contre les personalistes.* (Editions de l'Université Laval, 1943). Cf. also the author's reply to a criticism of his book: "In Defense of Saint Thomas: a Reply to Father Eschmann's Attack on the Primacy of the Common Good." *Laval Théologique et Philosophique,* I (1945), 9-109. We are indebted to de Koninck for a lot in the positive idea of the common good we are trying to develop here.

3. Cf. Herbert Marcuse, *One-Dimensional Man,* (Beacon Press, 1964).

4. *Op. cit.,* p. 230.

5. We refer here to the two types of dialectic we shall discuss below, after our elaboration of the idea of the common good, the dialectic of reason (cf. sections II and III of this chapter) and the dialectic of sensibility (cf. the next chapter, on justice and friendship).

6. We refer here to the well known principles operative in Adam Smith's economic theory on the one hand and in Jeremy Bentham's utilitarianism on the other. It is not surprising to find theologians still appealing to such principles, for example, Joseph Fletcher in his *Situation Ethics,* (Westminster Press, 1966), pp. 118 ff., because such ideas are only a secularized version of an ancient idea of divine providence akin to occasionalism which saw only God as working for the common good, leaving out any consideration of man's initiative in history.

7. Thomas Aquinas speaks of coming to maturity as finding oneself already communicating one's actions to others — *incipit jam communicare actiones suas ad alios.* Cf. *Summa of Theology,* Part III, quest. 72, art. 2.

8. See, for example, *The German Ideology,* Ed. R. Pascal, (International Publishers, 1947), pp. 16-19.

9. Cf. *Nicomachean Ethics,* Bk. VI, cc. 4-5.

10. Cf. *Leisure, the Basis of Culture,* Tr. Alexander Dru, (Pantheon Books, 1964).

11. Hegel never lost his early enchantment with Greek society as a prototype of the perfect coincidence between an individual and a

people, though he came to see it as only a moment in the development of the World Spirit. He did, however, retain the model of a particular people for his own Philosophy of Right, a philosophy of the State, while tending to belittle the idea of a universal society as too abstract, especially as this was stated in the ideals of the French Revolution. See, for example, *The Philosophy of Right,* # 330-340, especially the Zusatz to # 333; also # 209, # 258, # 322. Here, while recognizing the extreme difficulty of such a thing, we would like to maintain an idea of the common good that is absolutely universal, beyond the particularity of the state or the nation, and propose a way of approaching the idea concretely, that is, dialectically, without however passing through a mediation of war, as Hegel was still too ready to do.

12. Hegel saw the risking of one's life in war as the privilege reserved to the noblest class of citizens in Greek society (cf. *Werke,* Ed. Glockner, Vol. I, pp. 494-496). This attitude toward the nobility of risk in war perdured in his own philosophy (cf. *The Philosophy of Right,* # 321-329).

13. *Nic. Eth.,* Bk. I, c. 7.

14. *Ibid.,* c. 3.

15. Cf. Johannes Messner, *Social Ethics: Natural Law in the Western World,* (Herder, 1965), pp. 123 ff.

16. Cf. ch. 1, section III, pp. 21-25.

17. In this respect the Greeks and Hegel were entirely correct in insisting on the common good as specified in particular societies. These are essential moments in the dialectical elaboration of the universal common good. But they are only moments, not the end, only parts, not the whole.

18. Cf. *The Phenomenology of Mind,* Tr. J. B. Baillie, (Harper Torchbook, 1967), pp. 599 ff. See also Joachim Ritter, *Hegel und die Französische Revolution,* (Köln-Opladen, 1957).

19. For the dialectic we wish to present here, we are indebted to an excellent little book by Gaston Fessard, *Autorité et bien commun,* (2e. ed., Aubier-Montaigne, 1969). The connection between this dialectic and the emergence of both Nazism and Communism out of 19th century liberalism, as typified in Hegel, was developed further by the same author in an essay already referred to: "Esquisse du mystère de la société et de l'histoire," cf. notes 22 and 23, ch. 1.

20. See, for example, the definition of communism as the end of history in the "Economic and Philosophical Manuscripts," *Early Writings*, Tr. T. B. Bottomore (McGraw-Hill, 1964), pp. 155-157.

21. Hegel had real inklings of this man/woman dialectic. At one point in his courses at Jena he even spoke of a beginning of recognition (*erkennen*, and not yet *anerkennen*) in the relationship between man and woman, and he did so in terms of a breaking out from merely individual consciousness bent on the immediate satisfaction of its needs (cf. *Realphilosophie* I, Ed. Hoffmeister, (Leipzig, 1932), pp. 221 ff. But he then proceeded to think of this dialectic as still too immediate and only natural. He never saw it as belonging properly to history as such, like the dialectic of the master and the slave which gives rise to recognition on the political level. That is why Hegel's judgments on history always remained harsh and were never tempered by a more humane sense of the struggle which constitutes the movement of history. It is also this same harshness which Marxism inherited from Hegel, though Marx also had a moment when he saw something basically significant for history in the relation between man and woman (cf. "Economic and Philosophical Manuscripts," *op. cit.*, pp. 145-155).

22. *Ibid.*

23. Cf. ch. 1, section I and III, pp. 4-6, 19.

24. Cf. ch. 1, introduction and beginning of section III, pp. 3ff., 19ff.

25. Ch. 1, section II, pp. 11 ff.

26. Cf. above, in this ch., section I, p. 44.

27. Gibson Winter speaks of three foci of intersection: societal identity, cultural integrity, and historical fulfillment, to specify the responsible moral stance taken in history. Other elements or further specification could be added, but these three foci can serve as a model to interrelate the factors to be integrated in our move toward the future. Cf. *Elements for a Social Ethic*, (Macmillan, 1966), pp. 263 ff.

28. Cf. Preface to the new ed. of *Reason and Revolution*, (Beacon Press, 1960), pp. vii-xiv.

29. See, for example, Joseph Fletcher, *Situation Ethics*, (Westminster Press, 1966), *passim*, esp. pp. 60-61, 87-94.

30. Only when reason reaches the end, whether it be in death or in the end of history as such, does its decision become absolute. But such an act does not take place in history purely and simply. Though it starts in history, it is a passage out of history.

31. Cf. "Politics as a Vocation," *From Max Weber: Essays in Sociology,* Ed. Gerth and Mills, (Galaxy, 1958), pp. 118 ff.

32. The unification in question, of course, is not automatic, but dialectical. The reciprocity of projects between persons can give rise to a struggle as well as a collaboration. For an analysis of this means and end relationship in a reciprocity of projects, see J.-P. Sartre, *Critique de la raison dialestique,* (Gallimard, 1960), pp. 191 ff.

33. For a closer discussion of this "historical" fallacy in Marxism, see "History and Nature in Karl Marx," *The Philosophical Forum,* II (1970), pp. 24-35.

34. We spoke of this relation between a vertical and horizontal dimension earlier in speaking of the historical tension in social reality (ch. 1, section III). In his book, *Autorité et bien commun,* referred to above in this ch., note 19, G. Fessard goes into this theological dimension in terms of a symbolism required to meet the question of the common good in our time. This symbolism he finds neither in Nazism nor in Communism, but only in the Spiritual ideal of the common good proposed in Christianity (*op. cit.,* 89 ff.).

35. The reason why our idea alone of the common good cannot be the last word of history is that its content still remains too indeterminate. The form of the idea, however, is open to a more determinate content, but the question is whether such a determination can ever be given purely and simply from within history. This is where the question of the common good opens up into that of an Absolute Spirit, a Giver of Meaning in and yet beyond history — where philosophical reflection opens the way for theological reflection.

FOOTNOTES TO CHAPTER THREE

1. Cf. *Nic. Ethics,* Bk. VI, c. 5.

2. *One-Dimensional Man,* pp. 203 ff. The absence of serious consideration of moral virtue as part of historical consciousness is a deficiency in Marcuse's thought which has to be overcome. Here we shall try to do just that.

3. For a more detailed discussion of virtues and their role in the exercise of moral judgment, cf. Josef Pieper, *The Four Cardinal Virtues,* (Harcourt Brace, 1965) and George P. Klubertanz, S. J., *Habits and Virtues,* (Appleton-Century-Crofts, 1965).

4. The notion of general virtue, as distinct from particular, is something which has been somewhat lost in modern philosophy of ethics. It

was something basic to ancient Greek ethics, strange as it may sound for us with our modern notion of virtue. Our discussion of both justice and friendship as general virtues will illustrate what is meant by "general virtue" as a basic component in exercising moral judgment. It will be seen how dialectical such an understanding of virtue can become.

5. The question of relating specific virtues to particular faculties as their proper subject of inherence was an old Scholastic exercise that had its merits, though it might have been overdone. Even if we do not take the distinction of faculties as seriously as the Scholastics did, some of the ideas which they proposed in this sort of discussion have a real value for any view of the life of the spirit. See, for example, Thomas Aquinas' discussion of the will as the proper subject of inherence for the virtue of justice, *Summa of Theology*, Part II-II, quest. 58, art. 4.

6. It is Aquinas who insists on this external aspect of justice (*Ibid.*, Part I-II, quest. 60, art. 2; Part II-II, quest. 57, art. 1; quest. 58, art. 1, 9-12). In this he seems to have been much more explicitly clear than his master in this regard, Aristotle (*Nic. Eth.*, Bk. V). The following discussion of justice has been very heavily influenced by Aquinas both in form and in content.

7. The idea of the "happy medium" is basic to the classical idea of virtue. Cf. *Nic. Eth.*, Bk. II, c. 6; Bk. V, c. 3. It shows how important the role of virtue was in the proper exercise of moral judgment. Having to see it as something *objective*, by reason of justice, as well as *subjective*, shows how dialectical the idea could become in historical consciousness.

8. Cf. *Nic. Ethics*, Bk. V, c. 1, 15-20.

9. Cf. Richard B. Brandt (ed.), *Social Justice*, (Prentice-Hall, 1962), the essay by William K. Frankena, "The Concept of Social Justice," pp. 3-4, and that by Greg Vlastos, "Justice and Equality," pp. 31, 35, 53, 63.

10. Cf. *op. cit.*, the essay by Kenneth Boulding, Social Justice in Social Dynamics," pp. 80-81, 90-91, that by Paul Freund, "Social Justice and the law," p. 94, and that by Alan Gerwith, "Political Justice," pp. 121-122, 154-157. In the last pages referred to, Gewirth discusses the "common good" as the principle of "political justice," and objections to having the common good as such a principle. But he does not analyse the idea of the "common good" closely enough and tends to reduce it to the legal terms of government, thus leaving us caught between the horns of totalitarianism on the one hand

and *laissez-faire* on the other, without any way of getting beyond this abstract dilemma. Gewirth, however, does point out that the principle of the common good "requires a positive conception of human well-being and of the contribution which government can make to it," and he does distinguish between "distributive justice" and the common good as an "aggregative principle," that is, "political justice" as conducive to the common good. In this he returns to an ancient tradition of "general justice" which we are trying to restore here.

11. Cf. "the principle of the common good" as stated by Gewirth in the pages referred to in the preceding note.

12. Cf., for example, *The Phenomenology of Mind,* Tr. Baillie, (Harper Torchbook, 1967), pp. 375-382, 460-499.

13. Aristotle himself, however, did not take this simply for granted, though he saw this as posssible under an ideal constitution because, as he saw it, there could also be instances where a good man might not be a good citizen and support the constitution. Cf. *Politics,* Bk. III, cc. 3-4.

14. Cf. *The Phenomenology of Mind, loc. cit.* and pp. 501-679.

15. This is the division offered by William F. Drummond, S. J., *Social Justice,* (Bruce, 1955), pp. 15-16. Though we take exception to the approach of this book, we recognize that it was a pioneering work on the subject of social justice.

16. We are indebted here to another pioneering work on social justice by William Ferre, S.M., *The Act of Social Justice,* (Catholic University of America, 1943), esp. pp. 143-192.

17. For a development of this idea of restitution in function of social justice, see Josef Pieper, *Justice,* Tr. L. E. Lynch, (Pantheon Books, 1955), pp. 56-62.

18. Cf. *Nic. Ethics,* Bk. VIII, c. 1.

19. Cf. *Summa of Theology,* Part II-II, quest. 25-46, and Part I-II, quest. 26-29. For a study of the role of charity in the moral theology of Aquinas, see the excellent work of Gérard Gilleman, S.J., *The Primacy of Charity in Moral Theology,* Tr. W. F. Ryan and A. Vachon, (Newman Press, 1959).

20. Cf. *Situation Ethics,* pp. 61-62 and *passim* after that.

21. See the 'dialectic of the common good" above, ch. 2, sect. II. Gilleman's work on *The Primacy of Charity in Moral Theology,* referred to above (note 19), gives an excellent account of how love informs all exercise of virtue, starting from the end as the good to be realized.

22. *Summa of Theology*, Part II-II, quest. 23, art. 6, corpus, and quest. 24, art. 1, ad 2.

23. Once again, it is in Aristotle that we find one of the first systematic discussions of this division: *Nic. Ethics*, Bk. VIII, c. 3 ff.

24. In *Life Against Death: The Psychoanalytical Meaning of History*, (Vintage Book, 1959), Norman O. Brown argues that *repression*, rather than reason, is constitutive of history. Historical man thus appears as diseased and history is explained as neurosis. The cure would appear in what Brown speaks of as "the Resurrection of the Body," which is a sort of return to the free play of the polymorphous and "immortal" instincts experienced in childhood, beyond the re-pressions of adult life in civilization. What this would be concretely, Brown leaves open to discussion in this radical re-interpretation of Freud, but it does seem to be basically a kind of return to the "pleasure principle" or a re-affirmation of the "principle of life" over the "principle of death" which would evacuate human existence of all historical tension between social structure and communion. It fails to break out of the circle of need and satisfaction — a problem that dogs any therapeutic approach to the interpretation of history. The experience of love and friendship, however, as we wish to speak of it here does provide a ground for breaking out of that circle into a broader, more transcending view of history, one that takes us beyond a mere return to the "pleasure principle" even in its unre-pressed, resurrected form. This experience is love precisely as me-diated by reason, that is, a "love of benevolence" over and above the "love of concupiscence," which includes both the love of pleasure and the love of usefulness.

25. The distinction is classical but has recently been worked out bril-liantly in Freudian terms by Denis Vasse, a disciple of the struc-turalist Freudian, Jacques Lacan, in *Le temps du désir*, (Seuil, 1969), pp. 17-57.

26. We refer here to Herbert Marcuse's *Eros and Civilization: A Philo-sophical Inquiry into Freud*. (Vintage Books, 1961). Marcuse's ap-propriation of Freud is more authentically historical than Brown's in that it refuses the mystification through symbolism in which Brown indulges in the end (cf. Marcuse's critique of Brown in "Love Mystique of Norman O. Brown," *Commentary*, XL no. 3 (Feb., 1967), 71-74). Brown's re-affirmation of mystification through sym-bol in *Love's Body*, (Random House, 1966), and in his reply to Marcuse (*Commentary*, XL no. 4 (Mar., 1967), 83-84), may have a real point, but it is lost in the vague materialism in which it seems

to disappear. Ultimately the idea of the common good does require a symbolism, but the symbolism has to be beyond mystification, not in it. The debate between Brown and Marcuse is still caught in the vicious circle of needs and satisfaction. Marcuse wants to take death much more seriously than Brown does, as a historical reality, but he is still at a loss before death. With his mystifying symbolism Brown fails to take us beyond it. With the experience of actual love here we wish simply to face the issue both more positively and realistically, that is, more historically, than either one.

27. *Nic. Ethics*, Bk. VIII, c. e, *in fine;* c. 5, *in fine*.

28. It is because Hegel saw love and friendship only in terms of a natural, immediate relationship, centering in the family, that he did not think of it as relevant to the universal good of the state, or beyond the state. The best that he could do was to speak of a reciprocal recognition between states and a rather abstract "possibility of peace" in warlike relations ("so, for example, envoys must be respected"), while war itself must "not be waged against domestic institutions, against the peace of the family and private life" (*Philosophy of Right*, # 338). In its aspirations at least, Marxism goes beyond Hegelianism in this respect, though it still reflects the Hegelian propensity for war in its tactics for reaching the end of universal peace. In proposing friendship as a truly universal movement here, the most truly universal dialectic of historical reality, we are trying to propose a way out of the last vicious circle in human relations which is not just one of needs and satisfaction but rather one of violence and domination.

29. *Commentary on Nic. Ethics*, Bk. VIII, lect. 7, n. 1631; lect. 1, n. 1543.

30. Reinhold Niebuhr, *Love and justice*, Ed. D. B. Robertson, (Meridian Books, 1967), p. 26.

31. This dialectic between justice and friendship is found in Aristotle and was underlined in Aquinas' commentary on the *Nic. Ethics*. Cf. the article on which we depend considerably in the following presentation of this dialectic by André Hayen, S. J., "Note sur la dialectique de la justice et de l'amour selon Saint Thomas," *Archives de Philosophie*, XXI (1958), 76-91. Here, more specifically, we refer to the *Commentary on the Nic Ethics*, Bk. VIII, lect. 1, n. 1538.

32. *Com. on the Nic Ethics*, Bk. VIII, lect. 2, n. 1559.

33. *Ibid.*, lect. 5, n. 1605.

34. Cf. Robert Johann, *The Meaning of Love: An Essay towards a Metaphysics of Intersubjectivity*, (Deus Books, 1966), pp. 17-18 and *passim* (see index).

35. *Com. on the Nic. Ethics,* Bk. VIII, lect. 7, n. 1632.
36. Cf. *Nic. Ethics,* Bk. VIII, c. 11 and c. 14.
37. *Com. on the Nic. Ethics,* Bk. VIII, lect. 9, n. 1663.
38. Cf., for example, Reinhold Niebuhr, *Moral Man and Immoral Society: A Study in Ethics and Politics,* (Scribner, 1960), pp. ix and xi ff.
39. Cf. above, c., sec. II, pp. 15 ff.

FOOTNOTES TO CHAPTER FOUR

1. Here and throughout the following argument we are greatly indebted to Gaston Fessard's work, *Autorité et bien commun,* (2nd ed.; Aubier, 1969), esp. pp. 14 ff.
2. Cf. G. Fessard, *op. cit.,* p. 19.
3. The need for both radical fear and laborious service for the passage to self-conscious thought is clearly affirmed by Hegel himself. Cf. *The Phenomenology of Mind,* pp. 237-240.
4. Cf. ch. 3, sect. I and II, pp. 81 ff., 91 ff.
5. Cf. Johannes Messner, *Social Ethics,* Tr. J. J. Doherty, (Herder, 1965), pp. 201 ff.
6. In a truly Aristotelian perspective, the juridical order is never separated from a judge in the concrete. *Epikeia* is no exception, grudgingly allowed, but a high form of the exercise of justice, its ultimate refinement. Cf. *Nic. Ethics,* Bk. V, c. 10.
7. Cf. ch. 3, sec. III, p. 103.
8. Cf. the *Leviathan,* cc. 13 and 14.
9. *From Max Weber,* Ed. Gerth and Mills, (Galaxy, 1958), pp. 77 ff.
10. For Kojève and other Marxist interpreters of the master/slave dialectic, true historical leadership can only come through labor and the laboring class. Such an interpretation can be brought into question on two grounds. First, is the inflection of the Hegelian dialectic in the direction of a *class* struggle justified? Is it not rather a falsification of what is true in the Hegelian dialectic, because it separates into different segments of humanity elements of a struggle that is found in any man in his relation with any other man? Secondly, is there not another dialectic operative in this relation between men, one more basic than the master/slave dialectic, which gives a deeper sense to the process of recognition operative in the latter as well as a more universal meaning, one which introduces an element of love as well as fear and so opens the way to a different means to

rational life, the use of language as well as labor in the human dialogue, namely, the dialectic of man and woman?

11. *Summa of Theology,* Part I-II, quest. 91, art. 2.

12. Art. 3.

13. Quest. 94, art. 3.

14. Art. 4.

15. Art. 5.

16. Quest. 95, art. 2.

17. Quest. 94, art. 4.

18. Quest. 95, art. 4.

19. Part II-II, quest. 57, art. 3.

20. Book II, c. 4.

21. PartII-II, quest. 66, art. 2.

22. Cf. *Summa of Theology,* Part I-II, quest. 90, art. 2, ad 2. The manner of insisting on the end as the principle of community rather on the "species-being" is what distinguishes Aquinas and the ancients from moderns like Hegel and Marx in their common concern for a social spirit.

23. We refer here to the analytical school of philosophy in its attitude, not only to "ordinary language," but also to established institutions in general which has been rightly criticized by Herbert Marcuse, in *One-Dimensional Man.*

24. Cf. *Summa of Theology,* Part I-II, quest. 97, art. 1.

25. Cf. ch. 2, sec. II, pp. 50 ff.

26. Cf. sect I in this chapter, pp. 123 ff.

27. Cf. *Early Writings,* Tr. T. B. Bottomore, (McGraw-Hill, 1964), p. 155.

28. It was not a necessity based on the end, *ex suppositione finis,* as it had been for Aquinas and the ancients, but one based on mere process, on matter, as Marx did in fact insist.

29. Cf. ch. 3, sect. IV, p. 109 ff.

FOOTNOTES TO CHAPTER FIVE

1. Cf. Hannah Arendt, *On Revolution,* (Viking Press, 1963), esp. pp. 15 ff.

2. Cf. ch. 1, sect. I.

3. In this we are again following Hannah Arendt, *The Origins of Totalitarianism,* (Harcourt-Brace, 1966), pp. 308-311.

4. Cf. A. James Gregor, *The Ideology of Fascism,* (Free Press, 1969), 283 ff.

5. Besides Arendt, here we would cite also Hans Buchheim, *Totalitarian*

Rule, Tr. R. Hein, (Wesleyan, 1968), pp. 28 ff.; Waldemar Gurian, "Totalitarianism as Political Religion," in *Totalitarianism, Ed. C. J.* Friedrich, (Universal Library, 1964), pp. 119 ff.; Gaston Fessard, *De l'actualité historique,* (Desclée de Brouwer, 1960), Vol. I, pp. 30-40.

6. Cf. Hannah Arendt, *The Origins of Totalitarianism,* pp. 40 ff.

7. Cf. Carl J. Friendrich, *Totalitarianism,* pp. 52-53.

8. Cf. Arendt, *op. cit.,* pp. 395 ff.

9. Cf. *A Contribution to the Critique of Political Economy,* Tr. N. I. *Stone,* (Kerr, 1904), p. 11.

10. See, for example, Aristotle's Politics, Bk. I, c. 2; Bk. III, cc. 1-5; Bk. VII, cc. 13-14.

11. In the *Communist Manifesto,* Marx and Engels argued that the internationalization of economics arose as a development of bourgeois society which created world markets to provide outlets for its production. More basically, however, this universalization in Marxism has to be explained by its reversion to a priority of nature against Hegel's idea of the Spirit.

12. Arendt shows that totalitarian governments aspire to conquer the globe (*op. cit.,* pp. 415 ff.). The explanation for this lies not only in the will to power and domination, but also in the reduction of politics to process by means of economics. In the absence of any clear distinction between the two, history remains absorbed in nature at the moment when it should emerge on the international level. Arendt makes the same point when she argues for a "new law on earth," as a guarantee against totalitarianism (*op. cit.,* p. xxxi), a law which will not only be "Natural or Historical," but *positive,* in the creative sense of the term, and *external* in a body politic, providing an element of stability for human actions and motions in the flow of motion itself (cf. *op. cit.,* pp. 461-464). It should be noted that in the context, taking her cue from totalitarianism itself, Arendt identifies History with Nature. We have tried to maintain a distinction of history from nature as the proper realm of human liberty and politics.

13. Cf. our argument against this surreptitious, and hence false, insertion of a "divine" element in the realm of human responsibility, above ch. 2, sect. I, pp. 44 ff.

14. Arendt makes much of the fact that totalitarianism depends upon the rise of mass man, atomized and isolated in a massive organization (*op. cit.,* 311-326). One could ask whether our acceptance of mass

media, as they have developed, is a result of or a step toward totalitarianism, or both.

15. Arendt, pp. 419 ff.
16. Arendt, p. 375.
17. *Op. cit.*, pp. 404 ff.
18. Cf. ch. 4, sect. I, p. 119 ff.
19. Ch. 3, sect. III, pp. 103 ff.
20. Arendt, pp. 308 ff., 323 ff.
21. Arendt, p. 417.
22. The art of propaganda, one of the chief instruments of totalitarianism, along with terror, is perhaps more than anything else what has transformed the means of communication into mere mass media. The advent of the ad-men into political activities is only another sign of how we have reduced the political to the economic.
23. We refer here, once again, to the philosophy of language whose sole concern is with clarifying accepted usage in its lowest common denominator, which therefore empties philosophy of all *really* critical function and, worse still, of any creative intent.
24. Many protesters have a keen sense of the almost systematic confusion of language, the hypocrisy of speech, in our society. In trying only to shock people out of this hypocrisy, however, without bringing reason to it, they are only adding to the hypocrisy, their own as well as that of others.
25. Cf. A. James Gregor, *op. cit.*, pp. 3-4.
26. Ch. 2, sect. IV, pp. 71 ff.
27. Cf. Waldemar Gurian, "Totalitarianism as Political Religion," in *Totalitarianism*, Ed. C. J. Friedrich, pp. 122-123.
28. Any theory of "absolute right" for kings or dictators can be termed a worldly theology, but as long as any dictatorship still acknowledges the existence of God it cannot be absolutely totalitarian. This could be termed a "saving feature." For atheistic totalitarianism, however, there is no such limiting factor. It has to deify itself.
29. Cf. Alex Inkeles, "The Totalitarian Mystique," in *Totalitarianism*, Ed. C. J. Friedrich, pp. 87-108; Gaston Fessard, *De l'actualité historique*, Vol. I, pp. 32-40, 121-211 ("Esquisse du mystère de la société et de l'histoire").
30. Cf. Inkeles, *op. cit.*, pp. 102-105. Arendt sees the "amazingly swift recovery of the arts" in Russia after Stalin as a "sign that the Soviet Union can no longer be called totalitarian in the strict sense of the term" (*op. cit.*, p. xx).
31. Ch. 2, sect. II, pp. 60 ff.; ch. 1, sect. III, pp. 21 ff.

32. It is Aquinas who points out this partiality of mere usefulness, even if it be usefulness for the whole. Cf. *Summa of Theology*, Part I-II, quest. 92, art. 1. The point is similar to that made by Josef Pieper in *Leisure, the Basis of Culture*, when he distinguishes the common good from mere common needs. Cf. above, ch. 2, sect. I, p. 49.

33. Arendt speaks of totalitarianism as a radical revolution, but in this she is thinking of revolution as nothing more than a reduction of human actions and motions to a natural process. Here we wish to speak of revolution in a more properly historical sense, as something distinct from evolution and belonging to the political realm in the classical sense of, that term, as taken by Arendt.

34. Cf. Bk. V in its entirety.

35. *Pol.* Bk. III, c. 2. It should be noted that what Aristotle had in mind in this Book is any form of change in constitutions and not just the revolutionary ones. Indeed, Aristotle speaks not so much in terms of revolution, as we translate him today, but of *stasis* or sedition, the formation of groups for attaining political ends whether by legal or illegal means.

36. In her study *On Revolution*, (Viking Press, 1963), Hannah Arendt points out how the social question as a factor in revolution is proper to modern times (p. 15), how revolution has come to be motivated by concern for freedom for the poor people (p. 41), and how slavery has disappeared in connection with the social question (p. 66).

37. Ch. 1, sect. 2, pp. 13 ff.

38. We are thinking here of Gandhi's doctrine of *Satyagraha*, "force born of Truth and Love or non-violence." Cf. *The Gandhi Reader*, Ed. Homer A. Jack, (Indiana University, 1956), pp. 110-116, 136-144.

39. When Gandhi speaks of total adherence to the Truth, it is of the ultimate bond of communion that he is speaking, for Truth is not only what makes us free but also what brings us together. It is error that separates and alienates us.

40. Cf. ch. 1, sect. II, pp. 12 ff.

41. Cf. Robert Tucker, "Marx as a Political Theorist," in *Marx and the Western World*, Ed. N. Lobkowicz, (Notre Dame, 1967), pp. 126-131.

42. Paulo Freire has expressed this necessity of revolution to pass through the consciousness of the people to be liberated admirably and quite practically in his book on *The Pedagogy of the Oppressed*, Tr. M. Marcos, (Herder and Herder, 1970).

43. Ch. 3, sect. IV, pp. 109 ff.

44. Ch. 4, sect. I, pp. 125 ff.

45. John K. Galbraith's book, *The New Industrial State*, (Signet, 1967),

has shown how this can be done by sheer complexification of problems.

46. Cf. ch. 1, sect. III and ch. 2, sect. II, pp. 21 ff., 60 ff.
47. Arendt also speaks of revolution as a beginning: cf. *On Revolution,* p. 13.
48. Cf. our article, "History and Nature in Karl Marx, *The Philosophical Forum,* II (1970), pp. 32-34.
49. *Early Writings,* Tr. T. B. Bottomore, p. 154.
50. At Iena, Hegel saw the role of language and love in the dialectic of recognition, but he saw it only for a moment and as still too bound up with nature, not unlike what Marx was to do forty years later on his own, without any knowledge of this early Hegel. Cf. texts already referred to above, ch. 2, note 21: *Realphilosophie* I, Ed. Hoffmeister, (Leipzig, 1932), pp. 221 ff. Though he continued to view the relation of man and woman as part of the life of the Spirit, he always saw it only as too immediately bound up with nature to constitute a proper element of political life as such. His fixation on "bourgeois society" as necessary mediator between family and state perhaps distracted him from this insight of his youth and may have led him to his absolutization of the State.
51. *Politics,* Bk. I, c. 6 and c. 13.
52. Paulo Freire quite rightly places dialogue at the heart of his *Pedagogy of the Oppressed.*
53. Cf. Jean-Francois Revel, *Without Marx or Jesus: the New American Revolution has Begun,* Tr. J. F. Bernard, (Doubleday, 1971).
54. Cf. Charles A. Reich, *The Greening Of America,* (Bantam, 1971), pp. 322 ff., esp. pp. 380 & 395.
55. *Op. cit.,* p. 379.
56. *Op. cit.,* p. 388.
57. *Op. cit.,* pp. 341-342.
58. *Op. cit.,* p. 362.
59. *Ibid.*
60. *Op. cit.,* p. 394.

INDEX OF SUBJECTS

226

nature, 26 f.
nazism, *58* ff., 74, *162* ff.
obligation, 67 f., 85, 88 f., 193.
participation, *40-41,* 43, 45, 67, 83, 86, 169.
person, 25 f., 37-40, 63 f., 70, 81 f., 96, 106, 113 f., 154, 185 f.
politics, XV, 4, 11-13, 16-17, 81, 88, 121 ff., 155, 163, *167* f.
practice, XIV, 7, 19, 57.
pragmatism, 63 f.
principles, XI-XIV, XVI, XIX, 1-3.
prudence, *6-8,* 35, 62 f., 76 f., 79 f., 110, 138, 154, 168, 187.
purpose, *29* ff., 35.
reason, 24, *127* ff.
recognition, 22, 24, *45,* 60 f., *91, 95* f., 103 ff., 110, *120* ff., *137* ff., 155, 171, 189 f., 195, 198.
responsibility, XXII, *8* ff., 35, 47, 54 f., 62, 107, 154, 161 f., 168, 182, 187.
revolution, XXII, 24, 41, 59, 75, 102, 115, 119, 126 f., 151, 160 ff., *174* ff., 196.
American 9, 160, 182.
French 9, 58 f., 160, 182.

situationism, X-XIV, XVI, XIX, 15, 36.
social order, XXII, *19* ff., 84, 107 f., 125, 155 f., 168.
social science, XIV, XVIII-XIX, *19* ff., 35, 55 f., 63-65, 122, 125, 134, 163, 167 ff., 199.
social structure, *20* ff., 29-30, 77 ff., 82, *86* f., 89, 101, 108 f., 113 ff., 133 f., 135, *137* ff., 147 f., 160, 162, 171, 180, 190, 194, 197 f.
society, *25* ff., cf. social order.
stoicism, 10-11, 53.
technology, 43, 55, 63 f., 89, 94, 108, *111,* 128, 155, 159 f., 166 f., 168 f., 178, 195, 197 ff.
totalitarianism, XXII, 38 f., 41, 54, 82, 85, 115, *158* ff., 186, 196, 198.
transcendence, XIX, 21-24, 42 f., *44,* 49, 56, 63, 80, 89 f., 96 ff., 110, 121, 124, 152 f., 174, 180, 195 ff.
utilitarianism, XVII-XVIII, *45* ff., 66.
value, *35* ff., 64, 76.
violence, *183* ff., 190.
virtue, XIX, *75* ff., 88 f., 102, 114.

INDEX OF NAMES